MEDIA AND SOCIAL LIFE

ELECTRONIC MEDIA RESEARCH SERIES
Sponsored by the Broadcast Education Association
Robert K. Avery, Series Editor

SPORTS MEDIA
Transformation, integration, consumption
Edited by Andrew C. Billings

New in Paperback

MEDIA MANAGEMENT AND ECONOMICS
RESEARCH IN A TRANSMEDIA ENVIRONMENT
Edited by Alan B. Albarran

MEDIA AND THE MORAL MIND
Edited by Ron Tamborini

MEDIA AND SOCIAL LIFE

Edited by
Mary Beth Oliver
Arthur A. Raney

Routledge
Taylor & Francis Group

NEW YORK AND LONDON

First published 2014
by Routledge
711 Third Avenue, New York, NY 10017

and by Routledge
2 Park Square, Milton Park, Abingdon,
Oxfordshire OX14 4RN

First issued in paperback 2016

*Routledge is an imprint of the Taylor & Francis Group,
an informa business*

Library of Congress Cataloging in Publication Data
Media and social life / edited by Mary Beth Oliver, Arthur A. Raney.
pages cm
Consists of papers presented at a 2013 research symposium conducted by the
Broadcast Education Association.
1. Mass media—Social aspects—Congresses. 2. Social
media—Congresses. I. Oliver, Mary Beth, editor of compilation.
II. Raney, Arthur A., editor of compilation.
III. Broadcast Education Association (U.S.)
HM1206.M3875 2014
302.23—dc23
2013050797

Typeset in Sabon
by Swales & Willis Ltd, Exeter, Devon, UK

ISBN 13: 978-1-138-69215-2 (pbk)
ISBN 13: 978-0-415-82847-5 (hbk)

TO JENNINGS BRYANT AND
JOANNE CANTOR,
OUR MENTORS AND GUIDES
ON OUR SCHOLARLY JOURNEYS

CONTENTS

CONTENTS

FIGURES

CONTRIBUTORS

Markus Appel (Ph.D., University of Cologne) is an associate professor of psychology at the Johannes Kepler University of Linz, Austria, and a professor of psychology at the University of Koblenz-Landau, Germany (starting October 2013). He is interested in a range of topics, including the psychology of fictional stories, android robots, the Internet in the lives of adolescents, and stereotype threat. His recent work has been published in renowned communication and psychology journals such as *Journal of Communication, Media Psychology, Journal of Adolescence, Educational Psychology Review,* and *Political Psychology.*

Erin Ash (Ph.D., Pennsylvania State University) is an assistant professor in the Department of Communication Studies at Clemson University. Her research focuses on representations of social groups in media, with an emphasis on the psychological processes that explain media-based stereotyping. Her work examining race and gender in media has appeared in such journals as *Howard Journal of Communications, Mass Communication and Society,* and *International Review for the Sociology of Sport.*

Jennifer Stevens Aubrey (Ph.D., University of Michigan) is an associate professor of communication at the University of Arizona. Her research investigates the media's effects on emotional, mental, and physical health in young people, with an emphasis on issues related to sexuality and body image. Her recent publications on these topics have appeared such journals as the *Journal of Health Communication, Mass Communication and Society,* and *Communication Research,* among others.

Joseph B. Bayer is a Ph.D. student in communication studies at the University of Michigan. His current research centers on the psychological and social processes that emerge from the use of social and mobile media. His early work in this area was recently published in *Computers in Human Behavior.*

J. Alison Bryant (Ph.D., University of Southern California) is CEO and Chief Play Officer at PlayCollective, a strategy, research, and product group that helps organizations create educational media and programs. Her research and writings focus on how children and families interact with media, particularly emerging technologies; and how we can create sustainable products and programs that have a positive impact. She has published three edited books and over thirty research articles and chapters.

Scott W. Campbell (Ph.D., University of Kansas) is Pohs Professor of Telecommunications and an associate professor of communication studies at the University of Michigan. His research helps explain mobile communication behaviors and consequences. Campbell's work is published in *Journal of Communication, Human Communication Research, Communication Monographs, Communication Research, New Media & Society, Mobile Media & Communication*, and other scholarly venues. He has also co-edited two books (with Rich Ling) for the Mobile Communication Research Series and collaborated with the Pew Internet & American Life Project on a national study of teens and mobile communication. Campbell is an associate editor of *Human Communication Research* and serves on the editorial boards for *Journal of Communication, Journal of Computer-Mediated Communication, New Media & Society, Mobile Media & Communication, Communication Reports*, and *Revista Chilena de Communicacion*.

Jonathan Cohen (Ph.D., University of Southern California) is an associate professor in the Department of Communication at the University of Haifa, Israel. His research and teaching focus on narrative persuasion, audience relationships with media characters, and perceptions of media influence. His recent publications on these topics have appeared in such journals as the *Journal of Communication, Media Psychology*, and *Communication Research*, among others. He is currently an associate editor of *Communication Theory*.

Mun-Young Chung is a Ph.D. student in the College of Communications at Pennsylvania State University. His research interests center on psychological effects mediated by entertainment media.

Hilary Gamble is a Ph.D. student in communication at the University of Arizona. Her research integrates interpersonal and media effects theories to investigate the role media play in relationship functioning.

Jennifer Hoewe is a Ph.D. candidate and University Graduate Fellow within the College of Communications at Pennsylvania State University. Her research examines the psychological effects of news media consumption on individual beliefs, attitudes, and behaviors as well as public opinion. Specifically, she studies the news media's ability to create and perpetuate stereotypes and in-group, out-group relationships. Her work has earned top paper awards at the AEJMC, NCA, and BEA annual conferences and has appeared in journals such as the *Journal of Black Studies*, *Communication Teacher*, and the *Journal of Muslim Minority Affairs*, among others.

Brittney Huntington is a Ph.D. student in educational psychology at Fordham University. Her research focuses on media, health, youth and families, and education.

Sophie H. Janicke is a Ph.D. candidate in the School of Communication at Florida State University. Her research in media psychology focuses on media processes and effects as related to morality and spirituality within traditional and new media.

Keunyeong Kim is a Ph.D. candidate in the College of Communications at Pennsylvania State University. Her research area broadly focuses on the social and psychological effects of media creation and consumption within emerging media, with particular issues related to enjoyment, moral disengagement, and prosocial outcomes.

Christoph Klimmt (Ph.D., Hannover University of Music, Theater, and Media) is professor of communication science and director of the Department of Journalism and Communication Research at Hanover University of Music, Drama, and Media, Germany. His research interests range from the psychology of video gaming and media entertainment in general to other domains of audience responses to mass and online communication. He is currently an associate editor of *The Journal of Media Psychology*.

Marina Krcmar (Ph.D., University of Wisconsin-Madison) is an associate professor at Wake Forest University and recently completed a visiting associate professorship at Vrije Universiteit Amsterdam. Her research focuses on children, adolescents and the media as well as selective exposure to violent media. Her research has appeared in *Journal of Communication*, *Human Communication Research*, *Media Psychology*, *Communication Research*, and other journals.

Rich Ling (Ph.D., University of Colorado) is a professor at IT University of Copenhagen. He also works with Telenor Research and has an adjunct position at the University of Michigan. He has studied the social consequences of mobile communication for two decades. He has written several books including *The Mobile Connection* (Morgan Kaufmann, 2004), *New Tech, New Ties* (MIT, 2008) and most recently *Taken for Grantedness* (MIT, 2012). He is a founding co-editor of the journal *Mobile Media and Communication* (Sage) and the Oxford University Press series *Studies in Mobile Communication*.

Martina Mara is a media psychologist and senior researcher at the Ars Electronica Futurelab in Linz, Austria. Her work focuses on fundamental and applied questions of human–technology relationships, mainly regarding the acceptance of robots and social implications of the Internet. She teaches media psychology and media sociology at the Johannes Kepler University Linz and the University of Arts Linz.

Robin L. Nabi (Ph.D., University of Pennsylvania) is a professor of communication at the University of California, Santa Barbara. Her research interests focus on discrete emotions' influence on message processing and decision-making in response to media messages that concern health or social issues. She has published over 50 articles and book chapters and co-edited the *SAGE Handbook of Media Processes and Effects*. She has served on several editorial boards, as the chair of the Mass Communication Division of the International Communication Association, and as a co-editor of *Media Psychology*.

Mary Beth Oliver (Ph.D., University of Wisconsin-Madison) is a distinguished professor in the Department of Film/Video & Media Studies and co-director of the Media Effects Research Lab at Pennsylvania State University. Her research in media effects focuses on entertainment psychology and on social cognition. Her recent publications on these topics have appeared such journals as the *Journal of Communication, Human Communication Research*, and *Communication Research*, among others. She is currently an associate editor of the *Journal of Media Psychology*.

Zizi Papacharissi (Ph.D., University of Texas at Austin) is professor and head of the Communication Department at the University of Illinois-Chicago. Her work focuses on the social and political consequences of online media. She is author of three books, and over 40 journal articles, book chapters or reviews, and editor of the *Journal of Broadcasting and Electronic Media*. Zizi is presently working on a new book, titled *Affective Publics: Politics, Emotion and Twitter* (Oxford University Press, 2014).

Kelly Quinn (Ph.D., University of Illinois at Chicago) is a visiting assistant professor in the Department of Communication at the University of Illinois at Chicago. Her work focuses on new media and its intersection with the life course, social capital, friendship, and privacy. Her publications have been included in *Information, Communication & Society*, the *International Journal of Emerging Technologies and Society* and in edited volumes.

Srividya Ramasubramanian (Ph.D., Pennsylvania State University) is an associate professor and director of the Communication Research Lab in the Department of Communication at Texas A&M University. Her research focuses on cultural diversity, media literacy, and prosocial media effects. Her recent publications on these topics have appeared in such journals as the *Communication Monographs*, *Communication Research*, and *Journal of International and Intercultural Communication* among others.

Arthur A. Raney (Ph.D., University of Alabama) is the James E. Kirk Professor of Communication and director of doctoral studies in the School of Communication at Florida State University. His research primarily examines how and why we enjoy various media entertainment content, with specific attention to the role morality plays in those processes. His writings on these issues have been published in various anthologies, as well as *Journal of Communication*, *Media Psychology*, *Communication Theory*, and *Mass Communication and Society*.

Drew D. Shade is a Ph.D. candidate in the College of Communications at Pennsylvania State University. His research focuses on the positive effects of media, especially concerning perceptions of others and subsequent prosocial behaviors. He also studies mass media migration: the process in which media consumers move from one medium to another tied to a specific entertainment text. His work has been presented at conferences for ICA, AEJMC, and NCA, where he received a top paper award from the Mass Communication Division.

Carmen D. Stavrositu (Ph.D., Pennsylvania State University) is an assistant professor in the Department of Communication at the University of Colorado, Colorado Springs. Her research focuses on the social and psychological effects of new media. Her work has been published in the *Journal of Computer-Mediated Communication*, *Mass Communication and Society*, and *CyberPsychology, Behavior, and Social Networking*, among others.

Sonja Utz (Ph.D., Catholic University of Eichstätt) leads the research group Social Media at the Knowledge Media Research Center in Tübingen, Germany. Her research focuses on social media use in the interpersonal and organizational context, currently mainly on the informational and emotional benefits of social media use (financed by an ERC starting grant). Her research has been published in journals such as the *Journal of Computer-Mediated Communication*, *Communication Research*, *Computers in Human Behavior*, and *Public Relations Review*.

Silvana Weber is a psychologist and teaches work psychology and computer-mediated communication in the Department of Work, Organizational and Media Psychology at the University of Linz, Austria. Her research deals with the application of social psychological theories in educational settings, mainly focusing on social identity, stereotype threat and the promotion of well-being in a cross-cultural context.

SERIES EDITOR'S FOREWORD

Since its inception in 1948, the Broadcast Education Association (BEA) has fostered a serious commitment to scholarly research, though that commitment became more formalized with the publication of its first scholarly journal, *Journal of Broadcasting* (later *Journal of Broadcasting & Electronic Media*) in 1957. Over the Association's rich intellectual history, BEA's annual meetings have afforded both academics and professionals with a wide range of opportunities for the presentation of important scholarship focusing on broadcasting and the electronic media.

In 2008, BEA launched a new series of programs designed to advance original research initiatives under the direction of the Association's Research Committee. The name of this new scholarly venture within the framework of the annual conference is the BEA Research Symposium Series, and over the past six years it has served to advance the research agendas of our discipline and provide a forum for some of the leading scholars and latest ground-breaking research in our field. The first Research Symposium in 2008 was orchestrated by Professor Jennings Bryant with a focus on Media Effects. This was followed in 2009 with a Research Symposium on the subject of TechnoPolitics, under the direction of Professor Linda Kaid.

In response to these two highly successful symposia, discussions began in 2010 between BEA and the Taylor & Francis Group of Routledge to form a partnership to enable the publication of an annual volume resulting from the yearly BEA Research Symposium. That new scholarly publication venture is the Electronic Media Research Series, and is intended to serve as cutting-edge seminal publications that offer an in-depth cross section of significant research topics. The 2010 Research Symposium Chair was Andrew C. Billings and hence the first volume in the new series edited by Professor Billings was *Sports Media: Transformation, Integration, Consumption* published in 2011. The 2011 Research Symposium Chair, Ron Tamborini, edited the second volume, *Media and the Moral Mind*, released in 2012. The third volume growing out of the 2012 Research Symposium published in 2013 was edited by Alan B. Albarran and is titled, *Media Management and Economics Research in a Transmedia Environment*.

The present volume resulted from the 2013 Research Symposium under the direction of co-chairs Arthur A. Raney and Mary Beth Oliver, and is titled *Media and Social Life*. Professors Raney and Oliver serve as both coeditors and contributors to this landmark collection that illuminates how media content, consumption, and use touches virtually every aspect of our social life. The multidimensional intersections of media and social life suggest a symbiotic relationship between the transformation of media and our evolving social lives. The Broadcast Education Association and Routledge are proud to make this important volume available to scholars across the entire communication discipline and beyond.

Robert K. Avery
BEA Research Committee Chair
Symposium Series, Executive Editor

PREFACE

Communication represents the essence of our social lives. It is what forms the basis of virtually all of our relationships, including our intimate connections, our professional contacts, our family ties, our interactions with and perceptions of in- and out-group members, and ultimately, how we come to know and understand ourselves. We express love, we introspect and learn, we share secrets, we argue for our values, and we provide (or withhold) guidance in ways that build, sustain, and sometimes dissolve our relationships. But of course, as medium theorists have so aptly noted, the content of what we communicate cannot be separated from the channel through which we communicate and from what different channels do or do not afford, imply, and amplify. In short, our social lives are built upon communication, including what is communicated, why it's communicated, and how it's communicated.

When reflecting upon the myriad ways communication functions in our social lives, perhaps the examples that come to mind most readily are face-to-face, interpersonal interactions—a parent's loving touch of a newborn, the rough-and-tumble play of childhood friends, or the timid smiles shared in a budding romance. But these types of interactions, as vivid and important as they may be, represent what is arguably a very small proportion of our day-to-day social communication. Rather, the texts we send, the video games we play, the television programs we watch, and the social media sites we visit form the contemporary building blocks of our social realities. Media content, consumption, and use touch upon virtually all aspects of our social lives, including how we think of ourselves and others, and how we understand, create, and maintain relationships.

This volume was motivated by a recognition that almost all facets of our social lives are affected by media, including our emotional and moral selves, as well as our interactions with family members, romantic partners, friends, and work associates. Further, changes in media landscapes imply that our social lives are evolving as well. As such, we believe that it is a particularly opportune time to gather together scholarship that takes stock of the innumerable ways that our media use and our social lives intersect, what transformations in our media environments may foretell about subtle and large-scale changes in our social lives, and the important questions that scholars should be exploring as we look to the future.

We are delighted to have had the opportunity to bring together an international team of scholars to share their expertise on these issues from a diversity of perspectives and viewpoints. We chose three broad themes to frame this volume: (1) media and the self; (2) media and relationships; and (3) emerging media and social life. Though issues raised in these themes are neither mutually exclusive nor exhaustive, we believe they represent a thorough and up-to-date examination of some of the more pressing questions and issues related to media and social life.

Our theme pertaining to media and the self recognizes that an important part of our social lives rests in the self—that our interactions with others depend, in large part, on how we understand and experience the self. Robin Nabi begins this section by exploring the various interconnections between emotions and media use: how our emotions impact what content we consume, how that content leads to emotional responses, and how those emotional responses facilitate other effects of media. She also identifies an important set of next steps for scholars to take along the path to better understanding how the media–emotion nexus influences our daily social lives. Markus Appel, Martina Mara, and Silvana Weber's chapter then takes a look at media and identity, including both how people use the media as a means of self-presentation, as well as how media play a role in the development and priming of self-concepts. In the next two chapters we get insight into the moral and spiritual sides of ourselves. Art Raney and Sophie Janicke overview the ways that issues pertaining to morality serve to not only influence individuals' selection, preference, and responses to media messages, but also how media depictions may in turn affect individuals' moral emotions and judgments. Srividya Ramasubramanian's chapter follows up on this issue of morality by examining the emerging field of spirituality and media. Her chapter draws on theoretical perspectives from positive psychology, Eastern philosophy, and traditional communication scholarship to explore how positive media messages can serve to inform, inspire, heal, and transform our social lives. The final chapter in this theme focuses on how media content and technology are serving in the development of our intellectual selves. Brittney Huntington and Alison Bryant, from the industry-leading research firm PlayScience, give readers a first-hand account of how media technology can be used successfully (or not) in formal and informal student learning environments.

Our second theme moves from a focus on the self to our relationships with others—with "others" taking many different forms in our social lives. Mary Beth Oliver, Jennifer Hoewe, Erin Ash, Keunyeong Kim, Mun-Young Chung, and Drew Shade join forces in the first chapter of the section, examining how media may influence our perceptions of people with whom we come in contact on a daily basis. These authors provide an overview of how media portrayals of persons from various races and ethnic groups, men and women, and other social groups might promote certain viewer perceptions (often negative or incorrect) of those persons in reality. They also explore how media might be used as a way of bringing otherwise different people together, creating greater social connectedness. From there, the next chapters take a more socially intimate turn. Marina Krcmar examines how media technologies—both old and new—can simultaneously offer families a means to learn and laugh together and a way to isolate and watch and play alone. She also guides the reader to consider possible effects of near-constant media connectivity on family life. Sonja Utz's chapter examines media and friendships, and how multiple affordances in evolving technologies can serve to both facilitate and maintain relationships among friends. Jennifer Aubrey and Hilary Gamble then focus our attention on a particular type of friendship. In their chapter, they offer an excellent overview of studies that explore and theoretical perspectives that seek to explain the link between exposure to entertainment media use and attitudes about romance, sexuality, and the intimate relationships that involve them. The final chapter within this theme takes a look at the notion of relationships from yet another vantage point. The focus of Jonathan Cohen's chapter isn't on our relationships with other *people*, but rather with *media characters*. In this chapter, Cohen provides a detailed analysis and roadmap for future research on topics ranging from fandom, to identification, to parasocial relationships.

Within each of the chapters described above, our authors have carefully considered the important implications that evolving media technologies might have on our selves and on our social relationships. Yet these changes are so widespread and consequential that we believed a third theme—one devoted specifically to the role of new media technologies in social living—was warranted. Christoph Klimmt leads off this section of the volume by considering the myriad ways that video games intersect with our social lives. His chapter considers not only how game play allows for social interaction, but also how games have both deleterious and constructive effects on our social interactions. Scott Campbell, Rich Ling, and Joseph Bayer's chapter then presents a timely overview of the role of mobile communication on our social lives at both the individual and social levels. Their discussion of how these devices require a greater awareness of the connections between social and psychological theory is sure to be an inspiration to many scholars who investigate mobile technologies. Kelly Quinn and Zizi Papacharissi's subsequent chapter tackles the importance of social networking sites on our social relationships. These authors provide a nuanced and broad-based look at the diversity of approaches to studying this multifaceted issue, touching on topics such as privacy, sociality, and surveillance. Carmen Stavrositu rounds out this section by considering the role of blogging in social life. The importance of this new form of expression and interaction is expertly overviewed in this chapter, exploring *why* we may blog and the variety of ways that doing so may be associated with beneficial outcomes.

A book project such as this reflects the efforts of a multitude of talents, and we are very grateful to many people who were instrumental in bringing this volume to fruition. First, we are extremely grateful to Heather Birks, Bob Avery, Don Godfrey, and all of the additional wonderful folks at the Broadcast Education Association who motivated this project and made it run smoothly. We are also indebted to Linda Bathgate and Julia Sammaritano for their continued support and encouragement—you both make the trains run on time, and you do so with talent and good humor. We also owe a huge amount of gratitude to Sophie Janicke who has been an instrumental help in every single stage of this project—without Sophie, this volume would not have happened. And finally, we thank our families, and particularly our respective partners John and Laura. Your gentle encouragement, patience, and love inspire and sustain us.

Mary Beth Oliver
Arthur A. Raney

Part I

MEDIA AND THE SELF

1

EMOTION, MEDIA, AND OUR SOCIAL WORLD

Robin L. Nabi

Given the centrality of emotion to the human experience, it is reasonable to imagine that the role of emotion in media effects processes has been a major focus within the communication literature. Yet, a close reading of the literature reveals that the examination of emotion in this context has been rather disjointed, with certain issues receiving close consideration (e.g., the use of media for managing moods) and others of arguably equal import receiving scant attention (e.g., how media socializes us to emotional norms). In light of the inherent social implications and importance of emotional experiences, the purpose of this chapter is to simultaneously examine the ways in which emotion has been integrated into media effects research and expand our thinking to include the myriad of ways in which emotion may shed light on how media impact our personal and social lives. Specifically, this chapter first examines the questions that have traditionally been the focus of emotion and media research, including emotion as an impetus for message selection, an outcome of message exposure, and a mechanism by which other media effects emerge, along with their guiding theories. The chapter will then examine the ways in which the study of media and emotion may be expanded to give us a more complete view of how our social lives are shaped and directed by the intersection of these two prevailing influences.

Key Issues in the Study of Emotion and Media

Following the lead of the emphasis on cognitive, rather than emotional, phenomena in psychology, media effects research has historically focused more on the cognitive and behavioral effects of the media, and less on issues directly related to emotion or their implications for social interaction.

However, over the decades, several streams of research have emerged as forming the bedrock of emotion and media research, painting a picture of emotion as a critical factor in media selection and message processing as well as simply an outcome important in its own right.

Emotion as the Impetus for Media Selection

One of the more long-standing and important questions posed by media effects scholars is: Why do audiences select the media messages that they do? As it turns out, one of the most well-developed lines of research in this area offers an emotion-based answer. Zillmann's (1988, 2000) mood management theory (MMT) asserts that people use media to modulate their affective states. More specifically, Zillmann argues that people, driven by hedonistic desires, strive to alter negative moods as well as maintain and prolong positive ones. Consequently, they will, either consciously or subconsciously, arrange their environments to adjust "all conceivable moods" (1988, p. 328), using any genre or specific type of communication available. Zillmann goes on to note four message features that might impact mood-based message selection: excitatory potential, absorption potential, semantic affinity, and hedonic valence. For each, the underlying principle is the same. If a message reflects one or more features that might perpetuate the negative state, the message is likely to be avoided in favor of one that would interrupt the negative state.

Much research supports mood management theory's predictions (see Oliver, 2003, for a review). However, its boundaries have been challenged by paradoxes of media selection, like the enjoyment of watching horror movies or tearjerkers that are designed to evoke negative affect, seemingly in contradiction to MMT's assumption of hedonistic motivation. Thus, recent research has examined alternative motivations linking affect to media selection. For example, Knobloch's (2003) mood adjustment theory asserts that when anticipating a future activity, people might use media to achieve the mood they believe will be most conducive to completing that task. Thus, the focus is on mood optimization, which she argues is a more specific goal than mood regulation. Most recently, Oliver (2008) argued that media consumers are at times driven not by hedonism, but by eudaimonia, or happiness rooted in greater insight and connection to the human experience. This motivation, she argues, explains viewers' desires to consume more poignant or tragic fare.

Although the extant research on media message selection overwhelmingly emphasizes mood, rather than discrete emotions, some research has considered the unique role that discrete emotions might play in this process. For example, Nabi, Finnerty, Domschke, and Hull (2006) examined the effects of regret on media message preference and found, counter to MMT predictions, that people with lingering regret over a past experience

4

were more, not less, likely to want to see programming on the topic of their regret. This and other studies (e.g., Knobloch-Westerwick & Scott, 2006) suggest that discrete emotions may function differently than moods in that media selection may be driven by coping, rather than more basic regulation, needs. Clearly, moods and emotions impact media message selection, and given the necessity of message exposure to media effects, it is critical that we more fully explore emotion's role in media selection processes.

Emotion as Outcome of Media Exposure

Another dominant focus of media effects and emotion research has been on the emotions that *result* from message exposure—both specific emotions, like fear, as well as more general affect-laden states, like enjoyment. The lines of research that focus simply on emotion as an outcome of media exposure are examined below.

Affect-Based Responses to the Media

Media messages clearly have the capacity to evoke a wide range of emotions. Perhaps the most specific line of research in which the emotional response itself is of primary interest involves children's fright reactions to media fare (see Cantor, 2009; see also Wilson & Drogos, 2009). In essence, this line of research documents that children experience fear of their social and physical environments in response to the media content they consume, and examines the conditions under which such reactions emerge. Specific content that frightens children of different ages (e.g., monsters vs. abstract threats), the individual differences that moderate fright reactions (e.g., empathy and gender), and the effectiveness of coping strategies to manage potentially fright-inducing media exposure have all been explored. Given frightening media can result in nightmares, recurring negative thoughts, and persisting anxiety or stress, this line of research is unique in its recognition that simple emotional experiences are profound not just in the actual experience but in their implications for psychological well-being and how people operate within their social worlds.

Although there are no specific theories within the media corpus that focus on emotional evocation per se, there are two theories that help to explain, at a very general level, the intensity of the emotional reactions people have to the media they consume: excitation transfer theory and desensitization. Excitation transfer theory (Zillmann, 1983) highlights the role of physiology in the emotional experience, arguing that the physiological arousal associated with an emotional experience decays slower than the associated cognitions. Thus, if one is aroused physiologically, one's emotional response to subsequent events, including media exposure, is likely to be more intense. Therefore, if one feels fright watching a film protagonist running for her life, one will feel even more relief than they would have otherwise once she has reached safety (Oliver, 1994; Zillmann, 1980).

Desensitization, on the other hand, focuses on dampening the intensity of emotional experiences. Drawing from the therapeutic technique designed to help people overcome phobias (e.g., fear of spiders), media desensitization suggests that repeated exposure over time to messages that typically evoke strong emotionally-based physiological responses (e.g., those that contain violence) lose their capacity to do so (e.g., Carnagey, Anderson, & Bushman, 2007; Cline, Croft, & Courrier, 1973). Although a strict interpretation of desensitization focuses on physiological response, research has expanded to consider self-reported arousal along with emotional and cognitive reactions as outcomes of interest (e.g., Mullin & Linz, 1995). The concern associated with desensitization, of course, is that this emotional dampening will transfer to the real world such that people will have blunted emotional reactions to social situations that might benefit from action (e.g., offering aid to someone in need) or may minimize the disincentive to engage in anti-social behavior (e.g., aggressive behavior; Bartholow, Sestir, & Davis, 2005).

Ultimately, both excitation transfer and desensitization have implications for the intensity of emotional arousal, though the specifics in terms of the scope of these effects are remarkably unexplored. For example, the literature is mute on whether these processes work equally well for various negative or positive emotions or how these processes might be harnessed for positive effects (Nabi, 2009). To the extent emotional intensity has implications for outcomes like message attention, encoding, and recall as well as personal behavior and social interaction, a more complete understanding of these processes would be of great value.

Emotion as the Mechanism of Effect

Finally, there has been increasing attention to the role of emotion as a key mechanism through which other effects might emerge. Although there are several ways in which this point might be articulated, this section will focus on message processing and persuasion.

Emotion and Message Processing

Arguing from a dimensional view of emotion, Lang's (2000) limited capacity model of motivated mediated message processing (LC4MP) essentially suggests that media consumers allocate cognitive resources to the messages they choose to process. However, because they only have limited cognitive capacity to do so, their cognitive resources are spread among the processing tasks of attention, encoding, storage, and retrieval. Further, how those resources are allocated is argued to be driven by the message's characteristics, signal properties, and motivational relevance (see Lang, 2009, for a detailed model description). Drawing emotion into the equation, Lang argues that motivational activation underlies and enables emotional experiences which, in turn, influence the distribution of cognitive resources. More specifically, aversive (or avoid) system activation leads to negative emotional experience, and appetitive (or approach) system activation leads to positive emotional experiences. As the level of appetitive system activation increases, relatively more resources are thought to be allocated to encoding and storage of message information. As the level of aversive system activation increases, an increase, followed by a slight decrease, in allocation to encoding is expected.

The LC4MP serves as a useful guide toward understanding the message features that stimulate the motivational systems that, in turn, impact the information attention, encoding, storage, and retrieval that underlie media messages' effects on knowledge structures and decision-making. Thus, the LC4MP is poised to be a foundational model in the area of emotion and media effects.

Emotion and Persuasion

Perhaps the most well-known and well-researched issues regarding emotion as a moderator of media effects come from the domain of persuasion, fear appeals in particular, though increasing attention is being paid to the persuasive influence of other emotional states. The fear appeal literature has cycled through several theoretical perspectives over the past 50 years (see Nabi, 2007, for a more detailed discussion), including the drive model (e.g., Hovland, Janis, & Kelley, 1953), the parallel processing model (PPM; Leventhal, 1970), the protection motivation theory (Rogers, 1975), and the extended parallel process model (EPPM; Witte, 1992). Sadly, meta-analyses have yet to endorse any of these models as accurately capturing the process of fear's effects on decision-making (see Mongeau, 1998; Witte & Allen, 2000). However, such analyses have identified four cognitions generated in response to fear appeals—judgments of threat severity, threat susceptibility, and response and self-efficacy—that may be predictive of positive action in response to such messages. Further, evidence does support a positive linear relationship between fear and attitude, behavioral intention, and behavior change. Thus, to the extent message features evoke perceptions of susceptibility and severity, as well as response and self-efficacy, fear may moderate persuasive outcome, though there are still important questions about the interrelationships among these constructs that remain unanswered.

Extending beyond fear, there is growing interest in understanding the persuasive effects of a range of emotions within a media context (see Nabi, 2007, for a more extensive discussion), and emerging models attempt to examine those processes. For example, the cognitive functional model (CFM; Nabi, 1999) attempts to explain how message-relevant negative emotions (e.g., fear, anger, sadness, guilt, disgust) affect the direction and stability of persuasive outcome based on three constructs—emotion-driven motivated attention, motivated processing, and expectation of message reassurance. In a similar vein, Nabi (2003, 2007) posits an emotions-as-frames model to explain the effects of more general media exposure on attitudinal and behavioral outcomes. Specifically, emotions are conceptualized as frames, or perspectives, through which incoming stimuli are interpreted. First noting the message features likely to evoke various discrete emotions, the model then articulates how those emotional experiences, moderated by individual differences (e.g., schema development, coping style), may influence information accessibility, information seeking, and ultimately emotion-consistent decisions and action. As such, this model offers a better understanding of the potentially central role emotions may play in understanding how message frames in a range of media messages might impact attitudes and behaviors.

Despite the growing attention to the persuasive effect of discrete negative emotions, there is still surprisingly little attention to the persuasive effects of positive emotions. Humor has unquestionably received the most attention in this domain, though meta-analyses suggest inconsistent effects on measures of persuasion (Eisend, 2009, 2011). Specifically, humor has been found to increase message attention and produces positive affect, but does not meaningfully impact the valence of cognitive responses or source liking. Indeed, humor can actually detract from perceptions of the source's credibility. Especially important, humor associates with increased ad liking, brand liking, and purchase intention. However, there is no consistent evidence that humor impacts ad recall or purchase behavior, the ultimate goal of commercial advertisements. Thus, humor has the potential to enhance psychological states associated with persuasion, though the lack of behavioral effects suggests tempered enthusiasm for its persuasive benefit.

With the recent popularity of political satire programs, such as the *Daily Show* and the *Colbert Report*, there has been an upswing in interest in examining the process through which humor may be persuasive in entertainment contexts. For example, Nabi, Moyer-Guse, and Byrne (2007) argue that humor may not have immediate persuasive effects because though audiences attend closely to the message, they discount it as a joke that is not intended to persuade, thus minimizing the message content's immediate effects on their attitudes. However, they further argue that if humor serves as a discounting cue, a "sleeper effect" could emerge such that the persuasive effect of humor may be seen after some time has passed (see also Jensen, Bernat, Wilson, & Goonewardene, 2010; Young, 2008). In light of the influence such emotionally-arousing messages may have in significant social contexts, including those related to consumer, political, and health behavior, clearly future research would benefit from closer examination not only of the conditions under which humor may be persuasive but also the potential of other positive emotions, like hope and pride, to influence audiences' attitudes and behaviors.

Next Steps for Emotion and Media Research

Despite what appears to be a healthy consideration of emotion in the realm of media thus far, there are still many important issues that have received only scant attention and still others that are only now emerging in light of new technological developments. Further, it is clear that past research has focused on the intrapersonal aspects of emotional effects with far less attention to the social implications of emotional experiences engendered by media exposure. In response to these limitations in the literature, below are three areas of inquiry that represent the exciting and important directions research could develop to shed light on how media exposure influences our emotions and, in turn, our personal and social experiences: emotional learning, social sharing, and use of new media.

Media and Emotional Learning

It is well documented that media can evoke a range of emotions and that those emotions have effects on message processing and even behaviors. However, what about emotional *learning?* That is, do the media influence what we know about emotions, what we learn to be appropriate emotional responses to social situations, and how to manage our emotional states and thus stimulate more productive interactions and outcomes? A review of the literature reveals very little research speaking to these issues. However, in light of the extensive research on cultivation of beliefs and the social learning of behaviors generally, Nabi, So, and Prestin (2010) argue that media may very well likely influence emotional beliefs and expressions as well, especially given the dramatic events and emotionality that are frequently the hallmarks of media fare. As Nabi et al. (2010) note, there are many promising research directions related to these issues, though two that are particularly relevant to social interaction include how media consumption contributes to the development of emotional skills (e.g., emotion perception and regulation) as well as the development of norms of emotional expression and self-disclosure. If media consumption enhances (or detracts from) an audience's skills of emotional intelligence and their awareness of appropriate emotional articulation, there are exciting implications for media's indirect effect on a host of outcomes, like psychological well-being, relational satisfaction, success at work, and the like (Salovey,

Detweiler-Bedell, Detweiler-Bedell, & Mayer, 2008) that are not yet credited. Clearly, much remains to be uncovered regarding the role of media in emotional learning and socialization processes.

Media, Emotion, and Social Sharing

Another way in which emotions associated with media consumption can enrich or deepen our personal and social lives is through the social sharing that occurs as a result of exposure to emotionally-charged media content. Exploring the intersection between media consumption and interpersonal communication is a critical, yet often overlooked, area of media and emotion research. Although the social sharing of information obtained through the media is at the foundation of one of the earlier models of media effects (two-step flow model of communication; Katz & Lazarsfeld, 1955), the role of emotion was not of concern at that time.

Yet, there is a growing body of literature on the social sharing of emotions that indicates that people have an instinctive need to disclose to others when they experience emotionally-charged events, which has been widely documented across cultures, gender, and age groups (Rimé, 1995). Indeed, the more intense the emotional experience or the greater the emotional disruption, the more likely it is to be socially shared (Rimé, Mesquita, Philippot, & Boca, 1991; Rimé et al., 1994) and shared repetitively over an extended period of time (Rimé, 1995). There are multiple explanations for this need to share, including the need to verbalize our experiences to help make sense of them, to help validate the self or confirm that we are still ourselves despite this event, and to allow groups to develop collective social knowledge of emotional experiences.

Harber and Cohen's (2005) recently-proposed emotional broadcaster theory (EBT) of emotional disclosure suggests that this intrapsychic need to share emotional experiences results in both emotion and information traveling across social networks, and their research documents that the extent to which stories travel reflects the degree to which the original teller was affected by the experience shared. Given the emotional nature of much media content, it is only logical to imagine that media messages may be the source of much social sharing. Yet there is surprisingly little research that speaks directly to this issue.

Still, there is growing evidence in multiple media contexts indicating that the emotionality of media messages is associated with their diffusing through social networks, including tragic and shocking news stories (Kubey & Peluso, 1990; Ibrahim, Ye, & Hoffner, 2008), health messages (Dunlop, Kashima, & Wakefield, 2010; Dunlop, Wakefield, & Kashima, 2009), and viral videos (Berger & Milkman, 2012). To the extent such sharing influences audience behaviors, from health behavior change to political action, this question is of great social significance. Moreover, in light of technological innovations that allow for the mass sharing of media messages to one's social network via social media sites, like Facebook and Twitter, the opportunity for the rapid diffusion of emotionally-charged media messages is at a level heretofore unprecedented. Thus, exploring how emotion influences the spread of media messages, generates conversation about those messages, and prompts both individual as well as collective action is ripe for exploration.

Emotion and the New Media Environment

Finally, as suggested above, the rapid development of new technologies through which media are created and displayed demands that we consider a host of new questions, including emotion's role in these phenomena and their impact on a range of outcomes from knowledge acquisition to personal well-being to political action. For example, given the wealth of information available online, examining the role of emotion in information seeking, content selection, and decision-making within this context is fundamental (e.g., Nabi, 2003, 2007; Turner, Rimal, Morrison, & Kim, 2006; Valentino, Hutchings, Banks, & Davis, 2008).

Second, in the context of social networking sites, it would be worthwhile to consider how a range of affective states (e.g., boredom, depression, jealousy, anxiety) influence, and are influenced by, their use and the resulting implications for social relationships. Evidence suggests that emotional openness online associates with perceptions of receiving emotional support through Facebook (Zhang, Tang, & Leung, 2011). But do Facebook posts expressing anxiety actually generate supportive comments that build closer relationships? Do posts boasting of accomplishments produce feelings of jealousy and thus distance with online friends? As users learn about events in their friends' lives – relationship break-ups, engagements, illnesses and so on – not only are emotions likely to shift (e.g., Muise, Christofides, & Desmarais, 2009), but behaviors consistent with those emotions (e.g., offering or seeking social support) are likely to shift as well.

Third, given the explosion of user-generated content on the Internet in venues such as YouTube, it behooves us to consider how the emotions that people experience are expressed via the content they generate. For example, it is likely that blogging could serve as a relatively productive way to vent anger and frustration or generate feelings of well-being via social connection (e.g., McDaniel, Coyne, & Holmes, 2012), whereas excitement to express creativity may lead to the creation and posting of videos on YouTube. Further, not only are such messages vehicles for emotional expression, but they also become part of the media environment with the potential to spread those feelings to message consumers and perhaps even generate group cohesion around the shared beliefs and world views those messages represent.

Finally, and related to the above, the role of emotionality in the spreading of media messages via social networking sites and the impact of such messages on not only behaviors but also feelings of social connectedness is both timely and highly socially relevant. Of particular recent interest is the role of social media in capitalizing on or even generating public outrage to motivate political action, such as boycotting corporations (e.g., Kang, 2012) or organizing protests of perceived unjust corporate or political decision-making (e.g., Bennett & Segerberg, 2011).

These are just a few examples of the ways in which technological innovations open up an array of new research questions that directly implicate emotion as central to understanding media-based processes and effects, extending beyond the intrapersonal domain to appreciate the implication of media-generated emotion on social interactions and processes. The coming decade will be an exciting time as these questions and other related ones are hopefully addressed.

Conclusion

Emotion has long been a part of media-oriented communication research. Yet, only recently have scholars begun to more fully appreciate its centrality in influencing exposure to and processing of media messages and the outcomes that ensue. Further, while the extant research has adopted a largely intrapersonal focus, it is quite evident that media-generated emotion has significant implications for actions and interactions within the larger social world. With the rapidly changing media environment in which questions of message exposure, message sharing, and message generation are of increasing interest, examining the role of emotion in these processes has never been more critical. By deepening our understanding of the traditional lines of emotion and media research as well as initiating new paths of inquiry, like those articulated here, scholars will undoubtedly be poised to offer important insights into the ways in which media may influence the world in which we live and how we operate within it.

References

Bartholow, B. D., Sestir, M. A., & Davis, E. B. (2005). Correlates and consequences of exposure to video game violence: Hostile personality, empathy, and aggressive behavior. *Personality & Social Psychology Bulletin, 31,* 1573–1586. doi: 10.1177/0146167205277205

Bennett, W. L., & Segerberg, A. (2011). Digital media and the personalization of collective action: Social technology and the organization of protests against the global economic crisis. *Information, Communication & Society, 14,* 770–799. doi: 10.1080/1369118X.2011.579141

Berger, J., & Milkman, K. L. (2012). What makes online content viral? *Journal of Marketing Research, Vol. XLIX,* 192–205. doi: 10.1509/jmr.10.0353

Cantor, J. (2009). Fright reactions to mass media. In J. Bryant & M. B. Oliver (Eds.), *Media effects: Advances in theory and research* (3rd ed., pp. 287–303). New York: Routledge.

Carnagey, N. L., Anderson, C. A., & Bushman, B. J. (2007). The effect of video game violence on physiological desensitization to real-life violence. *Journal of Experimental Social Psychology, 43,* 489–496. doi: 10.1016/j.jesp.2006.05.003

Cline, v. B., Croft, R. G., & Courrier, S. (1973). Desensitization of children to television violence. *Journal of Personality and Social Psychology, 27,* 360–365. doi: 10.1037/h0034945

Dunlop, S. M., Kashima, Y., & Wakefield, M. (2010). Predictors and consequences of conversations about health promoting media messages. *Communication Monographs, 77,* 518–539. doi: 10.1080/03637751.2010.502537

Dunlop, S. M., Wakefield, M., & Kashima, Y. (2009). Something to talk about: Affective responses to public health mass media campaigns and behavior change. *Journal of Health & Mass Communication, 1*(3/4), 211–234.

Eisend, M. (2009). A meta-analysis of humor in advertising. *Journal of the Academy of Marketing Science, 37,* 191–203. doi: 10.1007/s11747-008-0096-y

Eisend, M. (2011). How humor in advertising works: A meta-analytic test of alternative models. *Marketing Letters, 22,* 115–132. doi: 10.1007/s11002-010-9116-z

Harber, K. D., & Cohen, D. J. (2005). The emotional broadcaster theory of social sharing. *Journal of Language and Social Psychology, 24,* 382–400. doi: 10.1177/0261927X05281426

Hovland, C. I., Janis, I. L., & Kelley, H. H. (1953). *Communication and persuasion.* New Haven, CT: Yale University Press.

Ibrahim, A., Ye, J., & Hoffner, C. (2008). Diffusion of news of the Shuttle Columbia disaster: The role of emotional responses and motives for interpersonal communication. *Communication Research Reports, 25,* 91–101. doi: 10.1080/08824090802021970

Jensen, J. D., Bernat, J. K., Wilson, K. M., & Goonewardene, J. (2010). The delay hypothesis: The manifestation of media effects over time. *Human Communication Research, 37,* 509–528. doi: 10.1111/j.1468-2958.2011.01415.x

Kang, J. (2012). A volatile public: The 2009 Whole Foods boycott on Facebook. *Journal of Broadcasting & Electronic Media, 56,* 562–577. doi: 10.1080/08 838151.2012.732142

Katz, E., & Lazarsfeld, P. (1955). *Personal influence.* New York: Free Press.

Knobloch, S. (2003). Mood adjustment via mass communication. *Journal of Communication, 53*(2), 233–250. doi: 10.1111/j.1460-2466.2003.tb02588.x

Knobloch-Westerwick, S., & Scott, A. (2006). Mood adjustment to social situations through mass media use: How men ruminate and women dissipate angry moods. *Human Communication Research, 32,* 58–73. doi: 10.1111/j. 1468-2958.2006.00003.x

Kubey, R. W., & Peluso, T. (1990). Emotional response as a cause of interpersonal news diffusion: The case of the space shuttle tragedy. *Journal of Broadcasting and Electronic Media, 34,* 69–76. doi: 10.1080/08838159009386726

Lang, A. (2000). The Limited Capacity Model of Mediated Message Processing. *Journal of Communication, 50*(1), 46–71. doi: 10.1111/j.1460-2466.2000tb02833.x

Lang, A. (2009). The Limited Capacity Model of Motivated Mediated Message Processing. In R. L. Nabi & M. B. Oliver (Eds.), *The SAGE Handbook of media processes and effects* (pp. 193–204). Thousand Oaks, CA: Sage.

Leventhal, H. (1970). Findings and theory in the study of fear communications. In L. Berkowitz (Ed.), *Advances in experimental social psychology* (Vol. 5, pp. 119–186). New York: Academic Press.

McDaniel, B. T., Coyne, S. M., & Holmes, E. K. (2012). New mothers and media use: Association between blogging, social networking, and maternal well-being. *Maternal and Child Health Journal, 16,* 1509–1517. doi: 10.1007/s10995-011-0918-2

Mongeau, P. (1998). Another look at fear-arousing persuasive appeals. In M. Allen & R. W. Preiss (Eds.), *Persuasion: Advances through meta-analysis* (pp. 53–68). Cresskill, NJ: Hampton.

Muise, A., Christofides, E., & Desmarais, S. (2009). More information than you ever wanted: Does Facebook bring out the green-eyed monster of jealousy? *CyberPsychology & Behavior, 12,* 441–444. doi: 10.1089/cpb.2008.0263

Mullin, C. R., & Linz, D. (1995). Desensitization and resensitization to violence against women: Effects of exposure to sexually violent films on judgments of domestic violence victims. *Journal of Personality and Social Psychology, 69,* 449–459. doi: 10.1037/0022-3514.69.3.449

Nabi, R. L. (1999). A cognitive-functional model for the effects of discrete negative emotions on information processing, attitude change, and recall. *Communication Theory, 9,* 292–320. doi: 10.1111/j.1468-2885.1999.tb00172.x

Nabi, R. L. (2003). The framing effects of emotion: Can discrete emotions influence information recall and policy preference? *Communication Research, 30,* 224–247. doi: 10.1177/0093650202250881

Nabi, R. L. (2007). Emotion and persuasion: A social cognitive perspective. In D. R. Roskos-Ewoldsen & J. Monahan (Eds.), *Social cognition and communication: Theories and methods* (pp. 377–398). Mahwah, NJ: Erlbaum.

Nabi, R. L. (2009). Emotion and media effects. In R. L. Nabi & M. B. Oliver (Eds.), *The SAGE handbook of media processes and effects* (pp. 205–221). Thousand Oaks, CA: Sage.

Nabi, R. L., Finnerty, K., Domschke, T., & Hull, S. (2006). Does misery love company? Exploring the therapeutic effects of TV viewing on regretted experiences. *Journal of Communication, 56,* 689–706. doi: 10.1111/j.1460-2466.2006.00315.x

Nabi, R. L., Moyer-Guse, E., & Byrne, S. (2007). All joking aside: A serious investigation into the persuasive effect of funny social issue messages. *Communication Monographs, 74,* 29–54. doi: 10.1080/03637750701196896

Nabi, R. L., So, J., & Prestin, A. (2010). Media-based emotional coping: Examining the emotional benefits and pitfalls of media consumption, In E. Konijn, K. Doveling, & C. von Scheve (Eds.), *Handbook of emotions and mass media* (pp. 116–133). New York: Routledge.

Oliver, M. B. (1994). Contributions of sexual portrayals to viewers' responses to graphic horror. *Journal of Broadcasting & Electronic Media, 38,* 1–17. doi: 10.1080/08838159409364242

Oliver, M. B. (2003). Mood management and selective exposure. In J. Bryant, D. Roskos-Ewoldsen, & J. Cantor (Eds.), *Communication and emotion: Essays in honor of Dolf Zillmann* (pp. 85–106). Mahwah, NJ: Erlbaum.

Oliver, M. B. (2008). Tender affective states as predictors of entertainment preference. *Journal of Communication, 58,* 40–61. doi: 10.1111/j.1460-2466.2007.00373.x

Rimé, B. (1995). The social sharing of emotion as a source for the social knowledge of emotion. In J. A. Russell et al. (Eds.), *Everyday conceptions of emotion:*

An introduction to the psychology, anthropology, and linguistics of emotion.
(pp. 475–489). Dordrecht, The Netherlands: Kluwer Academic Publishers.

Rimé, B., Mesquita, B., Philippot, P. & Boca, S. (1991). Beyond the emotional event: Six studies on the social sharing of emotion. *Cognition and Emotion, 5,* 435–465. doi: 10.1080/02699939108411052

Rimé, B., Philippot, P., Finkenauer, C., Legast, S., Moorkens, P., & Tornqvist, J. (1994). *Mental rumination and social sharing in current life emotion.* Unpublished manuscript, University of Louvain, Louvain-la-Neuve, Belgium.

Rogers, R. W. (1975). A protection motivation theory of fear appeals and attitude change. *Journal of Psychology, 91,* 93–114. doi: 10.1080/00223980. 1975.9915803

Salovey, P., Detweiler-Bedell, B. T., Detweiler-Bedell, J. B., & Mayer, J. D. (2008). Emotional intelligence. In M. Lewis, J. Haviland-Jones, & L. Feldman Barrett (Eds.), *Handbook of Emotions* (3rd ed., pp. 533–547). New York: Guilford.

Turner, M. M., Rimal, R., Morrison, D., & Kim, H. (2006). The role of anxiety in seeking and retaining risk information: Testing the risk perception attitude framework in two studies. *Human Communication Research, 32,* 130–156. doi: 10.1111/j.1468-2958.2006.00006.x

Valentino, N. A., Hutchings, V. L., Banks, A. J., & Davis, A. K. (2008). Is a worried citizen a good citizen? Emotions, political information seeking, and learning via the Internet. *Political Psychology, 29,* 247–273. doi; 10.1111/j.1467-9221.2008.00625.x

Wilson, B. J., & Drogos, K. L. (2009). Children and adolescences: Distinctive audiences of media content. In R. L. Nabi & M. B. Oliver (Eds.), *The SAGE handbook of media processes and effects* (pp. 469–485). Thousand Oaks, CA: Sage.

Witte, K. (1992). Putting the fear back into fear appeals: The extended parallel process model. *Communication Monographs, 59,* 329–349. doi: 10.1080/03637759209376276

Witte, K., & Allen, M. (2000). A meta-analysis of fear appeals: Implications for effective public health campaigns. *Health Education & Behavior, 27,* 591–615. doi: 10.1177/109019810002700506

Young, D. (2008). The privileged role of the late-night joke: Exploring humor's role in disrupting argument scrutiny. *Media Psychology, 11,* 119–142. doi: 10.1080/15213260701837073

Zhang, Y., Tang, L. S.-T., & Leung, L. (2011). Gratifications, collective self-esteem, online emotional openness, and traitlike communication apprehension as predictors of Facebook use. *Cyberpsychology, Behavior, and Social Networking, 14,* 733–739. doi: 10.1089/cyber.2010.0042

Zillmann, D. (1980). Anatomy of suspense. In P. H. Tannenbaum (Ed.), *The entertainment functions of television* (pp. 133–163). Hillsdale, NJ: Erlbaum.

Zillmann, D. (1983). Transfer of excitation in emotional behavior. In J. T. Cacioppo & R. E. Petty (Eds.), *Social psychophysiology: A sourcebook* (pp. 215–240). New York: Guilford.

Zillmann, D. (1988). Mood management through communication choices. *American Behavioral Scientist, 31*(3), 327–341.

Zillmann, D. (2000). Mood management in the context of selective exposure theory. *Communication Yearbook, 23,* 103–123.

2

MEDIA AND IDENTITY*

Markus Appel, Martina Mara, and Silvana Weber

"Who am I?"—While thinking about the question, several different aspects come to one's mind, including affiliations to social groups, personal qualities, and attributes such as "I am a student," "I'm in a soccer team," "I am an outgoing person," and "I am a little overweight."

The relationship between media use and what we think and feel about ourselves is a broad topic which involves a number of research threads. The current chapter provides a selection of important approaches relating to older and newer media. It starts with a brief introduction to some major concepts relating to self and identity. Next, we present theory and findings on the use of the Internet and social network sites which appear to be particularly relevant when it comes to establishing a firm sense of oneself in adolescence. One core aspect of identity is gender. For many years, public and scholarly attention has been devoted to the portrayal of women in the media and how these portrayals shape self-concepts, gender-related attitudes, and perceptions of the female body. Subsequently, we address recent research that points at the influence of fictional stories on perceptions about who we are.

Identity and Self

Before we focus on the association between media and identity, some introductory words on theory and findings regarding *identity* in general seem warranted (including theory and findings on the *self*, as both terms are largely overlapping, cf. Swann & Bosson, 2010). Identity is multifaceted: the picture we have about ourselves includes a number of associations to traits, social groups, and past experiences. Depending on the theoretical

*Preparation of this chapter was supported by the Austrian Science Fund (FWF): I 996-G22 and funds of the Austrian National Bank (Jubiläumsfonds der Österreichische Nationalbank), project number: 14994.

background, a person's identity has been described as more or less variable. Scholars who are interested in personality factors such as the Big Five (extraversion, neuroticism, openness, conscientiousness, and agreeableness) or the need for affect, for example, focus on the rather invariant part of one's self-concept (cf., Appel, Gnambs, & Maio, 2012). Other perspectives have emphasized the flexibility of the self. Goffman (1959) popularized the term *impression management* for conscious or unconscious attempts to influence the perceptions of other people about one's own person. He used the metaphor that social interaction is like acting, with different roles for different audiences. According to this perspective, the self-concept is very flexible and depends largely on the situation, as it may change completely with the role played and the reaction of the interaction partners.

Many newer psychological approaches suggest that one's self-concept is a function of both, rather invariant aspects and situational factors. Different aspects of our self are salient at different times. In an academic context a person might perceive and present herself as a hard-working scholar who highly identifies with the subject, whereas while interacting with her family she might perceive herself primarily as a caring mother. Depending on which aspects of the self are salient at a time, our self-related emotions, thoughts, and behaviors can vary (cf. *working self-concept*, Markus & Kunda, 1986; *active self*, Wheeler, DeMarree, & Petty, 2007).

The importance of reactions by others to develop a sense of one's self has been emphasized from early on (*looking glass self*, Cooley, 1902). Without other social beings reacting on our appearance, without possibilities to socially compare and specify characteristics of one's personality in relation to others, individuals would have difficulties identifying what they are like. During social interactions, individuals perceive the reactions of others in response to their attributes and behavior. The individual's interpretations of these reactions are key information the self-concept is based on. For the last thirty years, the relationship between the self and larger groups has been a focus of scholarly attention. *Social identity theory* (e.g., Tajfel & Turner, 1979) explains the relations between the self, groups, and society. It suggests that social categories (e.g., nationality, university, soccer team), which one identifies with and has a sense of belonging to, provide a framework to define one's self. Every person has multiple distinct category memberships at the same time (e.g., member of a punk band; woman; African American; lawyer; soccer player), and consequently multiple social identities as these group identities are typically linked to different attributes and behavior. In a given situation, an individual's experience and behavior depends on the salient social identity that is active (e.g., member of a punk band or lawyer).

Up to this point, a person's sense of his or her self has been introduced as a deliberate judgment of what is real, but there is more to it. A distinction in theory and research refers to the explicitness of self-knowledge. *Explicit* self-knowledge is deliberate and controllable whereas *implicit* self-knowledge is rather uncontrollable and not always accessible to deliberate reflections (cf., Swann & Bosson, 2010). Self-report measures such as personality scales or adjective lists assess the explicit self-knowledge, whereas reaction time tasks are employed to assess implicit aspects of an individual's self. Moreover, in addition to the *actual* or *real self*, people have concepts of their *ideal self* (i.e., who we want to be) and *ought self* (i.e., what we think others expect us to be, cf., Strauman, 1996). Self-discrepancy theory (Higgins, 1987) proposes that perceived discrepancies between the actual self and ideal self can lead to negative affect and depressive feelings, while discrepancies between actual self and ought self might lead to social anxiety. Vice versa, people experience more well-being if their actual self and their goals converge (cf., Swann & Bosson, 2010).

Identity on the Internet

Individuals strive for a consistent sense of one's self. This goal is particularly dominant in adolescence, a time in which individuals need to achieve psychosocial autonomy (Steinberg, 2008). Identity development is closely linked to the mastering of developmental tasks adolescents are faced with (cf. Havighurst, 1972; Subrahmanyam & Smahel, 2010). These tasks include dealing with a society's gender roles and the development of a gender role self-concept, accepting one's body, getting acquainted with prevalent concepts of ethnicity in a society and potentially the development of an ethnic identity, and developing a personal framework of values and of philosophical and political beliefs.

To master these kinds of tasks, adolescents need to engage in *self-exploration*, a process of search, discovery, and decision-making on relevant issues such as lifestyle, relationships, political or religious values, and future occupation. Today's media provide ample opportunities to gather information that can assist self-exploration. Moreover, self-exploration is typically a social activity; it takes place through interactions, with parents or teachers, but particularly with peers, as they are facing similar challenges as oneself. Self-exploration is facilitated when adolescents are skilled in *self-presentation* and *self-disclosure* (Schlenker, 1980; Valkenburg & Peter, 2011). Self-presentation is the selective demonstration of features of oneself to others (typically in order to guide others' impression about oneself), whereas self-disclosure has been defined as revealing aspects of one's actual self.

Research on the contribution of media on identity exploration, including adolescents' self-presentation and self-disclosure, has been fuelled by the advent of the Internet and the enormous popularity of social network sites. In October 2012, the social network site Facebook announced it had passed the one billion mark of monthly active users worldwide (Facebook,

2012), meaning that compared to real-life inhabitant numbers on our planet, Facebook would make the third largest country in the world, having available a population of more than three times the USA. Eighty-six percent of US Internet users between 18 and 29 years coevally report to have a personal profile on at least one social network site (Pew Research Center, 2012). The Intel Corporation even came up with an application called "Museum of Me" (Grobart, 2011) that virtually stages textual and visual data taken from a Facebook user profile in an animated exhibition gallery just like it was common practice with precious paintings before.

When creating their personal profile pages in communicative online environments, individuals are directly faced with crucial questions linked to who they are (Subrahmanyam & Smahel, 2010) and how they want to be perceived. Social network sites allow people to design virtual representations of themselves that are created with the explicit intention of being seen by others. Via the membership in online groups, for example by "liking" the Facebook profile of President Obama, people can indicate their feeling of belonging and identification with certain social categories, in this case the Democratic Party (cf. *social identity theory*, Tajfel & Turner, 1979). Issues regarding *online identity experiments* and *self-presentation*—who users "pretend" to be and who they "really" are in their offline lives—not only play an important role in public discussion about social network sites, but also in terms of our scientific investigation (see Anderson, Fagan, Woodnutt, & Chamorro-Premuzic, 2012; Wilson, Gosling, & Graham, 2012, for an overview): "On the Internet, nobody knows you're a dog" is the title of a meanwhile famous cartoon published by *The New Yorker* magazine in 1993 (see http://en.wikipedia.org/wiki/On_the_Internet,_nobody_knows_you%27re_a_dog). Back then, participating in early versions of web-based communities and multi-user games was more strongly associated with anonymity and thus facilitated experimenting with different identities, pretending to be someone dissimilar to oneself, for example to be someone with another gender (*gender swapping*). A virtual *persona* theoretically could be constructed as the complete opposite of an individual's offline identity. Neither the presence of physical characteristics such as sex, race, and looks, nor a shared knowledge of each other's social background prevented people from claiming fake identities or exposing otherwise hidden aspects of themselves (Turkle, 1995; Zhao, Grasmuck, & Martin, 2008).

Despite early assertions that identity experimentation is a common phenomenon (Turkle, 1995), empirical evidence for today's Internet users suggests that slipping into a non-self identity is rare (Gross, 2004; Subrahmanyam & Smahel, 2010). Communities like Facebook or LinkedIn rely on users displaying at least roughly accurate representations of their actual selves. Participation in social network sites seems to require a certain amount of authenticity not least because of the constant monitoring by online and offline friends who may give feedback on one's self-presentation (Back et al., 2010; Wilson et al., 2012). Moreover, social network site users have been found to be judged to a greater degree based on their friends' comments (e.g., wall posts) than by their self-statements (Walther, Van Der Heide, Hamel, & Shulman, 2009). "On the Internet of today, *everybody* knows you're a dog," one could reply to the 1993 cartoon. In line with this assumption, Back et al. (2010) collected personality impressions gained by a layperson when just looking at a stranger's Facebook profile and drew comparisons with the profile owner's actual reported personality traits as well as his or her imagined ideal self, each measured by the Big Five personality dimensions. The findings suggest that social network sites serve more as a medium for expressing and communicating the actual self than for constructing idealized virtual identities. Bargh, McKenna, and Fitzsimons (2002) and McKenna, Green, and Gleason (2002) even come to the conclusion that individuals are able to express their true personalities more accurately over the Internet than in face-to-face interactions. Other empirical results, however, suggest that Facebook selves mirror highly socially desirable expressions of identity that individuals have not yet been able to embody offline, that is, their *ideal self* or *ought self*, rather than their actual self (Zhao et al., 2008).

To what extent users of social network sites embellish their profiles and engage in *impression management* strategies (Goffman, 1959; Schlenker, 1980) has been associated with the users' personality. Narcissistic personalities, for instance, tend to eliminate cues that are at odds with their intended *self-presentation* (i.e., selective presentation of aspects of one's self) and more often than others "detag" themselves from posted photos in case the portraits don't help in enhancing their physical attractiveness (Buffardi & Campbell, 2008). Introverted users with low offline-popularity have been found to follow similar strategies to make themselves look more popular in the online world (Zywica & Danowski, 2008). Enhanced controllability in interpersonal interactions is particularly important for individuals with low self-esteem (Valkenburg & Peter, 2011). Contrary to the offline world where they usually are self-protective and fearful of being devalued, individuals with low self-esteem perceive the Internet to be an appealing and safe medium for *self-disclosure* (i.e., honest exposure of aspects of one's actual self). Unfortunately, people with low self-esteem have been found to make online comments (e.g., status updates on Facebook) that are higher in negativity than those of people with higher self-esteem, and therefore don't reap their potential social and identity-related benefits (Forest & Wood, 2012).

Mass Media, Gender Roles, and Body Self-Concept

Important facets of one's identity relate to given sociodemographic categories, such as gender, ethnicity, nationality, or age group. Within the scope of this chapter we focus on gender, as this category has attracted the most scholarly research. In fact, surprisingly little research has been conducted on the influence of media exposure on the self-concept regarding other sociodemographic categories, including ethnic minority members' self-concept (see Mastro, 2009, for a brief overview, and Appel, 2012, for experimental evidence on the influence of anti-immigrant propaganda on immigrant adolescents).

The relationship between media portrayals of women (and men) and the self-concept of the recipients with respect to their own gender roles has attracted a substantive amount of interest. Content-analytic research identified women or female characters to be underrepresented in popular media such as on TV (Signorielli, 1989) or in video games (Williams, Martins, Consalvo, & Ivory, 2009). When present at all, women are often portrayed in traditional gender roles (e.g., TV: Emons, Wester, & Scheepers, 2010; movies: Finger, Unz, & Schwab, 2010; novels: cf. Hayes-Smith, 2011; Kramer & Moore, 2001). Moreover, women are remarkably thin in popular mass media. A content analysis of prime-time TV in the USA, for example, showed that about 30 percent of female TV characters are underweight, whereas the prevalence of underweight women in the US is 5 percent (Greenberg, Eastin, Hofschire, Lachlan, & Brownell, 2003).

Several theoretical approaches suggest that these depictions in the media influence how recipients perceive the world, as well as themselves. Social learning theory and cultivation theory suggest that recipients perceive traditional role models and thin bodies as common, with mass-mediated behaviors and looks becoming ideals that recipients try to reach (cf., Harrison, 2003). Note that on principle, media portrayals of thinness could dominantly activate parts of the self that are consistent with what is seen ("A thin person, like me"). Often recipients tend to compare themselves with women in the media, which likely activates self-related content that is opposed to what is seen ("I am overweight"). The ideal of being thin (*ideal self*) and the feeling that one should be thin (*ought self*) are in conflict with perceptions of the actual self. These discrepancies are aversive and may initiate disordered eating (cf. Harrison, 2001).

Most of the research on the correlates and consequences of media use in this field have examined attitudes toward gender roles (e.g., the appropriateness of certain behaviors for each gender) rather than more direct measures of the gender role self-concept (e.g., the Bem Sex Role Inventory; Bem, 1974). However, several correlational and ethnographic studies suggest that consuming more mainstream media (which feature traditional gender roles) is related to a more traditional perception of gender roles (e.g., Milkie, 1994; Signorielli & Lears, 1992). Likewise, a meta-analytic review quantified the overall relationship between recipients' amount of TV-viewing and sexist or anti-feminist attitudes (Oppliger, 2006). The analysis of eighteen correlational studies identified a small but significant overall relationship suggesting that watching TV might cultivate negative attitudes towards women and gender equality. Several experiments have also examined the influence of media portrayals on gender role-related attitudes and beliefs. Unfortunately, the results are rather inconsistent (Durkin, 1985; Ward & Harrison, 2005). The hypothesis that the presentation of traditional roles leads to more sexist attitudes and/or that more egalitarian content yields less sexist attitudes was supported in some studies (Johnston, 1983; Lanis & Covell, 1995; MacKay & Covell, 1997), but there were also effects contrary to these expectations (Kilbourne, 1984; Matteson, 1991). Additionally, other studies found no treatment effects (e.g., Schwarz, Wagner, Bannert, & Mathes, 1987). Focusing on children's attitudes, Ward and Harrison (2005) summarized that "causal connections between media use and viewers' gender role attitudes are unconfirmed" (p. 6).

In contrast to studies of gender-role perceptions, there is stronger support for the influence of media exposure on recipients' body image. A number of experiments have obtained self-reports of physical attractiveness, body satisfaction, and related measures after female participants were or were not exposed to depictions of thin women (most often photos). Meta-analytic reviews of these studies (Grabe, Ward, & Hyde, 2008; Groesz, Levine, & Murnen, 2002) conclude that the participants' image of their body is more negative after viewing images of thin women than after viewing average size models or no pictures. This finding is particularly relevant, as a negative body self-concept is closely related to eating disorders.

Stories and the Self

Further evidence on the causal influence of media portrayals comes from recent studies that have focused on the short-term effects of fictional stories (see also Richter, Appel, & Calio, in press, for an overview). In part, these studies have used implicit and behavioral measures to examine the influence of media on the self. Gabriel and Young (2011) presented participants with an excerpt from one out of the two best-selling novel series in recent years, *Harry Potter* or *Twilight*. Afterwards, the readers were asked (among other things) about how strongly they felt they perceived themselves as having characteristics related to wizards and vampires (for example, one characteristic related to vampires was "How sharp are your teeth?"). Moreover, an implicit association test with "me" and "not me" words and words associated with vampires vs. wizards was conducted, a measure to tap into implicit aspects of the self-concept. The results show that the explicit as well as the implicit self-concept was influenced by the story: participants who read an excerpt of *Harry Potter* perceived themselves to be more like wizards as compared to the *Twilight* group. The latter participants perceived themselves to be more like vampires instead.

The particular power of fictional stories (as compared to less narrative and non-fictional formats) was highlighted in a study by Djikic, Oatley, Zoeterman, and Peterson (2009). Participants were to read a short story by Chekhov (*The Lady with the Toy Dog*) or a comparison text with the same content (adulterous love affair), but documentary in form. Before and after reading, the participants completed a Big Five personality questionnaire. Greater changes in the entire self-reported trait profile were observed for participants in the Chekhov group than for those who read the control text (the changes occurred across all five traits and did not follow a common pattern).

In another experiment that focused on personality traits as well (Sestir & Green, 2010), the mechanisms underlying changes in the self-concept were examined. Participants watched a movie clip; their identification with story characters and their transportation into the story world (cf., Green & Brock, 2000) were manipulated with the help of written instructions. Before and after watching the movie, participants were asked to work on a reaction-time task (me/not-me task). This measure assessed whether characteristics of the movie characters applied to themselves or not. The results showed that higher identification as well as higher transportation were associated with a greater likelihood that participants switched from not-me-judgments to me-judgments for character-relevant traits, indicating that both receptional states facilitate changes in the recipients' self-concept. The support for identification was somewhat stronger, as only identification affected reaction times, which served as a second measure to demonstrate story-cued changes in the self-concept (Richter et al., in press, provide further evidence on the role of transportation).

A fourth recent study investigated the short-term influence of reading a story about a stupid soccer hooligan on cognitive performance (Appel, 2011). Based on research on media priming and priming theories that emphasize the role of active self-concepts (Mussweiler, 2003; Wheeler et al., 2007), the author assumed that reading a story about a stupid person would activate self-related concepts of stupidity which would in turn influence behavior. When simply instructed to read the story carefully, participants performed worse in a subsequent knowledge test than participants who read a story that featured a person who behaved in neither smart nor stupid ways. When instructed to use the hooligan in the story as a standard of comparison and to find dissimilarities between the hooligan and the own person, the story had no influence on cognitive performance. The assumed role of activating information about oneself when following the mediated prime was further corroborated: For participants who read the story without a special reading goal instruction, the amount of self-activation (assessed with a self-report scale) was associated with lower performance. In contrast, self-activation was associated with higher performance when participants were explicitly instructed to find dissimilarities with the protagonist.

Conclusion and Outlook

An individual's self-concept and his or her media use mutually influence each other. On the one hand, the human tendency to establish a positive and coherent sense of the self directs media choice and related activities. Media fare is chosen that is consistent with one's self-views, and activities are preferred that allow for self-exploration. On the other hand, media content found online along with the stories encountered on TV or in books shape the concept about who we are.

The overview presented in this chapter was guided by our aim to delineate important threads in the literature on identity and the self, and to introduce recent research on the role of media. Most likely, the topic of media and identity will attract increasing scholarly attention in the future. Over the past decade the Internet and mobile digital tools have significantly widened individuals' opportunities to explore and present themselves in front of much larger and more divergent target groups than ever before. The importance of others' reactions to develop a sense of one's self has been emphasized from early on. Web-based social networks such as Facebook provide new stages for recognition, comparison, and the specification of one's personality in relation to others. As the popularity of social network sites is rather recent, there are many research questions to answer regarding the choice and the effects of these applications and related activities. This includes the role of social network sites on the development of users' gender role identity, the contribution of using social network sites on the clarity of the user's self-concept, and the role that parents can play to increase the benefits (and to decrease the risks) of Internet use with respect to adolescents' identity development.

The importance of social network sites notwithstanding, individuals engage in many different media activities: They enjoy watching TV, going to the movies, and reading books (such as the current issue). Interestingly, even if a story encountered is a piece of fiction, it can have a substantial impact on our self-views. In particular when recipients experience a state of high immersion into a story world, they are likely to apply characteristics of the narrative's protagonists to themselves or to activate facets of their self-concept that relate to the storyline (e.g., a more magician-like concept of one's personality after watching or reading *Harry Potter*). Even when reflecting upon situations in everyday life, individuals tend to think in narrative structures: "Our life stories are who we are. They are our identity" (Gottschall, 2012, p. 161). The role of mediated fictional stories on the self in relationship to the events that unfold in our non-media life is a fascinating direction for future research.

From a methodological perspective, much of the previous research on different types of media and identity aspects has been correlational or focused exclusively on one potential direction of causal influence (e.g., the experiments examining story effects on self-perceptions and behavior). However, aspects of the self (such as a discrepancy between the actual and ought self-concept of thinness) may lead to a particular choice and/or interpretation of media (e.g., watching *America's Next Top Model*) which in turn likely affects identity aspects (an even higher discrepancy between the actual and ought self-concept of thinness) which again guides media choice (reading magazines that promote dieting), and so forth. In that sense, the mutual relationships between aspects of the self and media use can be conceived as reinforcing spirals (cf. Slater, 2007). Future research is encouraged to elucidate the mutual patterns of influence between self and media use with the help of experiments (e.g., media effects studies with future media use as a dependent variable) and longitudinal, cross-lagged designs.

References

Anderson, B., Fagan, P., Woodnutt, T., & Chamorro-Premuzic, T. (2012). Facebook psychology: Popular questions answered by research. *Psychology of Popular Media Culture, 1*, 23–37. doi: 10.1037/a0026452

Appel, M. (2011). A story about a stupid person can make you act stupid (or smart): Behavioral assimilation (and contrast) as narrative impact. *Media Psychology, 14*, 144–167. doi:10.1080/15213269.2011.573461

Appel, M. (2012). Anti-immigrant propaganda by radical right parties and the intellectual performance of adolescents. *Political Psychology, 33*, 483–493. doi: 10.1111/j.1467-9221.2012.00902.x

Appel, M., Gnambs, T., & Maio, G. (2012). A short measure of the need for affect. *Journal of Personality Assessment, 94*, 418–426. doi:10.1080/00223891.2012 .666921

Back, M. D., Stopfer, J. M., Vazire, S., Gaddis, S., Schmukle, S. C., Egloff, B., & Gosling, S. D. (2010). Facebook profiles reflect actual personality, not self-idealization. *Psychological Science, 21*, 372–374. doi: 10.1177/09567976093 60756

Bargh, J. A., McKenna, K. Y. A., & Fitzsimons, G. M. (2002). Can you see the real me? Activation and expression of the "true self" on the Internet. *Journal of Social Issues, 58*, 22–48. doi: 10.1111/1540-4560.00247

Bem, S. L. (1974). The measurement of psychological androgyny. *Journal of Consulting and Clinical Psychology, 42*, 155–162. doi: 10.1037/h0036215

Buffardi, L. E., & Campbell, W. K. (2008). Narcissism and social networking web sites. *Personality and Social Psychology Bulletin, 34*, 1303–1314. doi: 10.1177/0146167208320061

Cooley, C. H. (1902). *Human nature and the social order.* New York: Charles Scribner's Sons.

Djikic, M., Oatley, K., Zoeterman, S., & Peterson, J. B. (2009). On being moved by art: How reading fiction transforms the self. *Creativity Research Journal, 21*, 24–29. doi:10.1080/10400410802633392

Durkin, K. (1985). Television and sex-role acquisition 2: Effects. *British Journal of Social Psychology, 24,* 191–210. doi: 10.1111/j.2044-8309.1985.tb00680.x

Emons, P., Wester, F., & Scheepers, P. (2010). He works outside the home, she drinks coffee and does the dishes: Gender roles in fiction programs on Dutch television. *Journal of Broadcasting and Electronic Media, 54,* 40–53. doi:10.1080/08838150903550386

Facebook (2012). *Facebook newsroom: Key facts.* Available online under http://newsroom.fb.com/content/default.aspx?NewsAreaId=20.

Finger, J., Unz, D., & Schwab, F. (2010). Crime scene investigation. The chief inspectors' display rules. *Sex Roles, 62,* 798–809. doi: 10.1007/s11199-009-9722-5

Forest, A. L., & Wood, J. V. (2012). When social networking is not working: Individuals with low self-esteem recognize but do not reap the benefits of self-disclosure on Facebook. *Psychological Science, 23,* 295–302. doi: 10.1177/0956797611429709

Gabriel, S., & Young, A. F. (2011). Becoming a vampire without being bitten: The narrative collective-assimilation hypothesis. *Psychological Science, 22,* 990–994. doi: 10.1177/0956797611415541

Goffman, E. (1959). *The presentation of self in everyday life.* New York: Doubleday.

Gottschall, J. (2012). *The storytelling animal: How stories make us human.* New York: Houghton Mifflin Harcourt.

Grabe, S., Ward, L. M., & Hyde, J. S. (2008). The role of the media in body image concerns among women: A meta-analysis of experimental and correlational studies. *Psychological Bulletin, 134,* 460–476. doi: 10.1037/0033-2909.134.3.460

Green, M. C., & Brock, T. C. (2000). The role of transportation in the persuasiveness of public narratives. *Journal of Personality and Social Psychology, 79,* 701–721. doi: 10.1037/0022-3514.79.5.701

Greenberg, B. S., Eastin, M. S., Hofschire, L., Lachlan, K., & Brownell, K. D. (2003). Portrayals of overweight and obese individuals on commercial television. *American Journal of Public Health, 93,* 1342–1348. doi:10.2105/AJPH.93.8.1342

Grobart, S. (2011). Intel's Museum of Me is about You. *The New York Times,* June 9, 2011.

Groesz, L. M., Levine, M. P., & Murnen, S. K. (2002). The effect of experimental presentation of thin media images on body satisfaction: A meta-analytic review. *International Journal of Eating Disorders, 31,* 1–16. doi: 10.1002/eat.10005

Gross, E. F. (2004). Adolescent Internet use: What we expect, what teens report. *Applied Developmental Psychology, 25,* 633–649. doi: 10.1016/j.appdev.2004.09.005

Harrison, K. (2001). Ourselves, our bodies: Thin-ideal media, self-discrepancies, and eating disorder symptomatology in adolescents. *Journal of Social and Clinical Psychology, 20,* 289–323. doi: 10.1521/jscp.20.3.289.22303

Harrison, K. (2003). Television viewers' ideal body proportions: The case of the curvaceously thin woman. *Sex Roles, 48,* 255–264. doi: 10.1023/A:1022825421647

Havighurst, R. J. (1972). *Developmental tasks and education* (3rd ed.). New York: McKay. (Original work published 1948.)

Hayes-Smith, R. (2011). Gender norms in the Twilight series. *Contexts, 10,* 78–79. doi: 10.1177/1536504211408960

Higgins, E. T. (1987). Self-discrepancy: A theory relating self and affect. *Psychological Review, 94,* 319–340. doi: 10.1037/0033-295X.94.3.319

Johnston, J. (1983). Using television to change stereotypes. *Prevention in Human Services, 2,* 67–81. doi: 10.1300/J293v02n01_06

Kilbourne, W. E. (1984). An exploratory study of sex-roles in advertising and women's perceptions of managerial attributes in women. *Advances in Consumer Research, 11,* 84–87.

Kramer, D., & Moore, M. (2001). Family myths in romantic fiction. *Psychological Reports, 88,* 29–41. doi: 10.2466/pr0.2001.88.1.29

Lanis, K., & Covell, K. (1995). Images of women in advertisements: Effects on attitudes related to sexual aggression. *Sex Roles, 32,* 639–649. doi: 10.1007/BF01544216

MacKay, N. J., & Covell, K. (1997). The impact of women in advertisements on attitudes toward women. *Sex Roles, 36,* 573–583. doi: 10.1023/A:1025613923786

Markus, H., & Kunda, Z. (1986). Stability and malleability of the self-concept. *Journal of Personality and Social Psychology, 51,* 858–866. doi: 10.1037/0022-3514.51.4.858

Mastro, D. (2009). Effects of racial and ethnic stereotyping. In J. Bryant and M. B. Oliver (Eds.), *Media effects: Advances in theory and research* (pp. 325–341). New York: Routledge.

Matteson, D. R. (1991). Attempting to change sex role attitudes in adolescents: Explorations of reverse effects. *Adolescence, 26,* 885–898.

McKenna, K. Y. A., Green, A. S., & Gleason, M. E. J. (2002). Relationship formation on the Internet: What's the big attraction? *Journal of Social Issues, 58,* 9–31. doi: 10.1111/1540-4560.00246

Milkie, M. A. (1994). Social world approach to cultural studies: Mass media and gender in the adolescent peer group. *Journal of Contemporary Ethnography, 23,* 354–380. doi: 10.1177/089124194023003005

Mussweiler, T. (2003). Comparison processes in social judgment: Mechanisms and consequences. *Psychological Review, 110,* 472–489. doi: 10.1037/0033-295X.110.3.472

Oppliger, P. A. (2006). Effects of gender stereotyping on socialization. In R. G. Preiss, B. M. Gayle, N. Burrell, M. Allen & J. Bryant (Eds.), *Mass media effects research: Advances through meta-analysis* (pp. 199–214). Mahwah, NJ: Erlbaum.

Pew Research Center (2012). *Pew Internet: Social networking. Online report.* http://pewinternet.org/Commentary/2012/March/Pew-Internet-Social-Networking-full-detail.aspx.

Richter, T., Appel, M., & Calio, F. (in press). Stories can influence the self-concept. *Social Influence.* doi: 10.1080/15534510.2013.799099

Schlenker, B. R. (1980). *Impression management: The self-concept, social identity, and interpersonal relations.* Monterey, CA: Brooks/Cole.

Schwarz, N., Wagner, D., Bannert, M., & Mathes, L. (1987). Cognitive accessibility of sex role concepts and attitudes toward political participation: The impact of sexist ads. *Sex Roles, 17,* 593–601. doi: 10.1007/BF00287738

Sestir, M., & Green, M. C. (2010). You are who you watch: Identification and transportation effects on temporary self-concept. *Social Influence, 5,* 272–288. doi: 10.1080/15534510.2010.490672

Signorielli, N. (1989). Television and conceptions about sex roles: Maintaining conventionality and the status quo. *Sex Roles, 21,* 341–360. doi: 10.1007/BF00289596

Signorielli, N., & Lears, M. (1992). Television and children's conceptions of nutrition: Unhealthy messages. *Health Communication, 4,* 245–257. doi:10.1207/s15327027hc0404_1

Slater, M. D. (2007). Reinforcing spirals: The mutual influence of media selectivity and media effects and their impact on individual behavior and social identity. *Communication Theory, 17,* 281–303. doi: 10.1111/j.1468-2885.2007.00296.x

Steinberg, L. (2008). *Adolescence.* New York: McGraw-Hill.

Strauman, T. J. (1996). Stability within the self: A longitudinal study of the structural implications of self-discrepancy theory. *Journal of Personality and Social Psychology, 71,* 1142–1153. doi: 10.1037/0022-3514.71.6.1142

Swann, W. B., Jr., & Bosson, J. K. (2010). Self and identity. In S. T. Fiske, D. T. Gilbert, & G. Lindzey (Eds.), *Handbook of social psychology, Vol 1* (pp. 589–628). Hoboken, NJ: John Wiley & Sons Inc.

Subrahmanyam, K., & Smahel, D. (2010). *Digital youth: The role of media in development.* New York: Springer.

Tajfel, H., & Turner, J. C. (1979). An integrative theory of intergroup conflict. In W. G. Austin & S. Worchel (Eds.), *The social psychology of intergroup relations* (pp. 33 – 48). Monterey, CA: Brooks-Cole.

Turkle, S. (1995). *Life on the screen: Identity in the age of the Internet.* New York: Simon & Schuster.

Valkenburg, P. M., & Peter, J. (2011). Online communication among adolescents: An integrated model of its attraction, opportunities, and risks. *Journal of Adolescent Health, 48,* 121–127. doi: 10.1016/j.jadohealth.2010.08.020

Walther, J. B., Van Der Heide, B., Hamel, L., & Shulman, H. (2009). Self-generated versus other-generated statements and impressions in computer-mediated communication: A test of warranting theory using Facebook. *Communication Research, 36,* 229–253. doi: 10.1177/0093650208330251

Ward, L. M., & Harrison, K. (2005). The impact of media use on girls' beliefs about gender roles, their bodies, and sexual relationships: A research synthesis. In E. Cole & J. H. Daniel (Eds.), *Featuring females: Feminist analyses of media* (pp. 3–23). Washington, DC: APA Books.

Wheeler, S. C., DeMarree, K. G., & Petty, R. E. (2007). Understanding the role of the self in prime-to-behavior effects: The active-self account. *Personality and Social Psychology Review, 11,* 234–261. doi: 10.1177/1088868307302223

Williams, D., Martins, N., Consalvo, M., & Ivory, J. (2009). The virtual census: Representations of gender, race and age in video games. *New Media & Society, 11,* 815–834. doi: 10.1177/1461444809105354

Wilson, R. E., Gosling, S. D., & Graham, L. T. (2012). A review of Facebook research in the social sciences. *Perspectives on Psychological Science, 7,* 203–220. doi: 10.1177/1745691612442904

Zhao, S., Grasmuck, S., & Martin, J. (2008). Identity construction on Facebook: Digital empowerment in anchored relationships. *Computers in Human Behavior, 24,* 1816–1836. doi: 10.1016/j.chb.2008.02.012

Zywica, J., & Danowski, J. (2008). The faces of Facebookers: Investigating social enhancement and social compensation hypothesis. *Journal of Computer-Mediated Communication, 14,* 1–34. doi: 10.1111/j.1083-6101.2008.01429.x

3

MORALITY AND THE SELECTION, RECEPTION, AND EFFECTS OF ENTERTAINMENT MEDIA

Arthur A. Raney and Sophie H. Janicke

Morality is a fundamental part of all social life. Living in a group with any hope of survival requires shared guidelines that establish boundaries around what is and what is not good, proper, and acceptable for communal living. Throughout history, moral codes have evolved around several key principles, including the basic tenet that group-benefitting behaviors should be praised and selfishness should be condemned. In fact, Haidt (2008) contends that the complex and intertwined set of factors that constitute a moral system necessarily all "work together to suppress or regulate selfishness and make social life possible" (p. 70). No doubt, societies negotiate the meaning and boundaries of selfishness differently; moreover, individuals within the same society can hold quite disparate positions on moral (or moralized) issues, reflecting diverse sensitivities toward the moral domains those issues represent. Nevertheless, morality's ultimate function in providing guiding principles for group maintenance is universally the same.

Narratives are likewise a fundamental part of social life and human existence. In fact, many contend that humans are narrative creatures, "story-telling animals" (MacIntyre, 1981, p. 201), "*homo narrans*" (Fisher, 1984, p. 6). As social creatures, the narratives that clutter our minds, fill our conversations, and inhabit out entertainment are unavoidably bound to and contextualized by our group living, built upon the same social superstructure as our "real world" daily lives. It follows then that all narratives—as statements about and reflections upon social living—contain morality. That is, stories are unavoidably social and are therefore, likewise, unavoidably moral.

Quite often—especially in entertainment—moral concerns and issues take center stage, with an existential competition between virtue and vice, good and evil, right and wrong at the heart of the narrative. Consequently, for media consumers, the points of intersection between morality and narrative are numerous. Our subjectively held perspectives on morality can guide the amount and types of media narratives we seek out. Likewise, those perspectives can influence the way that we interpret and enjoy narratives, as stories inescapably reference and offer de facto statements about morality. Finally, given that narratives construct frames around and serve to comment on social life—thus, necessarily the moral components of that life as well—they can prompt moral thinking, potentially leading to (re)consideration and (re)formulation of individual and social moral codes. In this chapter, we examine these three intersections of morality and entertainment narratives through the prism of media psychology.

Morality and Media Entertainment Selection

Numerous perspectives explain why people choose different media entertainment content at different times: mood management theory (e.g., Zillmann, 1988); self-determination theory and intrinsic needs satisfaction (e.g., Tamborini, Bowman, Eden, Grizzard, & Organ, 2010); social identity theory (e.g., Harwood, 1999); uses and gratifications (e.g., Katz, Blumler, & Gurevitch, 1974), to name a few. Moral considerations can also influence media selection. Anecdotally, for instance, those with certain religious (and, in turn, moral) beliefs avoid sexually explicit content; the same is true for some who hold strong moral convictions about gender equality or human rights. Instead, such persons may prefer "wholesome," "family friendly," or others-affirming fare. From a scientific perspective, Nabi and her collaborators (2003) reported that some viewers disliked (and presumably avoided) reality television shows because the shows were "misleading" in their editing, clearly a morally laden critique. Researchers have also examined how specific moral values might predict attraction to certain media that reflects those values, like Oliver and Armstrong (1995) who demonstrated how attitudes about harsh punishment and authoritarianism predicted exposure to crime shows.

From a more holistic perspective, Zillmann (2000) argued that people holding similar moral values constitute morality subcultures; he theorized that one's subculture membership likely predicted media exposure. Synthesizing these ideas with the principles of moral foundation theory, Tamborini (2011, 2013) recently introduced the model of intuitive morality and exemplars (MIME) to explain how sensitivity to certain moral foundations might predict attraction to and enjoyment of media content.

Moral foundation theory (Haidt & Joseph, 2008) purports that moral systems are universally built upon five basic domains: harm and care (issues dealing with compassion and alleviating the suffering of others), fairness (issues dealing with reciprocal altruism, justice, and equity), authority (issues dealing with the negotiation of and respect for social hierarchies), loyalty (issues dealing with bias for one's in-group and against out-groups), and purity (issues dealing with sanctity and concerns over contamination).[1] Although it is thought that moral systems within all cultures have as a foundation these five basic domains, the theory contends that the salience of each domain varies—both across and within cultures—based on socialization and other influences. As a result, people may differ on the relative salience of each domain (perhaps akin to Zillmann's morality subcultures), thereby leading to variation in moral appraisals. Further, moral foundation theory contends that those appraisals—guided by the salient domains—are primarily intuitive; that is, the domains help to shape a chronically accessible moral lens leading most moral evaluations to occur nearly automatically.

Ultimately, then, the MIME attempts to describe how variation in the salience of each of the five moral domains among viewers might predict media use and enjoyment. To be fair, the MIME aims to do much more than this: it is a highly complex attempt to outline the ongoing reciprocal influence of media and morality. But for the sake of the current discussion, we can focus on the elements in the model that explain how domain salience impacts media selection. Similar to previous work on selective processes and cognitive consistency (e.g., Festinger, 1957; Heider, 1958), the MIME assumes that people select, attend to, and enjoy media content that is consistent with and relevant to the moral domains most salient to them. And, given that domain salience guides automatic moral processing, it can be assumed that

> a user's intuitive affective reaction to media content will be positive (i.e., they will judge it moral, and find it appealing) to the extent that they perceive the content as consistent with their overall moral-domain system and negative to the extent they do not.
>
> (Tamborini, 2013, p. 55)

Of course, the model permits that individuals may also willfully seek out morally inconsistent (or challenging) material from time to time. However, according to the MIME, the default guide to media selection is thought to be automatic, based on moral consistency with the salient domains.

A few initial studies, based on the logic of MIME, have examined how domain salience might be associated with preference for certain genres or broad content categories (see Mastro et al., 2013, for a recent overview).

For instance, Tamborini, Eden, Bowman, Grizzard, and Lachlan (2012) found that high harm/care salience was negatively associated with enjoyment of violent media, while those with high fairness salience enjoyed narratives in which justice is restored. This pattern reflects the consistency expectations noted above. Bowman, Dogruel, and Joeckel (2012) also outlined how domain salience predicts the appeal of certain television genres in a study with both U.S. and German participants. In general, those respondents with high harm/care, fairness, and loyalty salience indicated greater preference for news programs, while those low in fairness (and high in authority) salience preferred reality programs more than others. Moving beyond genre appeal to specific narratives, Tamborini and his colleagues showed how patterns of domain salience (measured on the individual-viewer level) can predict the appeal of narratives varying along the five moral domains (i.e., narratives containing more violations of some or of different domains versus others). Not only did the variations in the salience of certain domains predict the appeal of morally consistent narratives, but they also predicted perceptions of character morality within those narratives (Tamborini, Eden, Bowman, Grizzard, Weber, & Lewis, 2013).

From this admittedly brief overview, one can perhaps begin to get a sense of the role that morality plays in the selection of media content on both a general (genre) and specific (narrative) level. A few broad patterns are beginning to emerge from recent work, but these relationships are undoubtedly complex. Domain salience may promote attraction to some content and avoidance of others. Thus, a better understanding is needed of how "conflicting" domains may interact with one another in the media selection process, and how and why the influence of one domain salience might override that of another. Further, we must acknowledge that our specific moral perspectives are not always consistent with the statements made about morality in the resolutions of narratives we chose to watch and enjoy (cf., justice sequences, Raney & Bryant, 2002). In other words, we do not merely seek out narratives that reflect our specific moral belief; in fact, several studies show and our own experiences testify that we enthusiastically seek out and enjoy violations of morality. A next step for scholars in this area is to better understand when media content is sought after because it is consistent with the viewer's real-world morality system and when it is selected specifically because it is not.

Morality and Media Entertainment Reception

As noted above, narratives are necessarily social and are, therefore, inescapably moral. Thus, it should come as no surprise that the narrative reception process occurs at the intersection of a viewer's subjectively held moral perspective and the representations of morality displayed by the characters in the narrative itself. Researchers have explored this intersection from three primary angles: character liking, character plights, and overall enjoyment.

Morality and Character Liking

As depictions of social living, entertainment narratives and the characters that inhabit them are governed by a certain moral code. Without a doubt, those codes are story- (or, possibly, genre-) specific; but as others have noted, narratives constitute and serve as individual statements about moral issues (cf., Carroll, 1990; Raney & Bryant, 2002; Zillmann, 2000). Of course, the moral statements made in narratives are done so through social actors: the characters.

Plenty of extant research establishes that users treat and respond to media characters as social beings (cf., Cohen, this volume). In fact, as media users, we generally respond to characters in the same way we do our real-world friends and enemies, discriminating between those who would help or harm us. To distinguish friend from foe in reality, "we observe others' deliberate action, morally evaluate them as *bad* or *good*, and habitually presume that these judged actions reflect a persistent trait or characteristic. In the world of fiction, moral assessments are likewise applied to form character impressions" (Zillmann, 2013, p. 133). Thus, morality serves as a guide in the relationships we form, real or fictional. Our socialized, moral nature requires that the favor we show to some and not to others be justified, ultimately in line with selfishness and cooperative-living concerns. Of course, partiality— and all moral thinking, for that matter— involves more than just a cognitive evaluation of others; such social judgments generate automatic and appraisal-directed emotional reactions as well. In fact, moral considerations govern the emotional bonds that we form toward others, with those judged to be friends receiving our emotional favor and enemies receiving our disdain.

The line of reasoning just described is at the heart of affective disposition theory (ADT; Zillmann & Cantor, 1976). However, we know that the friend–foe dichotomy is overly simplistic. The theory acknowledges this reality when it comes to the role of morality in character liking. According to ADT, our liking of—or affective dispositions toward— characters grows stronger the more we judge their actions and motivations to be morally proper. Similarly, our liking of characters decreases (and disdain increases) the more we judge their actions and motivations to be morally incorrect. In turn, we react emotionally to and in concert with the valence and intensity of our dispositions. Additional factors— such as character attractiveness, plot, genre, viewer mood—undeniably also influence character liking. But ADT studies have consistently demonstrated that moral considerations are central to the process of character liking (Raney, 2002, 2005; Zillmann & Bryant, 1975).

It logically follows, then, that variation in viewer morality impacts the formation of dispositions toward characters. Researchers have empirically demonstrated this in several studies. For instance, measures or markers of morality like religiosity (Tamborini et al., 2012) and authoritarianism (Oliver, 1996) have been shown to predict differences in character liking. Raney (2002, 2005) reported that moral attitudes concerning vigilante forms of justice and harsh forms of punishment predicted differences in sympathy experienced toward protagonist–victims in crime–punishment narratives. Research conducted within the MIME framework showed that increased salience in the fairness domain moderated the moral approbation of a protagonist's behavior when the fairness domain was violated, which in turn predicted liking of the character (Tamborini et al., 2012). Tamborini, Grizzard, Eden, and Lewis (2011) also demonstrated that character liking increases the more a character upholds certain moral domains.

Morality and Character Plights

Narrative characters—like our real-world friends—are not static; the unfolding plot or storyline in which they are involved constitutes their "lives." Life, of course, is filled with peaks and valleys, successes and failure, gains and losses. These highs and lows are often thought to represent an existential battle between good and evil, with the morally proper result being victory for ourselves and our friends and defeat of our enemies. This moral conflict between good and evil is also the crux of dramatic narrative entertainment (cf., Vorderer & Knobloch, 2000), with the plot revealing the ongoing plights of characters as they participate in moral battle. Media users develop and experience anticipatory (and morally consistent) emotions toward characters in line with the affective dispositions. That is, we hope for beloved characters to find happiness, experience success, reach fulfillment, and we dread the thought of our/their hated enemies doing the same. These anticipations are morally proper in our eyes because it is right and good for our friends to receive such and wrong and bad if our enemies do. As a result, media users constantly render judgments about how morally warranted or unwarranted outcomes within the narrative may be (cf., Raney & Bryant, 2002; Zillmann, 2000, 2013).

Several studies have shown how differences in viewer morality not only predict disposition formation but also judgments of within-narrative plot points and outcomes. For instance, Zillmann and Bryant (1975) found that children at different Piagetian stages of (moral) development reacted in different and predictable ways when a character in a fairy tale was punished too mildly or too severely. Raney (2005) also demonstrated how differences in certain social-justice attitudes predicted ratings of deservedness for harsh punishment doled out to a villain in a crime drama. Additionally, a recent study found that viewers of an antihero film in Germany and the United States—two countries that may reflect (at least slightly) different moral cultures—evaluated the immoral actions of the protagonists differently, with the U.S. sample evaluating the moral transgressions less harshly than their German counterparts (Janicke & Podwalski, 2012). Furthermore, Tamborini, Eden, Bowman, Grizzard, Weber, and Lewis (2013) found that domain salience predicted negative perceptions of media characters violating those respective domains, which consequently affected the appeal of the narrative.

Morality and Narrative Enjoyment

We have already noted the role of morality in the formation of dispositions toward media characters, as outlined by ADT. Further, we have noted how morality guides interpretations and reactions to the unfolding events in the narrative; though we did not state it above, this too is described in the ADT literature. But ultimately, the primary function of ADT is to explain the overall process of enjoying mediated narratives. The theory describes how overall enjoyment is a function of both the affective dispositions held toward characters and the outcomes associated with those characters in the unfolding story. Enjoyment is thought to increase when liked characters experience positive outcomes and/or when disliked characters experience negative ones. Conversely, enjoyment suffers when liked characters experience negative outcomes and/or disliked characters experience positive ones. In keeping with the discussion throughout, at the heart of this seemingly obvious formula is a complex set of moral-judgment ingredients.

As noted above, all narratives (as social scripts) can be seen as making statements about morality. Raney and Bryant (2002) perhaps addressed this reality most directly when describing crime–punishment narratives as a justice sequence, described as one or more scenes in which instigational and retributional actions are presented leading to an ultimate narrative resolution and resulting in a statement about justice being made. The application of these ideas to other dramatic genres is obvious. For every conflict there exists at least one resolution; and with most narratives, the resolution generally portrays a victor and a vanquished. Given the moral lens through which those labels are applied in the first place, it follows that narrative resolutions are moral statements. Enjoyment—arguably, in large part—boils down to an evaluation by the viewer of the moral acceptability of that statement. Media users generally think that it is morally proper for the protagonist to succeed and the antagonist to fail. Such a resolution is not simply what we want to happen, but what we think should happen. Enjoyment in turn increases in such cases, relative to the strength of the dispositions held toward the characters. The ADT literature supports this logic across a variety of genres: drama (e.g., Zillmann &

Cantor, 1976), soap operas (e.g., Weber, Tamborini, Lee, & Stipp, 2008), sports (e.g., Zillmann, Bryant, & Sapolsky, 1989), humor (e.g., Zillmann & Cantor, 1976), news (e.g., Zillmann, Taylor, & Lewis, 1998), fright-inducing entertainment (e.g., Oliver, 1993), action films (e.g., King, 2000), and reality-based programming (e.g., Oliver, 1996).

Nevertheless, as has been seen in other processes, variability in viewer morality should (and does) lead to differences in enjoyment. Many of the studies already cited also demonstrate this reality: stages of moral development predicted enjoyment of fairy tales among children (Zillmann & Bryant, 1975), authoritarianism predicted enjoyment of reality television (Oliver, 1996), and vigilantism and punitiveness predicted enjoyment of crime drama (Raney, 2002, 2005). Tamborini and his colleagues also demonstrated that the appeal of graphic and justified violent drama can be predicted specifically by the harm and fairness domains (Tamborini et al., 2012). Additionally, Lewis, Tamborini, Grizzard, Weber, and Prabhu (2012) showed that individuals high in harm and fairness appreciated (rather than enjoyed; cf., Oliver & Bartsch, 2010) a narrative with a mixed moral resolution more than participants at lower levels of those respective domains.

The research record is unequivocal that enjoyment is linked to the moral approval of the victorious character, who most often is the hero protagonist. However, not all protagonists are equally moral. In fact, films like *Natural Born Killers* and *V for Vendetta* and TV shows like *Dexter* and *Breaking Bad* celebrate decidedly immoral characters. And, as we all know, viewers still love them. Our own research on this phenomenon indicates that viewers actually enjoy these antihero or morally complex narratives differently than traditional hero ones (Raney & Janicke, 2013). In short, such narratives offer justification for the protagonists' moral failings through various plot cues (cf. Hartmann & Vorderer, 2010), which then permit the viewer to (re)interpret the actions and motivations as morally appropriate. The mechanism underlying this process is moral disengagement (Bandura, 1986, 1999), a set of attitude-defensive strategies that allow us to avoid moral self-condemnation when we behave in morally questionable ways ourselves (e.g., intentionally exceeding the speed limit, telling a fib).

Shafer and Raney (2012) reported evidence suggesting that frequent viewers of antihero narratives develop cognitive schema that permit ready activation of the moral-disengagement process via the in-story cues, thereby facilitating enjoyment. But despite the (perhaps misleading) term moral *dis*engagement, the authors argue that moral considerations are in fact quite engaged during antihero narratives. These stories instead create scenarios wherein a different set of behaviors and motivations are (at least temporarily) judged to be morally permissible. Additional studies have lent support to this general argument (Hartmann & Vorderer, 2010; Janicke

& Podwalski, 2012; Krakowiak & Tsay, 2011; Krakowiak & Tsay-Vogel, 2013).

As the level of detail in this section may suggest, a good amount of scientific attention has been paid to the role of morality during the reception of entertainment. However, the field is still fairly young. The coming years will certainly see, for instance, the MIME applied to a variety of contents and in a variety of contexts. As alluded to earlier, one possible area of inquiry is how competing moral domains may be activated during viewing. For example, a storyline in which a young, heavily tattooed, dark-skinned male is racially profiled by a police officer is rife with multiple moral considerations, including fairness and care (which might lead to a negative moral–emotional response in some) and authority (which might lead to a less negative/even positive moral–emotional response in others). Researchers should strive to understand such complex interactions.

Further, virtually all of the research outlined in this section has measured *in situ* moral considerations *post situ*. That is, online measurement of moral activation and contemplation is rare. And when it has been attempted, it unavoidably introduced artificiality to the viewing situation. Put plainly: Because morality is pervasive and constant, one can naturally respond to moral questions when posed about any social situation. But it remains unclear whether those moral considerations and evaluation were generated during the course of the situation—in this case, while consuming media—or only generated after the fact, in response to the line of questioning. Researchers should explore ways to examine moral reactions to media in an unobtrusive, naturalistic manner. Raney (2013) offered one possible approach: Content analyses of social media feeds during first-run television broadcasts. Such an approach, and others like it, should be developed and utilized in the coming years.

Morality and the Effects of Media Entertainment

For centuries, entertainment's effect on individual morality has been questioned and debated by philosophers, religious leaders, parents, educators, and politicians. Consensus opinion has been that entertainment (potentially and predominately) breeds moral corruption and decay. In many ways, the entire effects tradition within media psychology has served to empirically examine, verify, or refute such claims. As such, one could argue that the bulk of media effects scholarship primarily examines morality: increased aggressive thoughts and behaviors, perpetuation of racial and ethnic stereotyping, promotion of unhealthy sexual attitudes and practices, biased (or unfair) processing of messages, adoption of prosocial behaviors modeled in children's educational television. However, taking such a broad, brushstroke perspective on this issue is perhaps of little benefit to the current discussion. In recent years, two new lines of research—inspired by and related to moral foundation theory—have emerged and have begun to paint a more fine-grained picture of the potential effects of entertainment on morality and moral thinking.

Media Entertainment and Moral Domain Salience

One line of this research centers on the question: Does consuming media narratives lead to moral thinking/processing? Undoubtedly, we have all had the experience of walking out of a movie theater after watching films like *Schindler's List, Juno,* or *Django Unchained,* talking about the moral dilemmas faced by the characters. Such examples provide an obvious answer to the question. But what about narratives in which morality is less overtly a part of the plot? If all narratives involve morality, then is your individual moral sense activated when consuming *all* entertainment?

As noted above, the MIME attempts to outline the potential reciprocal effects of morality and media consumption, with moral foundation theory serving as an underlying theoretical structure. With regard to effects, the model seeks to explain (among other things) how media exposure may increase the salience of the five moral domains. This is indeed a difficult task as moral foundation theory argues that domain salience/activation is intuitive and, as a result, extremely difficult to measure. MIME researchers have recently used implicit measures in an attempt to gauge the priming effect of media messages on intuitive morality and domain salience. Their efforts have been met with tentative success.

In one study, participants were primed with either a morally positive media exemplar (Superman, superheroes in general), a morally negative media exemplar (The Joker, supervillains in general), or neither (Tamborini, Grizzard, Eden, & Lewis, 2011). An affective misattribution procedure (AMP) was used to examine whether the morally laden media character activated affective moral evaluations in general (i.e., not specific domains). The AMP required participants to rate a series of neutral targets—in this case, Chinese characters—as either pleasant or unpleasant, following the brief display of a morally positive or negative picture. The researchers predicted that those primed with a morally positive media character would rate the neutral targets as pleasant significantly more often following morally positive images. Results trended in this direction, seeming to suggest that a morally laden media character can activate intuitive morality (though perhaps only weakly and for a short period of time).

Several follow-up studies—using similar procedures but relying on morally laden words in the AMP rather than images—have lent additional and somewhat stronger support to this claim. These studies have demonstrated that media narratives highlighting specific moral domains (especially in the climactic scene) may, at least temporarily, increase the salience of those domains in viewers (Grizzard, Tamborini, Lewis, & Wang, 2012;

Tamborini, Lewis, Prabhu, Grizzard, & Eden, 2012; Tamborini, Lewis, Prabhu, Grizzard, & Wang, 2012). Furthermore, one study in which moral salience was primed with news stories rather than entertainment content revealed that repeated moral priming may increase domain salience for at least 24 hours (Tamborini, Prabhu, Wang, & Grizzard, 2013).

Observing the increased salience of certain domains after exposure is definitely one step in a positive direction toward examining media content's direct impact on morality. Further, finding that media can activate domain salience for extended periods of time certainly holds promise for us better understanding the cumulative and long-term effects of exposure. But activation of intuitive morality may not necessarily equate with conscious moral thinking. It remains to be understood how media portrayals can prompt moral contemplation. Under what conditions do media make us *think* morally? Further, literature on selective perception and biased processing of messages consistently reports how different viewers can form quite disparate attitudes and draw completely different conclusions after exposure to the same media content (e.g., Houston & Fazio, 1989; Vidmar & Rokeach, 1974). It stands to reason that activation of moral domains may occur simultaneously across many viewers, but the interpretation of the moral messages that trigger such activation may result in quite different moral processing, moral thought, and moral impacts in both the short and long term. Scholars are encouraged to begin tacking these issues as well.

Media Entertainment and Moral Emotions

The second line of research deals with media's ability to elicit social emotions, or more specific to our current discussion, the subset known as moral emotions. These emotions are those "linked to the interests or welfare either of society as a whole or at least persons other than" ourselves (Haidt, 2003, p. 853); they are activated as a result of our ability to understand the mental states of others. Moral psychologists disagree over which emotions are or are not moral, but many typologies include anger, compassion, contempt, disgust, embarrassment, empathy, guilt, and shame, among others. Many of the emotional responses we experience toward media are moral in nature, with empathy arguably receiving the most scholarly attention (Hoffmann, 1987; Zillmann, 1994).

One longstanding line of research dealing with moral emotions has examined the conscious-numbing (or desensitizing) role of exposure to various forms of media. In truth, this phenomenon is typically measured as a decrease over time in physiological arousal in response to otherwise emotion-inducing media; however, assumptions about accompanying (or resulting) psychological effects are also often made. For instance, many studies suggest that repeated exposure to media violence is associated with a dampening of emotional—often conceptualized as empathic—response to such fare, with the fear that such effects might transfer to less sensitivity toward real-world violence or even increased likelihood of actual aggression (for a recent summary, Bushman, Huesmann, & Whitaker, 2009). Similarly, researchers have noted that long-term exposure to sexually explicit materials can lead to decreased arousal toward the material, increased callousness toward women—again, seemingly related to empathy—and recommendations of less severe punishments for those convicted of (fictional) rape (Zillmann & Bryant, 1984). Finally, repeated video game play has been associated with decreased feelings of guilt about immoral in-game decisions and actions (Grizzard & Tamborini, 2013).

But not all effects of media on moral emotions are negative. Oliver and Raney (2011) demonstrated how users are at times motivated to consume media for the purpose of truth seeking and contemplating human meaningfulness. Such research highlights how viewers can and do seek out entertainment experiences that are more than simple, pleasurable diversions and means to escape. The content associated with those experiences

> can be understood as increasingly meaningful when it focuses to a greater extent on questions of human moral virtues, it demonstrates such virtues (or the ramifications of the lack thereof), it teaches or inspires insight into these virtues, or it causes the viewer to contemplate them and what it means to live a "just" or "true" life.
>
> (Oliver & Bartsch, 2011, p. 31)

Further, such media encounters offer an opportunity to experience positive moral emotions—like awe, gratitude, and elevation—that simultaneously encourage users to explore the humanity within themselves and also to acknowledge and appreciate their connections to the larger social structure. Keltner and Haidt (2003) argued that "songs, symphonies, movie, plays, and paintings" (p. 310) can lead people to experience awe. Moreover, Oliver, Hartmann, and Woolley (2012) reported how viewers find some sad and tragic films to be "meaningful" because they portray moral virtue and beauty, promote heightened feelings of the moral emotion elevation, and even motivate people to think about leading a more moral and meaningful life themselves. The exploration of media's role in promoting positive moral emotions has truly just begun. But given the increased availability of "good news" (e.g., HuffingtonPost.com/goodnews) and inspiring viral videos (e.g., Upworthy.com) across the Internet, many important years of work in this area lie ahead.

Concluding Thoughts

The purpose of this chapter was to identify various points of intersection between morality and entertainment media use. In closing, we mention one point that we hope is not lost herein: These intersections are ultimately important because they reflect, maintain, reinforce, and perhaps even alter our social lives. As noted above, the meaning and boundaries of morality are constantly being negotiated within all societies. Your individual view of those boundaries is likewise a work in progress, informed by the stories (both real and fictional) that fill your days. Those moral parameters—reflected in the relative salience of moral domains and in the moral attitudes you hold dear—influence what entertainment you consume and how you receive and interpret those messages. Ultimately, those experiences reify, challenge, or perhaps encourage you to think about those parameters, which necessarily guide your social interactions.

Note

1 Recently, a sixth moral foundation—liberty/oppression—has been added to the theory, although to our knowledge no media-related research has examined this domain.

References

Bandura, A. (1986). *Social foundations of thought and action: A social cognitive theory*. Englewood Cliffs, NJ: Prentice Hall.

Bandura, A. (1999). Moral disengagement in the perpetuation of inhumanities. *Personality and Social Psychology Review, 3*, 193–209. doi: 10.1207/s15327957pspr0303_3

Bowman, N. D., Dogruel, L. & Joeckel, S. (2012). A question of morality? Moral salience and nationality on media choices. *Communications: A European Journal of Communication Research, 27*, 345–369.

Bushman, B. J., Huesmann, L. R., & Whitaker, J. l. (2009). Violent media effects. In R. L. Nabi & M. B. Oliver (Eds.), *The SAGE handbook of media processes and effects* (pp. 361–376). Thousand Oaks, CA: Sage.

Carroll, N. (1990). *The philosophy of horror or paradoxes of the heart*. New York: Routledge.

Festinger, L. (1957). *A theory of cognitive dissonance*. Stanford, CA: Stanford University Press.

Fisher, W. R. (1984). Narration as a human communication paradigm: The case of public moral argument. *Communication Monographs, 51*, 1–22. doi: 10.1080/03637758409390180

Grizzard, M., & Tamborini, R. (2013, June). *Video games, moral emotions, and repeated play: The desensitizing effect of repeated play on the ability of virtual behaviors to elicit guilt*. Paper presented at the annual meeting of the International Communication Association, London, UK.

Grizzard, M., Tamborini, R., Lewis, R. J., & Wang, L. (2012, November). *Being bad in a video game makes us more morally sensitive: Video game play, moral emotions, and moral intuitions*. Paper presented at the annual meeting of the National Communication Association, Orlando, FL.

Haidt, J. (2003). The moral emotions. In R. J. Davidson, K. R. Scherer, & H. H. Goldsmith (Eds.), *Handbook of affective sciences* (pp. 852–870). Oxford: Oxford University Press.

Haidt, J. (2008). Morality. *Perspectives on Psychological Science, 3*, 65–72. doi: 10.1111/j.1745-6916.2008.00063.x

Haidt, J., & Joseph, C. (2008). The moral mind: How five sets of innate intuitions guide the development of many culture-specific virtues, and perhaps even modules. In P. Carruthers, S. Laurence, & S. Stich (Eds.) *The innate mind*, Vol. 3. (pp. 367–391). New York: Oxford.

Hartmann, T. & Vorderer, P. (2010). It's okay to shoot a character: Moral disengagement in violent video games. *Journal of Communication, 60*, 94–119. doi: 10.1111/j.1460-2466.2009.01459.x

Harwood, J. (1999). Age identity and television viewing preferences. *Communication Reports, 12*, 85–90.

Heider, F. (1958). *The psychology of interpersonal relations*. New York: Wiley.

Hoffmann, M. L. (1987). The contribution of empathy to justice and moral judgment. In N. Eisenberg & J. Strayer (Eds.), *Empathy and its development* (pp. 47–80). Cambridge, UK: Cambridge University Press.

Houston, D. A., & Fazio. R. H. (1989). Biased processing as a function of attitude accessibility: Making objective judgments subjectively. *Social Cognition, 7*, 51–66. doi: 10.1521/soco.1989.7.1.51

Janicke, S. H., & Podwalski, P. (2012, November). *Differences in antihero enjoyment between Germany and the US.* Paper presented at the annual meeting of the National Communication Association, Orlando, FL.

Katz, E., Blumler, G., & Gurevitch, M. (1974). Utilization of mass communication by the individual. In J. G. Blumler & E. Katz (Eds.), *The uses of mass communications* (pp. 19–34). Beverly Hills, CA: Sage.

Keltner, D., & Haidt, J. (2003). Approaching awe, a moral, spiritual, and aesthetic emotion. *Cognition & Emotion, 17*, 297–314. doi: /10.1080/02699930302297

King, C. M. (2000). Effects of humorous heroes and villains in violent action films. *Journal of Communication, 50*, 5–24. doi: 10.1093/joc/50.1.5

Krakowiak, K. M., & Tsay, M. (2011). The role of moral disengagement in the enjoyment of real and fictional characters. *International Journal of Arts and Technology, 4*, 90–101. doi: 10.1504/IJART.2011.037772

Krakowiak, K. M., & Tsay-Vogel, M. (2013). What makes characters' bad behaviors acceptable? The effects of character motivation and outcome on perceptions, character liking, and moral disengagement. *Mass Communication and Society, 16*, 179–199. doi: 10.1080/15205436.2012.690926

Lewis, R. J., Tamborini, R., Grizzard, M., Weber, R., & Prabhu, S. (2012, May). *Reactions to moral conflict in narrative entertainment: The moderating influence of moral intuitions.* Paper presented at the annual meeting of the International Communication Association Conference, Boston, MA.

MacIntyre, A. (1981). *After virtue: A study in moral theory.* South Bend, IN: University of Notre Dame Press.

Mastro, D., Enriquez, M., Bowman, N. D., Prabhu, S., & Tamborini, R. (2013). Morality subcultures and media production: How Hollywood minds the morals of its audience. In R. Tamborini (Ed.), *Media and the moral mind* (pp. 75–109). London: Routledge.

Nabi, R. L., Biely, E. N., Morgan, S. J., & Stitt, C.R. (2003). Reality-based television programming and the psychology of its appeal. *Media Psychology, 5,* 303–330. doi: 10.1207/S1532785XMEP0504_01

Oliver, M. B. (1993). Adolescents' enjoyment of graphic horror: Effects of attitudes and portrayals of victim. *Communication Research, 20,* 30–50. doi: 10.1177/009365093020001002

Oliver, M. B. (1996). Influences of authoritarianism and portrayals of race on Caucasian viewers' responses to reality-based prime dramas. *Communication Reports, 9,* 141–150.

Oliver, M. B., & Armstrong, B. G. (1995). Predictors of viewing and enjoyment of reality-based and fictional crime shows. *Journalism and Mass Communication Quarterly, 72,* 559–570. doi: 10.1177/107769909507200307

Oliver, M. B., & Bartsch, A. (2010). Appreciation as audience response: Exploring entertainment gratifications beyond hedonism. *Human Communication Research, 36*(1), 53–81. doi:10.1111/j.1468-2958.2009.01368.x

Oliver, M. B. & Bartsch, A. (2011). Appreciation of entertainment. The importance of meaningfulness via virtue and wisdom. *Journal of Media Psychology, 23,* 29–33. doi: 10.1027/1864-1105/a000029

Oliver, M. B., & Raney, A. A. (2011). Entertainment as pleasurable and meaningful: Differentiating hedonic and eudaimonic motivations for entertainment consumption. *Journal of Communication, 61,* 984–1004. doi: 10.1111/j.1460-2466.2011.01585.x

Oliver, M. B., Hartmann, T., & Woolley, J. K. (2012). Elevation in response to entertainment portrayals of moral virtue. *Human Communication Research, 38,* 360–378. doi: 10.1111/j.1468-2958.2012.01427.x

Raney, A. A. (2002). Moral judgment as a predictor of enjoyment of crime drama. *Media Psychology, 4,* 307–324. doi: 10.1207/S1532785XMEP0404_01

Raney, A. A. (2005). Punishing media criminals and moral judgment: The impact on enjoyment. *Media Psychology, 7,* 145–163. doi: 10.1207/S1532785XMEP0702_2

Raney, A. A. (2013, April). *Morality, moral thinking, and media entertainment.* Keynote address presented at the Broadcast Education Association 2013 Research Symposium (Media and Social Life), Las Vegas, NV.

Raney, A. A., & Bryant, J. (2002). Moral judgment and crime drama: An integrated theory of enjoyment. *Journal of Communication, 52,* 402–415. doi: 10.1093/joc/52.2.402

Raney, A. A., & Janicke, S. (2013). How we enjoy and why we seek out morally complex characters in media entertainment. In R. Tamborini (Ed.), *Media and the moral mind* (pp. 152–169). London: Routledge.

Shafer, D. M. & Raney, A. A. (2012). Exploring how we enjoy antihero narratives. *Journal of Communication, 63,* 1–19. doi: 10.1111/j.1460-2466.2012.01682.x

Tamborini, R. (2011). Moral intuition and media entertainment. *Journal of Media Psychology: Theories, Methods, and Applications, 23*(1), 2011, 39–45. doi: 10.1027/1864-1105/a000031

Tamborini, R. (2013). A model of intuitive morality and exemplars. In R. Tamborini (Ed.), *Media and the moral mind* (pp. 43–74). London: Routledge.

Tamborini, R., Bowman, N. D., Eden, A., Grizzard, M., & Organ, A. (2010). Defining media enjoyment as the satisfaction of intrinsic needs. *Journal of Communication, 60,* 758–777. doi:10.1111/j.1460-2466.2010.01513.x.

Tamborini, R., Eden, A., Bowman, N. D., Grizzard, M., & Lachlan, K. (2012). The influence of morality subcultures on the acceptance and appeal of violence. *Journal of Communication, 62,* 136–157. doi:10.1111/j.1460-2466.2011.01620.x

Tamborini, R., Eden, A., Bowman, N. D., Grizzard, M., Weber, R., & Lewis, R. J. (2013). Predicting media appeal from instinctive moral values. *Mass Communication and Society, 16,* 325–346. doi: 10.1080/15205436.2012.703285.

Tamborini, R., Grizzard, M. N., Eden, A., & Lewis, R. J. (2011, November). *Priming intuitive morality: The effect of heroes and villains on immediate affective response to moral stimuli.* Paper presented at the annual meeting of the National Communication Association, New Orleans, LA.

Tamborini, R., Lewis, R. J., Prabhu, S., Grizzard, M., & Eden, A. (2012, May). *Priming morality: The influence of media exposure on moral intuitions.* Paper presented at the annual meeting of the International Communication Association, Phoenix, AZ.

Tamborini, R., Lewis, R.J., Prabhu, S., Grizzard, M., & Wang, L. (2012, October). *Media's influence on the salience of moral intuitions and egoistic motivations.* Paper presented at the annual meeting of the National Communication Association, Orlando, FL.

Tamborini, R., Prabhu, S., Wang, L., & Grizzard, M. (2013, June). *Setting the moral agenda: News exposure's influence on the salience of moral intuitions.* Paper presented at the annual meeting of the International Communication Association, London, UK.

Vidmar, N. and Rokeach, M. (1974). Archie Bunker's bigotry: A study in selective perception and exposure. *Journal of Communication, 24,* 36–47. doi: 10.1111/j.1460-2466.1974.tb00353.x

Vorderer, P., & Knobloch, S. (2000). Conflict and suspense in drama. In D. Zillmann & P. Vorderer (Eds.), *Media entertainment: The psychology of its appeal* (pp. 59–72). Mahwah, NJ: Erlbaum.

Weber, R., Tamborini, R., Lee, H. E., & Stipp, H. (2008). Soap opera exposure and enjoyment: A longitudinal test of disposition theory. *Media Psychology, 11,* 462–487. doi: 10.1080/15213260802509993

Zillmann, D. (1988). Mood management: Using entertainment to full advantage. In L. Donohew, H. E. Sypher, & E. T. Higgins (Eds.), *Communication, social cognition, and affect* (pp. 147–171). Hillsdale, NJ: Erlbaum.

Zillmann, D. (1994). Mechanisms of emotional involvement with drama. *Poetics, 23,* 33–51. doi: 10.1016/0304-422X(94)00020-7

Zillmann, D. (2000). Basal morality in drama appreciation. In I. Bondebjerg (Ed.), *Moving images, culture and the mind* (pp. 53–63). Luton, UK: Luton University Press.

Zillmann, D. (2013). Moral monitoring and emotionality in responding to fiction, sports, and the news. In R. Tamborini (Ed.), *Media and the moral mind* (pp. 132–152). London: Routledge.

Zillmann, D., & Bryant, J. (1975). Viewer's moral sanction of retribution in the appreciation of dramatic presentations. *Journal of Experimental Social Psychology, 11,* 572–582. doi: 10.1016/0022-1031(75)90008-6

Zillmann, D., & Bryant, J. (1984). Effects of massive exposure to pornography. In N. M. Malamuth & E. Donnerstein (Eds.), *Pornography and sexual aggression* (pp. 115–138). Orlando, FL: Academic Press.

Zillmann, D., Bryant, J., & Sapolsky, B. S. (1989). Enjoyment from sports specta-
torship. In. J. H. Goldstein (Eds.), *Sports, games, and play: Social and psychological viewpoints* (2nd ed., pp. 241–278). Hillsdale, NJ: Erlbaum.

Zillmann, D., & Cantor, J. (1976). A disposition theory of humor and mirth. In
A. J. Chapman & H. C. Foot (Eds.), *Humour and laughter: Theory, research
and applications* (pp. 93–115). London: John Wiley & Sons.

Zillmann, D., Taylor, K., & Lewis, K. (1998). News as nonfiction theater:
How dispositions toward the public cast of characters affect reactions.
Journal of Broadcasting and Electronic Media, 42, 153–169. doi: 10.1080/
08838159809364441

4

MEDIA AND SPIRITUALITY

Srividya Ramasubramanian

Although most of the research on media and social life has focused on negative media effects such as aggression, dependency, stereotyping, inter-group conflict, and addiction, media can also serve as a tool for self-enhancement, community development, and a sense of connectedness. They can enhance positive human values such as dignity, love, compassion, respect, resilience, and gratitude. They can lead us towards higher aspirations to thrive and blossom to our fullest abilities. Media can help us go beyond our mundane existence to expand our circle of belongingness, to see the humanity in all while still appreciating diversity, to admire the beauty and awe of nature, to serve selflessly for the common good, and to enable us to experience transcendence. This chapter on media and spirituality sheds more light on the transformative, inspirational, prosocial, and informative aspects of media and social life.

Millions of people around the world are seeking various types of spiritual media content on a regular basis. Meditation sites online, spiritual television channels, soul-stirring songs, books by spiritual leaders, meaningful movies, "apps" for spirituality, web-based quizzes about sacred texts, online prayer exchanges, comics on spiritual leaders, and inspirational quotes shared on social networks are some of the ways in which spirituality is incorporated into media. While specific statistics for websites, Twitter accounts, or apps related to spirituality are not readily available, they certainly occupy a significant space in contemporary new media environments.[1] For instance, spiritual leaders such as the Dalai Lama and Deepak Chopra and daily quotes from sacred texts such as the Bible, Zen Buddhism, and Sufi poetry have millions of followers on Twitter and Facebook. News aggregators such as *Huffington Post* have started incorporating "good news" on their sites. Elevating videos of people's random acts of extreme kindness—such as the picture of a New York Police Department (NYPD) officer giving away his boots to a homeless needy person—routinely go viral on social networks. Educational videos for social good are being produced by social entrepreneurs such as the Khan Academy. Research shows that 1.7 million webpages online host religious/spiritual content, and of these, 51 million are devoted to religion/spirituality (Hojsgaard & Warburg, 2005). Several spiritual organizations have set up websites online that offer electronic services such as virtual blessings from enlightened masters, live streaming of sacred temples/pilgrimage sites, video/podcasts of spiritual leaders, and information about services/community activities around the world, thus merging the real with the mediated, and the sacred with the secular in interesting ways.

Despite the prevalence of spirituality-oriented messages in the media, the research topic of media and spirituality has received very little attention within the field of communication, especially from empirical, social scientists working in the media-effects tradition. In fact, Roxanne Parrott (2004) calls this a "collective amnesia." Academics are often uncomfortable talking about spirituality and religion, which may be seen as a personal, subjective, and value-laden experience. Some scholars might consider spirituality to be the opposite of science, thus putting their scientific, rational thinking in conflict with their religious, spiritual beliefs. However, there is no denying that spiritual media content is very popular amongst audiences and warrants systematic, objective, and critical analyses by media scholars. In fields such as medicine, nursing, and management, spirituality has already received considerable research attention. Spirituality and science need not be seen as opposites. Indeed, new areas of research such as positive psychology, contemplative sciences, and inner sciences take a systematic, scientific approach to the study of spirituality.

Of the very little research on spirituality that has been conducted within the field of communication, most of it has been in the context of health communication and organizational communication. Media and spirituality is a broad and untapped area of research study. In this chapter, I will examine the conceptual and empirical definitions of spirituality, review various theoretical approaches in the study of media and spirituality, consider the role of new media for the study of spirituality, and point to some future directions for this important yet under-studied topic area.

Conceptualizing Spirituality

Spirituality is a complex, multifaceted, and much-contested term. Within the scholarship on media and spirituality, there is a lack of clarity about how spirituality is defined, in what ways it is different from or similar to religion, and a theoretical framework to study this topic. Bash (2004) contends that spiritual experiences are too personal and subjective. From

this perspective, spirituality cannot be categorized, generalized, or measured empirically. Therefore, examining spirituality using "scientific models and the language of empiricism are simply not relevant" (Bash, 2004,
p. 14). Along with fellow scholars of contemplative sciences, interiority
studies, and positive psychology, I argue that spirituality is a valid area
of inquiry. Qualitative methodological approaches can be used to capture
these personalized spiritual experiences. Quantitative measures should be
developed to group, measure, and classify spirituality.

Non-Theistic and Theistic Definitions of Spirituality

In this section, I distinguish non-theistic and theistic definitions of spirituality. Theistic definitions of spirituality are further divided into Abrahamic
and Dharmic forms of spirituality (see Figure 4.1).

The non-theistic definition of spirituality focuses on belongingness
(Howse, 1999), meaningfulness (Gilmartin, 1996), connectedness, and
self-transcendence by shifting the focus from the self to serving others for
the common good (Gilmartin, 1996). This idea of focusing on the meaning
and purpose of life and on positive values such as appreciation and altruism
is also emphasized in positive psychology (Seligman & Csikszentmihalyi,
2000). Bringing these various aspects of spirituality together, non-theistic
spirituality has been defined as purpose or meaning in life, transcendence,
connectedness, a search for the sacred, connectedness, and self-sacrifice
(Emmons, 2006; Klenke, 2007).

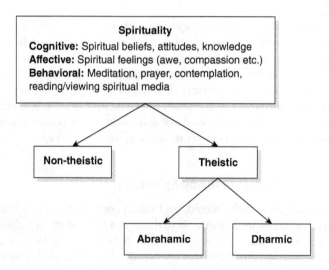

Figure 4.1 Conceptualizing the various dimensions of spirituality

The theistic approach, on the other hand, focuses on recognizing a higher power or force in the universe with which one forms a personal relationship (King, Speck, & Thomas, 1999; Scherurs, 2002). Within theistic traditions, there are slight differences between Abrahamic and Dharmic forms of spirituality. Abrahamic (Judeo-Christian-Islamic) perspectives on spirituality differ from the Dharmic (Buddhist, Hindu, and Jain) traditions in how the self is perceived in relation to the universe and to the higher power (Tsai, Miao, & Seppala, 2007).[2] Dharmic traditions have pioneered interiority studies and contemplative sciences for several millennia by focusing on ideas such as mindfulness, inner sciences (*adyaatmika vidyaa* in Sanskrit), and *samyama* (a Sanskrit word roughly translated as the union of concentration, contemplation, and equanimity) (Malathi, Damodaran, Shah, Patil, & Marathe, 1999; Schreiner, 2009). From the Dharmic perspective, spirituality is about connecting with the divine within one's own self and also about celebrating the communion between the individual spirit and the universal consciousness. In Abrahamic traditions, spirituality is about the existence of a transcendental force beyond the self and truth is based on gospels revealed to prophets. Meditation, contemplation, and individual inquiry are central to Dharmic traditions, whereas prayer, scriptural knowledge, and religious authority are central to Abrahamic traditions.

Theistic approaches are often taken by scholars studying media and religion, with *spirituality* and *religion* often being used as interchangeable terms (Campbell, 2005; Helland, 2000). The media scholarship on religion has largely examined religious practices and rituals, especially in online religious communities. However, there are many ways in which religion and spirituality might have different meanings for media users. Religion is often seen as institutionalized and organized and also responsible for intergroup violence, conflict, and tribalism today. In contrast, spirituality is increasingly perceived as a transformative identity for social change and personal growth. It is envisioned as a purer, more personalized form of religion without its dogma, politics, and institutional authority. Some others consider New Age spirituality as consumerist, neoliberal, and capitalistic in that it serves elitist interests without reaching out to a broader base of people. It is important for communication scholars to take into account such differences in how individuals conceptualize spirituality while taking a global, transnational, and spiritually pluralistic approach to the study of spirituality and the media. These distinctions in the approaches to spirituality also have implications for how spirituality is conceptualized, operationalized, and theorized for media studies.

Cognitive, Affective, and Behavioral Dimensions of Spirituality

As noted above, spirituality is a multifaceted construct that can be further divided into many dimensions. At the individual level, it can be divided into three primary dimensions: cognitive (spiritual beliefs), affective (spiritual feelings), and behaviors (spiritual behaviors).

Cognitive Dimension of Spirituality

The cognitive dimension of spirituality focuses on spiritual beliefs, attitudes, and knowledge. These relate to meaning/purpose in life, mindfulness, connectedness, belongingness, transcendence, inner peace, wholeness, virtue, social responsibility, and wisdom. Media content has the potential to shape, activate, reinforce, or change one's spiritual beliefs, knowledge, and opinions. However, research on these topics has not yet been examined with much depth. Some studies have examined meaningfulness (Oliver & Bartsch, 2011; Oliver & Hartmann, 2010; Oliver & Raney, 2011) and moral beliefs in understanding how audiences engage with entertainment (Krakowiak & Oliver, 2012; Raney, 2011; Raney & Bryant, 2002; Tamborini, 2011). Research in this area could examine how spiritual beliefs, knowledge, and values might influence media choices and experiences.

Another line of research has examined how situational mindfulness (through mindfulness meditation task exercises) and trait mindfulness (through scales such as MAAS – Mindfulness Awareness Assessment Scale) influences a variety of behaviors (Baer, Walsh, & Lykins, 2009; Dorjee, 2010; Frewen, Lundberg, MacKinley, & Wrath, 2011; Kabat-Zinn, 2003; Kass, VanWormer, Mikulas, Legan, & Bumgarner, 2011; Langer, 1989). This type of research can also be applied to the media context. For example, some researchers have started examining how mindfulness interventions influence media multitasking and texting-while-driving (Kass et al., 2011; Marcello-Serafin, 2008; Pike, 2009; Timmerman, 2002).

Affective Dimension of Spirituality

Spiritual feelings are those that help individuals express and experience the core of who they are. Feelings such as hope, optimism, appreciation, gratitude, resilience, elevation, inspiration, awe, courage, peace, strength, love, generosity, compassion, and empathy would be categorized under this dimension of spirituality. Maslow has described peak experiences of intense ecstasy, wonder, awe, and euphoria where one feels deeply interconnectedness with others, experiencing transcendence (Maslow, 1961). Media experiences such as awe-inspiring nature scenes, deeply moving meditative music, or touching expressions of love could possibly facilitate or enhance such peak experiences (Maslow, 1971).

Spiritual feelings can be negative, positive, or mixed. For instance, so-called "darker, disturbing" media content (such as Ingmar Bergman movies) can lead to deeply spiritual experiences of meaningfulness and connectedness. Narratives of resilience and courage during adversity can also be very inspiring (Park, 2012; Yates, 2004). On the other hand, a seemingly mundane but touching photo—like the one called the "Obama Hug" showing President Barack Obama and his wife Michelle Obama hugging right after the 2012 U.S. presidential election results were announced—can became the most "liked" image on Facebook and also the most re-tweeted one.

Spiritual feelings can be self-directed, other-directed, or both. Feelings of hope, elevation, and peace are self-directed or basic spiritual feelings. Research on news has examined stories about hope, courage, and resilience, which would fit into this category (Park, 2012; Yates, 2004). Compassion, empathy, generosity, and gratitude are examples of other-directed or social spiritual feelings. Entertainment scholars have examined appreciation, empathy and perspective-taking as audience characteristics while engaging with narratives (Oliver & Bartsch, 2011; Oliver & Hartmann, 2010; Oliver, Dillard, Bae, & Tamul, 2012; Zillmann, 1991). Some other feelings such as awe and inspiration may be either self-directed or other-directed. When directed outwards, they may be expressed towards people or experienced as nature-connectedness with animals, birds, and plants (Howell, Dopko, Passmore, & Buro, 2011).

Behavioral Dimension of Spirituality

Spiritual behaviors and actions constitute this third dimension of spirituality. There are several studies within social psychology that have examined altruistic or prosocial behaviors in general and in association with religiosity (Krause, 2007; Piliavin, 2009; Simpson, 2008; Tweed et al., 2011). In such studies, religiosity is often measured using behaviors such as frequency of church visits and prayer. Similar approaches could be taken to examine behavioral dimensions of spirituality within media contexts, such as how they serve as predictors of media exposure, genre preferences, and content avoidance.

Representations of spiritual behaviors in media narratives could also be examined. For instance, how are activities such as meditation, contemplation, deep breathing, yoga, and creative/artistic expressions depicted in media? Content analytical techniques could be used to examine behaviors that lead to characters being categorized as spiritual (or not) by the audience. It is possible that portrayals of (so-called) spiritual people might actually perpetuate stereotypes, if the behaviors that lead them to be classified as "spiritual" are actually unidimensional or emphasize certain exaggerated mannerisms, attire, and speech patterns. Hardly any research has been conducted within this realm of study. Finally, media content can lead to spiritual behaviors as well by inspiring smiles, hugs, comforting words, helping behaviors, random acts of kindness, and creativity/artistic expressions.

Recently, a viral video, "Making the Bus Monitor Cry," moved viewers to contribute more than US$600,000 to an anti-bullying fund. Media scholars should seek to understand how content can lead to positive social behaviors and spiritual actions.

Theoretical Perspectives on Media and Spirituality

Whatever little research has been conducted within the realm of media and spirituality has not necessarily been categorized or labeled thus. Using the broad definition of theistic and non-theistic spirituality described above, I have reviewed and consolidated relevant theoretical perspectives from a variety of disciplines such as positive psychology, wellness studies, organizational communication, and meaning-making. These theories can help guide further research in the area of media and spirituality.

Positive Psychology

Generally speaking, positive psychology is the study of positive subjective experiences that help individuals, organizations, and communities to flourish in ways that make life worthwhile and meaningful (Peterson, 2009; Seligman & Csikszentmihalyi, 2000). Positive psychology offers several useful concepts such as appreciation, gratitude, hope, authentic happiness, meaningfulness, empathy, awe, moral beauty, elevation, and so on, that would be invaluable in the future study of media and spirituality. This is not to suggest that media scholars should focus only on utopian, sugar-coated positive images that are far from the unpleasant sufferings of everyday reality. In fact, positive psychologists contend that authentic happiness also includes ideas such as resilience, altruism, compassion, and wisdom (Hutchinson, 2009; Oliver et al., 2012; Park, 2012; Piliavin, 2009). Some positive psychology approaches such as flow theory have been applied to media use (Jin, 2012; Sherry, 2004) but others such as the broad-and-build theory of positive emotions (Fredrickson, 2001), resilience (Seligman, 2011), and flourishing (Keyes & Haidt, 2003) have not been fully explored in media contexts.

Some initial research on positive *media* psychology has been conducted by Oliver and colleagues, emphasizing the role of media entertainment in inspiring meaningfulness, appreciation, and elevation in viewers (Oliver, 2008; Oliver & Bartsch, 2011; Oliver & Hartmann, 2010; Oliver et al., 2012). Oliver and Raney (2011) distinguished between hedonic (or pleasure-based) and eudaimonic (or meaning-based) viewer motivations for seeking out certain media and characters. Whereas some viewers might seek pure enjoyment from media in terms of increasing their sensory/aesthetic pleasure for hedonic motivations, others seek to engage with media characters for eudaimonic purposes of meaningfulness. While eudaimonic motivations focus on psychological well-being, virtues, and concern for others, chaironic happiness refers to a sense of gratitude, awe, and connectedness with a higher power (Wong, 2011). It reflects an attitude of open inquiry, mindfulness, and transcendence. Although chaironic media motivations are yet to be studied, they promise to provide insights into spiritual content selection.

Klimmt suggests that, along with meaning in life, a related theory that would be useful to consider is the terror management theory (Klimmt, 2011). He argues that one's search for meaning is closely related to mortality salience. When the realization comes that death is inevitable, it could act as a powerful motivator for media users to seek a deeper, more purposeful, meaningful life by shifting their focus to social groups and values that are meaningful to them. However, this conjecture has not been empirically tested.

Morality and Ethics

Another theoretical perspective from which one can approach the study of media and spirituality is the existing literature on morality and ethics that informs us about the meaning of "good" and "positive." Whereas morality focuses on implicit judgment and condemnation when someone is not following moral codes, ethics is more about aligning one's inner compass to core principles regardless of external judgments and consequences. Several scholars have focused on moral dimensions of good versus evil within the context of media effects traditions. The foundation for this tradition was laid by Zillmann in his affective disposition theory that focused on how good versus evil characters in media narratives elicit different emotional responses from audiences (Zillmann, 1985). Audience members experience euphoria when good characters win challenges and dysphoria when these characters lose. Through processes such as identification and perspective-taking, viewers might derive media enjoyment but also meaning and appreciation from characters.

Researchers have more recently examined morally ambiguous characters that might not fit with the traditional good versus bad dichotomy (Krakowiak & Oliver, 2012; Raney, 2004; Shafer & Raney, 2012). Tamborini and colleagues have explored the reciprocal relationship between media and morality through a dual processing model that tries to understand intuitive moral choices as well as a more rational, thoughtful judgment of media characters (Tamborini, 2011; Tamborini, Weber, Eden, Bowman, & Grizzard, 2010). They have tested the five dimensions of Haidt's moral foundations theory—care, fairness, liberty, authority, and sanctity—in various media contexts (Haidt & Craig, 2008). Oliver's research has also examined Haidt's concept of moral beauty as it relates to eliciting feelings of elevation and connectedness (Oliver et al., 2012).

Mindfulness and Eastern Philosophies

Eastern Dharmic traditions have long studied the inner life or interiority in a scientific, systematic manner, offering us deep insights that are relevant to the study of media and spirituality (Malathi et al., 1999; Schreiner, 2009; Tsai et al., 2007; Varambally, 2012). Central to these traditions is a focus on mind–body–spirit connectedness, peaceful coexistence, belongingness, and contemplative practices that help clarify the meaning of life and existence. Being in harmony with one's own personalized and subjective code of ethical principles is emphasized rather than a universal set of morality. Many of these ideas have now been applied and tested in several contexts.

Extant research on mindfulness, a central Dharmic principle, offers a rich avenue and a strong theoretical basis from which to approach the study of media and spirituality (Kabat-Zinn, 1992, 2003; Langer, 1989, 2009). Mindfulness emphasizes being in the present moment and responding to the world around us through non-judgmental openness. It emphasizes total awareness from a space of acceptance that goes beyond tolerance.

Similarly, the philosophy of yoga elaborates a state of contemplative awareness where the individual is focused and attentive but also connected to one's true nature—loving, caring, compassionate, and balanced (Kang & Whittingham, 2010). According to the words of Patanjali, the author of the foundational yoga text *Yogasutras*, passed down through the generations by word of mouth, contemplative awareness can be established in many ways, including meditation, exposure to inspiring messages, and nature-connectedness. From this state of contemplative awareness, individuals may use the media as a tool to express and experience their authentic selves, to create meaning, and to be connected with others while also staying connected with their inner selves. From this space of harmony, audience members may process and respond to media in ways that are consistent with and serve their authentic self.

Uses and Gratifications/Sense-Making

Another theoretical perspective from which to approach this topic is the analysis of audiences' motivations to seek gratifications from spiritual media. Such work could be informed by the uses and gratifications (e.g., Blumler & Katz, 1974) and selective exposure (e.g., Zillmann & Bryant, 1985) perspectives. For example, spiritual needs (such as belongingness and self-actualization) can be distinguished from material needs (such as shelter and food). Emerging digital media contexts may provide new opportunities for audiences to use media to actively seek spiritually enlightening and religiously meaningful experiences. Thus far, very limited research exists on this topic. The existing body of work has largely been produced by scholars using qualitative methods such as descriptive and ethnographic accounts of online religious media content. Researchers have studied how audiences access, seek, and engage with media texts from an audience reception perspective, with an emphasis on spiritual and religious rituals that promote a sense of community (Campbell, 2006; Campbell & Lövheim, 2011; Helland, 2000).

Wellness and Holistic Health

Spirituality has been studied most extensively in health/wellness contexts (King et al., 1999; Koenig, 2000, 2006; Krause, 2007; Parrott, 2004). There is much in terms of theoretical richness to be gathered from these existing studies for scholars interested in media and spirituality. One of the few research studies relating to media and spirituality is a content analysis that examines holistic health in newspaper coverage in Australia (Bonevski, Wilson, & Henry, 2008). In this study, spirituality is conceptualized as a complementary/alternative healing practice as part of what the authors define as "mind-body medicine" (p. 2).

Prior research shows that spirituality is positively correlated with greater quality of life including measures of physical health, psychological health, mental health (such as depression and anxiety), better health attitudes, and lower mortality rates (Gilmartin, 1996; Koenig, 2000, 2006; Parrott, 2004; Varambally, 2012). Some authors note a negative relationship between spirituality and depression, which in turn could influence overall physical, psychological, and mental health (Koenig, 2006). Scales such as spirituality, religion, and personal beliefs (SRPB) have been widely used within medicine and nursing contexts to measure spiritual connection, meaning of life, awe, wholeness and integration, spiritual strength, inner peace/serenity/harmony, hope and optimism, and faith (Koenig, 2006). However, this measurement has been criticized as being confounded with mental health indicators and psychological well-being such as cheerfulness and optimism. Social capital and family support could also influence the relationships between spirituality and the ability to cope with negative health situations. Applying these well-tried approaches and measures to issues of media and spirituality might prove fruitful.

Organizational Spirituality

Organizational communication as a field has contributed greatly to our understanding of spirituality and communication. Interestingly, it is within the organizational communication literature that we come across terms such as "e-spirituality" (Klenke, 2007), which would be a term that new media scholars would like to further explicate and apply in their own scholarship. Given the increase in occupational stress, higher number of work hours, and greater exposure to spirituality in developed countries such as the U.S., organizations are appreciating the importance of incorporating spiritual practices into their workplace environment (Klenke, 2007; Mohamed, Wisnieski, Askar, & Syed, 2004). Spirituality has been shown to decrease everyday stressors and deal with failures more easily, better task involvement and goal identification, and greater commitment to the organization (Klenke, 2007; Mohamed et al., 2004). Several organizations offer yoga classes, meditation lessons, and spirituality workshops to help their employees feel a sense of belongingness and to nourish positive human values in the workplace (Mohamed et al., 2004). Extending this work to examine, for instance, whether spiritual media content can lead to equally beneficial effects would seemingly be a natural step for media scholars to take.

Spirituality and New/Digital Media

For those seeking spiritual experiences, the media richness, speed of access, and anonymity offered by cyberspace makes it an ideal alternative to the physical, material world (Klenke, 2007). Some have argued that cyberspace represents a "sacramental place" (Campbell, 2005) that allows people to bring back the spiritual, immaterial dimension into their everyday lives. The seemingly timeless, seamless, and anonymous nature of the Internet allows those who are otherwise isolated and disconnected to seek religious and spiritual virtual spaces online. Klenke (2007) refers to this phenomenon as "e-spirituality."

The diversity of religious traditions and expressions available in the virtual environment offers e-pilgrims the opportunity to experience varied spiritual practices and rituals from the privacy and convenience of their own homes or virtually anywhere through mobile devices. This technologically mediated space allows for spiritual seekers to experiment with lesser known spiritual/religious traditions and to adapt non-mainstream, New Age, techno-friendly spirituality. As an example, social media such as Facebook provide an opportunity for those who share similar spiritual beliefs from around the world to use cyberspace to form spiritual communities where they share, express, and learn from one another.

Helland (2000) argued for a distinction between religion-online and online-religion; a similar approach can also be applied to spirituality. Spirituality-online might refer to spiritual organizations that use cyberspace as a mass medium to communicate spiritual information to their members through the online environment. The Internet here serves as a tool for transmitting spiritual knowledge and beliefs. In contrast, online-spirituality is the adaptation and re-presentation of spirituality in a networked, many-to-many environment. Examples of online-spirituality could be a virtual spirituality chat room, a Facebook fan site for a spiritual leader, a meditation group in Second Life, daily inspirational quotes on a social media site, and so on. Here, newer forms of innovative spiritual practices are evolving to fit the virtual new media environment. The Internet is, thus, a tool for spiritual networking to cultivate both personal spiritual experiences as well as communal identity.

Future Directions

The study of media and spirituality is a vitally important yet unexplored area of research within media-effects scholarship. From an even broader perspective, the study of spirituality and communication has also not received much research attention, except in health communication and organizational communication. Although spiritual media content is popular and is sought out by millions of people across the world, such content and its effects on audiences have not been studied systematically. Many theoretical approaches from positive psychology, mindfulness and Eastern philosophies, morality and ethics, organizational spirituality, holistic health and wellness, and uses and gratifications offer multiple perspectives from which to examine media and spirituality. However, much of the research on media and spirituality is currently being conducted by scholars interested in religion and theology whose work has largely been descriptive and qualitative in nature. The limited research within media effects on this topic has been conducted from a positive psychological perspective that examines meaningfulness, appreciation, elevation, and morality.

The field is ripe for many types of methodological approaches such as ethnography, audience reception, surveys, experiments, textual analysis, rhetorical criticism, and content analysis. Content analyses of spiritual books, websites, and social networks would help greatly in our understanding the prevalence and categories of spiritual media content that exist. Not only do we need to examine traditional media outlets such as books, audio CDs, radio shows, and television channels, but we also need to understand spirituality in new media contexts such as social network groups, websites, email, Second Life, and video games. Understanding who is accessing these types of media and for what purposes would be within the purview of scholars who study media uses and gratifications. This research will help us understand what kinds of motivations and needs are being satisfied by spiritual media content. Similarly, more widespread empirical research using survey methods could help us answer questions about the audience characteristics that relate to usage of such content. Experimental research will help us understand what kinds of spiritual messages in the media are helpful in eliciting spiritual cognitions, emotions, and behaviors. Research on mindfulness and yogic meditation offer another very important avenue for research exploration. How do audiences approach media from a state of mindful or contemplative awareness? What kind of media messages help audiences get established in this state of awareness? Apart from the transformative nature of media spirituality, scholarship should also examine the ways in which media access, literacy, and competence could serve as barriers to spiritual experiences. These are all interesting, socially-relevant, and important questions that we as media scholars should be addressing.

In conclusion, this chapter contributes to our understanding of media and spirituality in at least three key ways. First, it defines and categorizes spirituality as non-theistic and theistic spirituality that has three dimensions: spiritual beliefs, spiritual feelings, and spiritual behaviors. Second, it pulls together relevant literature on media and spirituality through a variety of theoretical perspectives such as positive psychology, morality, mindfulness and Eastern philosophies, wellness and health, uses and gratifications, sense-making, and organizational communication. Finally, it lays out a research agenda for scholars interested in both "traditional media" such as television and media as well as "new media" such as Internet, video games, and social networks to examine various dimensions of spirituality using experimental, survey-based, content analytical and qualitative research methods.

Notes

1 There does not seem to be any reliable source on the number of spiritual and/ or religious apps available. Some scholars put the number at around 5,000 or so apps that focus on spirituality. If we include apps specific to various faiths, this number would be much larger. A report by Zokem and GSMA (January 2011 as cited in http://readwrite.com/2011/02/21/apps-continue-to-overtake-mobile-web-study#awesm=~on5eKlC7lBSwTQ) analyzed 2,100 smartphone users in the US and UK using a device metering technique and found that about 7 percent used some type of Bible reader. However, this does not capture other religious apps and non-theistic spiritual apps.
2 Only major world religions have been considered in this classification. Future researchers should also include marginalized folk religions such as shamanism, Native American religions, Aboriginal spiritual traditions as well as Shintoism and Baha'I traditions.

References

Baer, R. A., Walsh, E., & Lykins, E. L. (2009). Assessment of mindfulness. In *Clinical handbook of mindfulness* (pp. 153–168). Springer: New York.

Bash, A. (2004). Spirituality: The emperor's new clothes? *Journal of Clinical Nursing, 13*(1), 11–16. doi: 10.1046/j.1365-2702.2003.00838.x.

Blumler, J. G., & Katz, E. (1974). *The uses of mass communications: Current perspectives on gratifications research* (Vol. 3). Beverly Hills, CA: Sage Publications.

Bonevski, B., Wilson, A., & Henry, D. (2008). An analysis of news media coverage of complementary and alternative medicine. *PLoS ONE, 3*(6), e2406. doi: 10.1371/journal.pone.0002406.

Campbell, H. (2005). Considering spiritual dimensions within computer-mediated communication studies. *New Media & Society, 7*(1), 110–134. doi: 10.1177/1461444805049147.

Campbell, H. (2006). Religion and the Internet. *Communication Research Trends, 25*(1), 3–24.

Campbell, H., & Lövheim, M. (2011). Introduction: Rethinking the online–offline connection in the study of religion online. *Information, Communication & Society, 14*(8), 1083–1096. doi: 10.1080/1369118X.2011.597416.

Dorjee, D. (2010). Kinds and dimensions of mindfulness: Why it is important to distinguish them. *Mindfulness, 1*(3), 152–160. doi: 10.1007/ s12671-010-0016-3.

Emmons, R. (2006). Spirituality: Recent progress. In M. Csikszentmihalyi & I. S. Csikszentmihalyi (Eds.), *A life worth living: Contributions to positive psychology*. Oxford and New York: Oxford University Press.

Fredrickson, B. (2001). The role of positive emotions in positive psychology: The broaden-and-build theory of positive emotions. *The American psychologist, 56*(3), 218–226. doi: 10.1037/0003-066X.56.3.218.

Frewen, P., Lundberg, E., MacKinley, J., & Wrath, A. (2011). Assessment of response to mindfulness meditation: Meditation breath attention scores in association with subjective measures of state and trait mindfulness and difficulty letting go of depressive cognition. *Mindfulness, 2*(4), 254–269.

Gilmartin, R. J. (1996). *Pursuing wellness, finding spirituality*. Mystic, CT: Twenty-Third Publications.

Haidt, J., & Craig, J. (2008). The moral mind: How five sets of innate intuitions guide the development of many culture-specific virtues, and perhaps even modules. In J. Haidt & J. Craig. *The innate mind Volume 3: Foundations and the future* (pp. 367–391). New York: Oxford University Press.

Haidt, J., & Kesebir, S. (2010). Morality. In J. Haidt & S. Kesebir. *Handbook of social psychology, Vol 2 (5th ed.)* (pp. 797–832). Hoboken, NJ: John Wiley & Sons Inc.

Helland, C. (2000). Online-religion/religion-online and virtual communitas. In J. K. Hadden & D. E. Cowan (Eds.), *Religion on the Internet: Research prospects and promises* (pp. 205–223). New York: JAI Press.

Hojsgaard, M., & Warburg, M. (2005). Introduction: Waves of research. In M. Hojsgaard & M. Warburg (Eds.), *Religion and cyberspace* (pp. 1–11). London: Routledge.

Howell, A. J., Dopko, R. L., Passmore, H., & Buro, K. (2011). Nature connectedness: Associations with well-being and mindfulness. *Personality and Individual Differences, 51*(2), 166–171. doi: 10.1016/j.paid.2011.03.037.

Howse, K. (1999). *Religion, spirituality and older people*. London: Centre for Policy on Ageing.

Hutchinson, J. (2009). Ordinary and extraordinary narratives of heroism and resistance: Uncovering resilience, competence and growth. *Counselling Psychology Review, 24*(3–4), 9–15.

Jin, S. (2012). Toward integrative models of flow: Effects of performance, skill, challenge, playfulness, and presence on flow in video games. *Journal of Broadcasting & Electronic Media, 56*(2), 169–186.

Kabat-Zinn, J. (1992). Effectiveness of a meditation-based stress reduction program in the treatment of anxiety disorders. *American Journal of Psychiatry, 149*(7), 936–943.

Kabat-Zinn, J. (2003). Mindfulness-based stress reduction (MBSR). *Constructivism in the Human Sciences, 8*(2), 73–107.

Kang, C., & Whittingham, K. (2010). Mindfulness: A dialogue between Buddhism and clinical psychology. *Mindfulness, 1*(3), 161–173. doi: 10.1007/s12671-010-0018-1.

Kass, S. J., VanWormer, L. A., Mikulas, W. L., Legan, S., & Bumgarner, D. (2011). Effects of mindfulness training on simulated driving: Preliminary results. *Mindfulness, 2*(4), 236–241.

Keyes, C. L. M., & Haidt, J. (2003). Introduction: Human flourishing—The study of that which makes life worthwhile. In *Flourishing: Positive psychology and the life well-lived* (pp. 3–12). Washington DC: American Psychological Association.

King, M., Speck, P., & Thomas, A. (1999). The effects of spiritual beliefs on outcome from illness. *Social Science and Medicine, 48*, 1291–1299. doi: 10.1016/S0277-9536(98)00452-3.

Klenke, K. (2007). E-spirituality: Spirituality at the confluence of affect and technology. *Journal of Management, Spirituality & Religion, 4*(2), 234–268. doi: 10.1080/14766080709518659.

Klimmt, C. (2011). Media psychology and complex modes of entertainment experiences. *Journal of Media Psychology, 23*(1), 34–38. doi: 10.1027/1864-1105/a000030.

Koenig, H. (2000). Religion, spirituality, and medicine: Application to clinical practice. *JAMA, 284*(13), 1708.

Koenig, H. (2006). Annotated bibliography on religion, spirituality and medicine. *Southern Medical Journal, 99*(10), 1189–1196.

Krakowiak, M., & Oliver, M. B. (2012). When good characters do bad things: Examining the effect of moral ambiguity on enjoyment. *Journal of Communication, 62*(1), 117–135. doi: 10.1111/j.1460-2466.2011.01618.x.

Krause, N. (2007). Altruism, religion, and health: Exploring the ways in which helping others benefits support providers. In N. Krause & S. G. Post (Eds.), *Altruism and health: Perspectives from empirical research* (pp. 410–421). New York: Oxford University Press.

Langer, E. J. (1989). *Mindfulness*. Reading, MA: Addison-Wesley/Addison Wesley Longman.

Langer, E. J. (2009). *Counterclockwise: Mindful health and the power of possibility*. New York: Ballantine Books.

Malathi, A., Damodaran, A., Shah, N., Patil, N., & Marathe, A. (1999). Self-actualization and practice of yoga. *NIMHANS Journal, 17*(1), 39–44.

Marcello-Serafin, G. (2008). *Media mindfulness: Developing the motivation and ability to process advertisements*. Doctoral dissertation, Rutgers University Graduate School-New Brunswick.

Maslow, A. H. (1961). Peak experiences as acute identity experiences. *The American Journal of Psychoanalysis, 21*, 254–262. doi: 10.1007/BF01873126.

Maslow, A. H. (1971). Peak experiences in education and art. *Theory into Practice, 10*(71), 149–153.

Mohamed, A. A., Wisnieski, J., Askar, M., & Syed, I. (2004). Towards a theory of spirituality in the workplace. *Competitiveness Review, 14*(1&2), 102–107. doi: 10.1108/eb046473.

Oliver, M. B. (2008). Tender affective states as predictors of entertainment preference. *Journal of Communication, 58*(1), 40–61. doi: 10.1111/j.1460-2466.2007.00373.x.

Oliver, M. B., & Bartsch, A. (2011). Appreciation of entertainment: The importance of meaningfulness via virtue and wisdom. *Journal of Media Psychology, 23*(1), 29–33. doi:10.1027/1864-1105/a000029

Oliver, M. B., & Hartmann, T. (2010). Exploring the role of meaningful experiences in users' appreciation of "good movies." *Projections: The Journal of Movies and Mind, 4*(2), 128–150. doi: 10.3167/proj.2010.040208.

Oliver, M. B, & Raney, A. A. (2011). Entertainment as pleasurable and meaningful: Identifying hedonic and eudaimonic motivations for entertainment consumption. *Journal of Communication, 61*(5), 984–1004. doi: 10.1111/j.1460-2466.2011.01585.x.

Oliver, M. B, Dillard, J. P., Bae, K., & Tamul, D. J. (2012). The effect of narrative news format on empathy for stigmatized groups. *Journalism & Mass Communication Quarterly, 89*(2), 205–224. doi: 10.1177/1077699012439020.

Park, N. (2012). Adversity, resilience, and thriving: A positive psychology perspective on research and practices. In R. A. McMackin, E. Newman, J. M. Fogler, & T. M. Keane (Eds.), *Trauma therapy in context: The science and craft of evidence-based practice* (pp. 121–140). Washington, DC: American Psychological Association. doi: 10.1037/13746-006.

Parrott, R. (2004). "Collective amnesia": The absence of religious faith and spirituality in health communication research and practice. *Health Communication, 16*(1), 1–5. doi: 10.1207/S15327027HC1601_1.

Peterson, C. (2009). Positive psychology. *Reclaiming Children and Youth, 18*(2), 3–7.

Pike, R. E. (2009). *Attribution formation, media effects, and communication mindfulness in virtual world environments: An application of Brunswik's Lens Model.* Doctoral dissertation, Washington State University.

Piliavin, J. A. (2009). Altruism and helping: The evolution of a field: The 2008 Cooley-Mead presentation. *Social Psychology Quarterly, 72*(3), 206–209. doi:10.1177/019027250907200304.

Raney, A. A. (2004). Expanding disposition theory: Reconsidering character liking, moral evaluations, and enjoyment. *Communication Theory, 14*(4), 348–369. doi: 10.1111/j.1468-2885.2004.tb00319.x

Raney, A. A. (2011). The role of morality in emotional reactions to and enjoyment of media entertainment. *Journal of Media Psychology: Theories, Methods, and Applications, 23*(1), 18–23. doi: 10.1027/1864-1105/a000027. doi: 10.1111/j.1468-2885.2004.tb00319.x

Raney, A. A. & Bryant, J. (2002). Moral judgment and crime drama: An integrated theory of enjoyment. *Journal of Communication, 52*(2), 402–415.

Scherurs, A. (2002). *Psychotherapy and spirituality: Integrating the spiritual dimension into therapeutic practice.* Philadelphia, PA: Jessica Kingsley Publishers.

Schreiner, P. (2009). Yoga in the modern world: Contemporary perspectives. *Numen, 56*(5), 591–595.

Seligman, M. E. (2011). Building resilience. *Harvard Business Review, 89*(4), 100.

Seligman, M. E., & Csikszentmihalyi, M. (2000). Positive psychology: An introduction. *The American Psychologist, 55*(1), 5–14. doi: 10.1037/0003-066X.55.1.5

Shafer, D. M., & Raney, A. A. (2012). Exploring how we enjoy antihero narratives. *Journal of Communication, 62*(6), 1028–1046. doi: 10.1111/j.1460-2466.2012.01682.x

Sherry, J. (2004). Flow and media enjoyment. *Communication Theory, 14*(4), 328–347. doi: 10.1111/j.1468-2885.2004.tb00318.x.

Simpson, B. (2008). Altruism and indirect reciprocity: The interaction of person and situation in prosocial behavior. *Social Psychology Quarterly, 71*(1), 37–52. doi: 10.1177/019027250807100106.

Tamborini, R. (2011). Moral intuition and media entertainment. *Journal of Media Psychology, 23*(1), 39–45. doi: 2048/10.1027/1864-1105/a000031.

Tamborini, R., Weber, R., Eden, A., Bowman, N. D., & Grizzard, M. (2010). Repeated exposure to daytime soap opera and shifts in moral judgment toward social convention. *Journal of Broadcasting & Electronic Media, 54*(4), 621–640. doi: 10.1080/08838151.2010.519806.

Timmerman, E. C. (2002). The moderating effect of mindlessness/mindfulness upon media richness and social influence explanations of organizational media use. *Communication Monographs, 69*(2), 111–131.

Tsai, J. L., Miao, F. L., & Seppala, E. (2007). Good feelings in Christianity and Buddhism: Religious differences in ideal affect. *Personality and Social Psychology Bulletin, 33*(3), 409–421.

Tweed, R. G., Bhatt, G., Dooley, S., Spindler, A., Douglas, Kevin S., & Viljoen, J. L. (2011). Youth violence and positive psychology: Research potential through integration. *Canadian Psychology, 52*(2), 111–121. doi: 10.1037/a0020695.

Varambally, S. (2012). Yoga: A spiritual practice with therapeutic value in psychiatry. *Asian Journal of Psychiatry, 5*(2), 186–189. doi: 2048/10.1016/j.ajp.2012.05.003.

Wong, P. (2011). Positive psychology 2.0: Towards a balanced interactive model of the good life. *Canadian Psychology, 52*(2), 69–81. doi: 10.1037/a0022511.

Yates, T. M. (2004). Fostering the future: Resilience theory and the practice of positive psychology. In P. Linley & J. Stephen (Eds.), *Positive psychology in practice*. Hoboken, NJ: Wiley.

Zillmann, D. (1985). The experimental exploration of gratifications from media entertainment. In K. E. Rosengren, L. A. Wenner & P. Palmgreen (Eds.), *Media gratifications research: Current perspectives* (pp. 225–239). Beverly Hills, CA: Sage Publications.

Zillmann, D. (1991). Empathy: Affect from bearing witness to the emotions of others. In J. Bryant & D. Zillmann (Eds.), *Responding to the screen: Reception and reaction processes* (pp. 135–167). Hillsdale, NJ: Lawrence Erlbaum.

Zillmann, D., & Bryant, J. (1985). Affect, mood, and emotion as determinants of selective exposure. In D. Zillmann & J. Bryant (Eds.), *Selective exposure to communication* (pp. 157–190). Hillsdale, NJ: Lawrence Erlbaum Associates.

5

INTEGRATING TECHNOLOGY AND MEDIA AND THE SOCIAL LEARNING ECOSYSTEM

The Evolving State of Formal Learning

Brittney Huntington and J. Alison Bryant

A growing body of literature and practical observation has indicated that children and young adults (from preschool to 24 years old) are digital natives that live in a constantly "connected" world. Global penetration rates and access to technology have been exponentially increasing over the past five years, especially for the younger generations. A recent online survey of U.S. families indicated that access is widespread, with most parents reporting children using shared devices for individual activities: 75 percent owned a gaming console, 60 percent a smartphone, 54 percent a handheld gaming device, and about 40 percent an iPad/iPhone/iPod touch respectively (PlayScience, 2013). Children and young adults appear to be a driving force behind parents purchasing technology for the home, with households with kids owning an average of ten media devices (including smartphones, TVs, game systems and laptops) (Purcell, 2012). And there is evidence that this will increase over time, since homes with toddlers now have even more devices than kids ages six+ (Purcell, 2012). The average eight to eighteen year old now spends twice as much time interacting with screens at home as they do in school on a weekly basis (Rideout, Foehr, & Roberts, 2010)

These children, aptly titled "iChildren" by Michelle Druin (2009), are "interactive, independent and international in their media and technology use," and they expect to interact with their environment in this way (p. xix). They are living in societies where technology and media are commonplace and expected, both in the entertainment and the education realms. Unfortunately, though, education often seems to lag behind. Previous attempts to create such "integrated, independent, and international" educational experiences for these students have not always been successful, as technology and media are typically not integrated into the student learning experience but are given a supporting role to traditional teaching methods. Today's iChildren seek the stimulation of more sophisticated and student-centric learning environments than have been provided for students in previous years.

In contrast to the more traditional practice of trying to predict "optimal" learning environments to benefit all types of students, student-centric learning theories ascribe to the idea that all students are different and ideally need varying environments based on their individual characteristics to thrive (Christensen, Horn, & Johnson, 2008). In the 1980s, Howard Gardner (1983) introduced his theory of multiple intelligences and challenged the idea of a uniform "best practices" for learning experiences by shedding light on the fact that different learners have varying strengths. He began to identify how learning environments and educational settings can be tailored to the individual to produce optimal learning for that person (Christensen et al., 2008; Gardner, 2006). Gardner suggested that there must be a balance between the characteristics of the environment and the individual learner (intelligences). Learning can be intrinsically motivating and optimal when students are exposed to educational environments that are aligned with their individual strengths (Gardner, 2006).

Around the same time as the development of Gardner's theory of multiple intelligences, Dunn and Dunn also identified a need for student-centric learning environments in their work with the development of the Learning-Style Model (Dunn & Dunn, 1978). The Learning-Style Model indicates that there are various student learning dimensions—learning environments, emotional, sociological, physiological, and psychological—that must be assessed before the diagnosis of an ideal learning environment for each student. In more than forty-two experimental studies examining the effects of student-centered teaching styles and accommodating student learning preferences, the researchers found that students who learned in environments and with teachers conducive to their individual learning styles had higher academic achievement than those who learned in environments that did not match their preferences (Dunn & Dunn, 1978). Given our knowledge of today's children and the proven efficacy of student-centric approaches, it stands to reason that the creation of more student-centric learning environments in which media and technology are successfully integrated may provide ideal conditions for iChildren learning.

This chapter explores this proposal by examining relationships within the *social learning ecosystem*, a system in which learning is fostered as a product of the various relationships among stakeholders and learning

environments. To that end, we examine past unsuccessful attempts to utilize technology and media in learning systems. Keeping in mind the lessons
learned, we identify why shifting toward an integration of media and technology is optimal for student learning; we also isolate core areas to focus
on in learning interventions or platform selection.

Stakeholder Relationships in the
Social Learning Ecosystem

Figure 5.1 outlines the interrelationships between key stakeholders involved
in the social learning ecosystem. In this section, we examine the roles the
primary stakeholder relationships play in the social learning ecosystem, as
well as briefly provide context for the secondary relationships.

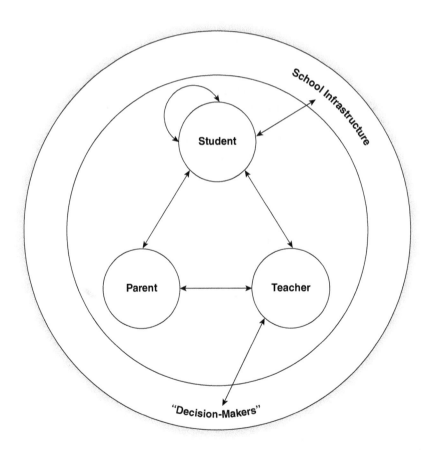

Figure 5.1 The social learning ecosystem

Primary Relationships

Student–Teacher

One of the most central and important relationships in the social learning ecosystem is between students and instructors. These relationships can have a positive impact on student attitudes about their classroom connectedness and academic achievement (Crosnoe, Kirkpatrick Johnson, & Elder, 2004; Frisby & Martin, 2010). In traditional and non-traditional learning environments, the teacher is often seen as the leader or facilitator in the group. Students will interact with this figure in various ways that are supported and encouraged by the learning environment the teacher provides. For instance, Martin, Myers, and Mottet (1999) identified five motives students reported for interacting with their instructors, including relational (i.e., to develop personal relationships with their instructor), functional (i.e., to offer reasons regarding material and course assignments), excuse making (i.e., to provide explanation for why work is late or not turned in), participatory (i.e., to demonstrate interest in the class), and sycophantic (i.e., to make favorable impressions on the instructor). These motives vary based on the way the teacher structures the learning environment (Young, Kelsey, & Lancaster, 2011). Teachers who encourage more collaborative environments for students (with instructors and peers) show increases in classroom connectedness and more positive individual student outcomes, such as better attendance, more hours of studying at home, retention, school satisfaction, academic engagement, and higher efficacy (Frisby & Martin, 2010).

Student–Student

Traditional learning environments focus more on the individual student, encouraging student–student relationships (both cooperative and competitive) mostly in small group-based projects. Alternatively, more collaborative learning environments where students are encouraged to interact help bolster peer relationships in the social learning ecosystem. Dwyer and his colleagues (2004) defined a connected classroom environment as one which encourages "student-to-student perceptions of a supportive and cooperative communication environment" (p. 267), as well as one which focuses on the interactions of peers within a classroom environment (Frisby & Martin, 2010). In such educational settings, students help co-create their learning environment by taking active roles as models and peer support for other students, participating and engaging more deeply with the content, and expanding their problem-solving skill set (Frisby & Martin, 2010). Positive peer interactions in learning environments have been shown to predict achievement, feelings of belongingness, and improve academic efficacy of students (Frisby & Martin, 2010).

In addition to classroom environments, student–student relationships can extend into home life. With the development of synchronous (e.g., chat, texting, IMing) and asynchronous (e.g., e-mail, forums, discussion boards) communication technology, students are able to expand the boundaries of the classroom and increase learning-related communications with other students and instructors (Wei, Wang, & Klausner, 2012). However, as student use of these communications rise inside and outside of the classroom, many instructors and administrators are concerned that the communication is not facilitating learning as often as it is providing entertainment and serving as a means for peer socializing (Wei, Wang, & Klausner, 2012).

Student–Parent

The relationship between students and parents (and other key adults in their lives) helps supplement the other two primary relationships within educational settings by reinforcing learned concepts outside of the school setting (school-to-home) and providing the foundation for informal learning (Hoover-Dempsey et al., 2001). Greater parental involvement in the school-to-home activities of K-12 students through modeling, concept reinforcement, and instruction has been shown to predict higher student achievement, student efficacy, student self-regulation, and academic competence (Hoover-Dempsey et al., 2001).

Unfortunately, the bulk of the literature focuses on the parent–student relationship in early educational settings, likely because parental involvement in learning has been thought to decrease for middle, high school, and college students as they become more autonomous (Hill & Taylor, 2001). However, more recent reports indicate that parents do not stop caring about monitoring progress of students as they age, even into college years. Although parents may not be as active in helping with homework, their involvement continues to be associated with student future educational aspirations (e.g., getting into college) and positive student outcomes (e.g., increased time spent on homework, increased homework completed) throughout high school and beyond (Hill et al., 2004).

Parent–Teacher

The parent–teacher relationship is especially important in the K-12 education system because the quality of this connection can allow the important adults in a student's life to work together to construct a child's learning environment to their individual needs (Trumbull, Rothstein-Fisch, & Hernandez, 2003). Research has shown that parent involvement can be a component of student success (Amundson, 1988; Chavkin & Garza-Lubeck, 1990; Love, 1996). Most of the research, however, has focused on more traditional forms of interpersonal or mediated communication, such as parent–teacher meetings, phone calls, or written notes and newsletters (Swap, 1987; Williams & Cartledge, 1997).

Secondary Relationships

The social learning ecosystem is also made up of secondary relationships between students, teachers, and parents with outside entities that contribute to the learning environment (Figure 5.1). Within the educational community, peer communication among teachers in the teacher–teacher relationship has been seen as a way for teachers to serve as models for other—especially, novice—teachers through both formal and informal means and to collaborate on best practices for teaching (e.g., sharing lesson plans, exchanging creative ideas). The most macro of the secondary relationships are the teacher– "decision-maker" and the student–school/infrastructure relationships. The teacher– "decision-maker" relationship here refers to the communication between teachers and school administrators, board members, and greater policy makers within the school community. This relationship comes to the forefront when teachers and "decision-makers" are determining the best teaching practices, course and curriculum design, and budgets for educational technology and media. The student–greater school network/infrastructure relationship applies mostly to high school, college, and adult learner populations, and relates to the ability of the student to navigate through the greater school network to communicate and advocate for their individual needs. The school network, in turn, can communicate with individual students regarding university- or network-wide issues.

Previous Attempts to Integrate Media and Technology

Attempting to integrate technology and media into classroom education is by no means a new phenomenon. Beginning with "old media" (i.e., books), as soon as new platforms and products become available, teachers and students have dabbled with them in, and at times adopted them into, the learning experience. A sampling of how media and technology offerings are currently being integrated into the social learning ecosystem is shown in Figure 5.2. Without a doubt, over the past twenty years of rapid technological innovation, significant lessons have been learned when it comes to integrating technology and media into formal education.

In the late 1990s President Clinton proposed a new vision for putting more technology in schools: Students should have modern computers and learning devices made available to them; classrooms should have the ability to communicate within and outside of the school; educational software should be an integral part of the curriculum; and teachers should be equipped with the tools and resources to use and teach with technology (Christensen, Horn, & Johnson, 2008). Computer technology immediately began entering

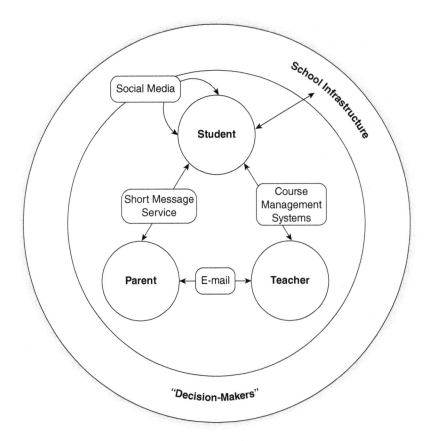

Figure 5.2 The social learning ecosystem with examples of integrated technology and media

classrooms and continued to pour in for the next several years. By 2000, the computer–student ratio was 1:5, up from 1:125 in 1981. By 2009, 97 percent of teachers had at least one computer in their classrooms (Gray, Thomas, & Lewis, 2010; Maher, Phelps, Urane, & Lee, 2012). In addition to computers, SMARTboard penetration rates in U.S. classrooms reached nearly 30 percent by 2009 (Gray, Thomas, & Lewis, 2010).

Despite this surge, teachers were often un- or under-prepared to success-fully utilize the technologies themselves or with students. Teachers were not trained properly to use the available media, and thus were unable to inte-grate them into their existing curriculum per Clinton's decree. Bers (2008) described teachers and school personnel at this time as "technocentric," focusing all of their energy and resources on *obtaining* technology for the classroom, while neglecting to develop a plan to integrate the platforms into existing educational goals and to overcome obstacles and challenges to learning. Instead of teaching students *with* available technology, teachers often resorted to teaching *around* the technology by using the platforms as an elective activity to supplement core learning. For instance, in 2008, fifth graders reported using computers in school only twenty-four minutes per week; eighth graders reported slightly more in-class use, but still only 38 minutes per week (Christensen, Horn, & Johnson, 2008). A recent international study suggests that things have not changed that much. According to the report, only 10 percent of teachers used the media provided (virtual learning environments) and less than one quarter (22 percent) had attempted to establish online learning environments of any kind. Of the few teachers who had done so, only 56 percent intended to use them for instruction (Maher et al., 2012). These findings suggest a significant lack of impact for teacher–student communication through these technologies.

As alluded to above, a lack of teacher training undoubtedly contributes to the gap in technology and media integration in learning, but so does a teacher's attitude about that integration. Teachers who are "resistant" to technology/media integration in the classroom are less likely to utilize them. Inan and Lowther (2010) showed that both teacher-readiness and positive beliefs about technology and media uses for learning significantly affected integration of technology in the classroom. Those teacher attitudes are greatly influenced by the attitudes toward technology and media integration held by decision-makers within the school environment (especially regarding overall support, technical support, and teacher professional development) (Inan & Lowther, 2010).

An additional hurdle to overcome in the successful application of media in learning environments is the issue of teacher presence. Teacher presence has been a point of contention for many years in the educational community. The term is related to the perspective that the teacher must serve (1) as a designer of the student educational experience; (2) as a subject matter expert who can be used to scaffold learning experiences; and (3) as a facilitator of the social environment of the class (Anderson, Rourke, Garrison, & Archer, 2001). It has been assumed that "presence" plays a role in the teacher meeting these expectations.

The introduction of online learning environments such as Second Life (2003) required researchers to consider how teacher presence might be extended beyond the traditional classrooms and into media platforms. Second Life promised the opportunity for residents to "digitize everything" including educational experiences; educational institutions that began holding lectures, courses, and even virtual campuses in Second Life were hailed for being early adopters (Jennings & Collins, 2007). Because teacher–student interaction and teacher presence has been seen as more important to educational outcomes than peer interaction, Second Life was poised to allow instructors to provide more individualized feedback and personalized attention (Garrison & Cleveland-Ives, 2005). Here instructors could "hold class" online or in a physical classroom and allow students to customize their learning experiences and interactions with both the instructor and peers (Huvila, Holmberg, Ek, & Widén-Wulff, 2010). Initial research indicated that college students reported no preferences between traditional or online learning environments, with online components being seen as complementary to in-person instruction and as allowing teachers to be hyper-aware of fulfilling student/teacher interaction needs (Garrison & Cleveland-Ives, 2005; Huvila et al., 2010).

Despite the initial buzz among academics and industry leaders, Second Life failed to make a lasting impression on today's educators. Many educators and students who initially used Second Life felt it was not the most "accessible or stable" platform, required too much training to become proficient, and was not strong enough to be a stand-alone asset, best used in tandem with more traditional class settings (Jarmon, Traphagan, Mayrath, & Trivedi, 2009). In truth, although Second Life was poised as having educational applications, it was never intended to serve the academic community; instead, it became a reminder that industry buzz does not guarantee successful applications for learning.

So even with considerable uptake in technology in schools (and in homes), we still have a long way to go in harnessing the power of media in the learning experience; and specifically to impact teacher–student and student peer communication. And as new platforms emerge more rapidly, it will become even more critical to reflect on the past successes (and failures) in order to develop appropriate and impactful platforms and content.

Emerging Media: Things to Consider

Without a doubt, with the emergence of new technology and media, the concept of a "learning environment" has shifted dramatically. As history attests, simply introducing emerging technology has not been enough to create new learning experiences. New models must use these tools and services to engage students on a deeper level (Johnson et al., 2013). Product developers are beginning to design more sophisticated media to use in tandem with existing and emerging technology platforms, and educators are attempting to integrate technology and media to supplement and replace traditional learning environments for all types of students. Through the lens of the lessons learned from previous attempts, below we examine current technology trends. Figure 5.3 provides an overview of how some current and emerging technology and media is being integrated into the social learning system.

Platforms Should Augment Existing Behavior, Not Change It

One of the biggest lessons learned from previous attempts was the importance of integrating technology into existing learning environments. The best cases have been those in which media have been implemented to augment

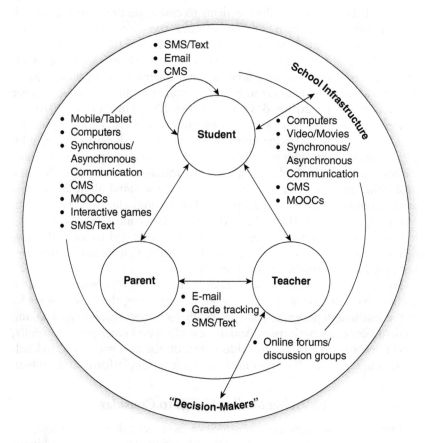

Figure 5.3 The social learning ecosystem and emerging technology and media

the learning experience, not replace in-classroom teaching. For example, Johnson et al. (2013) reported that many schools have increased their availability of providing tablet computing and associated educational media (via apps and games) to students. Tablet computing is important as an augmenting technology because it provides the potential for students to have their own device that can be used for personalized learning both within and outside the classroom, as well as enhances communication between teachers and students and student peers through ready access to social communication features such as email and chat. These devices: (1) have a built-in connection to a network of other devices (computer, mobile, iPod); (2) are portable, allowing them to move between classrooms and be taken home; and (3) allow students to load their own content and physically manipulate their device. This movement to tablets provides the technological potential for more individual student-centric learning environments in which educators can monitor and track educational progress. These specialized—even individualized—learning environments can be used with any student population where tablets can also supplement traditional classroom experiences with productivity apps, e-textbooks, and file-sharing capabilities for collaboration with peers (Johnson et al., 2013).

Other educators, especially those working with college populations, have adopted even more technology and media into their classrooms by including online course management systems (CMS) into learning experiences. CMS such as Blackboard, WebCT, or Moodle provide students, instructors, and the greater school infrastructure a shared online space where students can interact asynchronously (via discussion board or e-mail functions), interact with the instructor, and access greater resources provided by the school (Mullen, 2002). These platforms allow educators and students to generate and track discussions outside the classroom to supplement the in-class experience. In CMS, students have reported most frequently using the assignment-tracking, individual instruction, and grade-tracking features. However, the same students reported individualized learning record, assignment tracking, software downloads, system announcements, and user guidance as most *useful* for learning (Chou, Peng, & Chang, 2010). These key functionalities, in most cases, are simply digital versions of offline behaviors, such as using a paper planner or receiving text-based materials. The key, however, is that they make these behaviors easier and provide ways for them to be coordinated, easily accessed, and completed on one (or a couple) of devices. In addition, the communication features of these systems need to provide means of *improved* (or at least equal) communication between teachers and students, not just easier ways to send messages.

Integrating Formal and Informal Learning Environments

It is also important to consider the broad range of environments in which students gather and assimilate knowledge. Some learning environments are more formal (e.g., traditional classrooms, college settings), and some are more informal (e.g., at home, at churches/temples/mosques, at camp). More formal learning environments have a predefined curriculum set by state standards that can guide teachers to the desired learning objectives for a student group, and that must also be considered when choosing a platform to help teach those objectives. For instance, teachers may teach math concepts to preschoolers using tablet apps and games defined to teach numbers, counting, and sequencing; or use interactive e-books to reinforce literacy. In addition to traditional kids-focused media brands, such as PBS or Nick Jr., there are now entire app-focused brands being developed in the education space, such as Duck Duck Moose, Mindshapes, and Toca Boca.

Additionally, students learn a wide variety of information in informal settings through exploring, making and creating, and playing with peers, informal educators (e.g., parents, counselors, mentors), and even by them- selves. Educational technology built for use in these informal environments can address a wider variety of learning objectives—social–emotional learn- ing, creativity and abstract thinking skills, language and literacy skills—than formal education settings (Barker & Ansorge, 2007). Tablet and smartphone apps exist to help parents and other informal educators identify media that will help children learn various skills. For example, Storypanda allows chil- dren and parents to read, create, and share their stories with others. Toontastic allows children to tell stories through animation. Minecraft is a virtual world that allows students to develop user-generated content, navigate social con- texts, and creatively solve problems within the world. These types of media help facilitate both student–student and student–parent communication and collaborations, while drawing on a breadth of skills.

Even teachers have begun to acknowledge the power of informal learn- ing environments on student outcomes, making "homework" the new classwork (i.e. the "flipped classroom"). The flipped classroom approach (Strayer, 2007) allows students to use in-classroom time to complete home- work, projects, and other experiential and conceptual learning using the teacher as a guide, and to view teacher-selected or recorded lecture videos at home. This approach supports active learning of key concepts in class through student–student and student–teacher collaborations and practical concept exploration, while allowing students to take a more student-centric approach to homework by going at their own pace (Tucker, 2012).

Most of this content and these tools are being developed *only* for informal learning environments, however. There has been movement to provide more of an overarching national framework in the U.S. for certain subjects (such as the Common Core State Standards Initiatives for math and language arts), and some content/platform developers are using these standards in an effort to provide a closer link between informal and formal learning. In general, however, there is still a significant disconnect between informal learning experiences and a student's classroom learning.

In higher education, new informal learning providers, such as the Kahn Academy, are garnering huge student user audiences (over 10 million by 2012 for the Kahn Academy) (Noer, 2012). The curricula for these systems (or for students' individual experience within these systems), and the tieback into stu- dent's more traditional classroom experience, is not yet clear. Professors, for example, do not have a record of additional content being studied by students in these informal environments, and therefore cannot gauge the impact of the available learning there versus their more formal curriculum and lecture.

Conclusion

It is clear that today's students are fundamentally different in their expecta- tions and experiences with technology than those of previous generations, and they require a much more evolved social learning ecosystem that is facilitated by emerging technology to reflect this shift. Previous attempts to utilize emerging technology have left us with lessons learned: To be prepared to be always iterating, to acknowledge that technology integration is essential, and to not believe the hype surrounding every new consumer technology or platform as an educational panacea. All stakeholders in the social learning ecosystem are beginning to embrace integrating technology and media to create more customized and student-centric learning experiences in formal and informal learning environments. However, as new technologies and media develop, the potential for educational applications require the educational system to be constantly adapting and changing.

In addition to considering the core areas outlined above, there are a few more ways that those in the social learning ecosystem can keep up with ever-changing technology and media and choose platforms wisely: Teacher training/ efficacy research and positive technology development. Helping educators across all age groups feel more prepared to integrate technology includes increasing teacher trainings and in-services, providing "tech support" to provide check-ups/troubleshoot, researching the efficacy of various digital learning systems on student achievement and outcomes, and help in creating an integrated curriculum. In addition to teacher training, various experts in the world of educational media have started to pool resources and create an update-table guidebook or "best practices guide" to help designers and producers develop educational tools that are relevant to the target student audience (PlayScience, 2012; Sesame Workshop, 2013). Students will continue to be the center of the social learning ecosystem, and it is essential that other stakeholders (teachers, parents, decision-makers, and infrastructure) begin to find ways to utilize the technology and media available to best facilitate their learning needs.

References

Amundson, K. J. (1988). First teachers: Parent involvement in the public schools. Alexandria, VA: NSBA.

Anderson, T., Rourke, L., Garrison, R., & Archer, W. (2001). Assessing teaching presence in a computer conferencing context. *Journal of Asynchronous Learning Networks, 5*(2), 1–17.

Barker, B., & Ansorge, J. (2007). Robotics as means to increase achievement scores in an informal learning environment. *Journal of Research in Technology on Education, 39*, 229–243.

Bers, M. (2008). *Blocks to robots: Learning with technology in the early childhood classroom.* New York: Teachers College Press.

Chavkin, N., & Garza-Lubeck, M. (1990). Multicultural approaches to parent involvement: Research and practice. *Social Work in Education, 13*(1), 22–33. doi: 10.1093/cs/13.1.22

Christensen, C., Horn, M., Johnson, C. (2008). *Disrupting class: How disruptive innovation will change the way the world learns.* New York: McGraw Hill.

Chou, C., Peng, H., & Chang, C. (2010). The technical framework of interactive functions for course-management systems: Students' perceptions, uses, and evaluations. *Computers & Education, 55*, 1004–1017. doi: 10.1016/j.compedu.2010.04.011

Crosnoe, R., Kirkpatrick Johnson, M., & Elder, G. (2004). Intergenerational bonding in school: The behavioral and contextual correlates of student–teacher relationships. *Sociology of Education, 77*, 60–81. doi: 10.1177/003804070407700103

Druin, A. (2009). *Mobile technology for children: Designing for interaction and learning*. Burlington, MA: Morgan Kaufman, Elsevier.

Dunn, R., & Dunn, K. (1978). *Teaching students through their individual learning styles: A practical approach*. Reston, VA: Reston Publishing Company.

Dwyer, K. K., Bingham, S. G., Carison, R. E., Prisbell, M., Cruz, A. M., & Fus, D. A. (2004). Communication and connectedness in the classroom: Development of the connected classroom climate inventory. *Communication Research Reports, 21*, 264–272. doi: 10.1080/08824090409359988

Frisby, B., Martin, M. (2010). Instructor–student and student–student rapport in the classroom. *Communication Education, 59*, 146–164. doi: 10.1080/03634520903564362

Gardner, H. (1983) *Frames of mind: The theory of multiple intelligences*. New York: Basic Books.

Gardner, H. (2006). *Multiple intelligences*. New York: Basic Books.

Garrison, R., & Cleveland-Ives, M. (2005). Facilitating cognitive presence in online learning: Interaction is not enough. *The American Journal of Distance Education, 19*, 133–148. doi: 10.1207/s15389286ajde1903_2

Gray, L., Thomas, N., & Lewis, L. (2010). *Teachers' use of educational technology in US public schools: 2009*. First Look. NCES 2010-040. Washington, DC: National Center for Education Statistics.

Hill, N., & Taylor, L. (2001). Parental school involvement, and children's academic achievement. *Current Directions in Psychological Science, 13*, 161–164. doi: 10.1111/j.0963-7214.2004.00298.x

Hill, N. E., Castellino, D. R., Lansford, J. E., Nowlin, P., Dodge, K. A., Bates, J., & Pettit, G. (2004). Parent-academic involvement as related to school behavior, achievement, and aspirations: Demographic variations across adolescence. *Child Development, 75*, 1491–1509. doi: 10.1111/j.1467-8624.2004.00753.x

Hoover-Dempsey, K., Battiano, A., Walker, J., Reed, R., DeJong, J., & Jones, K. (2001). Parental involvement in homework. *Educational Psychologist, 36*, 195–209. doi: 10.1207/S15326985EP3603_5

Huvila, I., Holmberg, K., Ek, S., & Widén-Wulff, G. (2010). Social capital in Second Life. *Online Information Review, 34*, 295–316. doi: 10.1108/14684521011037007

Inan, F., & Lowther, D. (2010). Laptops in the K-12 classrooms: Exploring factors impacting instructional use. *Computers in Education, 55*, 937–944. doi: 10.1016/j.compedu.2010.04.004

Jarmon, L., Traphagan, T., Mayrath, M., & Trivedi, A. (2009). Virtual world teaching, experiential learning, and assessment: An interdisciplinary communication course in Second Life. *Computers in Education, 53*, 169–182. doi: 10.1016/j.compedu.2009.01.010

Jennings, N., & Collins, C. (2007). Virtual or virtually u: Educational institutions in Second Life. *International Journal of Social Science, 2*, 180–186.

Johnson, L., Adams Becker, S., Cummins, M., Estrada, V., Freeman, A., & Ludgate, H. (2013). *NMC horizon report: 2013 Higher education edition.* Austin, TX: The New Media Consortium.

Love, F. (1996). Communicating with parents: What beginning teachers can do. *College Student Journal, 30*(4), 440.

Maher, D., Phelps, R., Urane, N., & Lee, M. (2012). Primary school teachers' use of digital resources with interactive whiteboards: The Australian context. *Australasian Journal of Educational Technology, 28*, 138–158.

Martin, M. M., Myers, S. A., & Mottet, T. P. (1999). Students' motives for communicating with their instructors. *Communication Education, 48*(2), 155–164.

Mullen, M. (2002). "If you're not Mark Mullen, click here": Web–based courseware and the pedagogy of suspicion. *Radical Teacher, 63*, 14–20.

Noer, M. (2012, November 19). One man, one computer, 10 million students: How Kahn Academy is reinventing education. *Forbes.* http://www.forbes.com/sites/michaelnoer/2012/11/02/one-man-one-computer-10-million-students-how-khan-academy-is-reinventing-education.

Purcell, K. (2012). *Teens 2012: Truth, trends, and myths about teen online behavior.* Paper presented at the 27th Annual ACT Enrollment Planners Conference. Pew Research Center, Pew Internet & American Life Project, July, 11.

PlayScience (2012). *Best Practices Guide.* Internal White Paper.

PlayScience (2013). *Casual Gaming Report.* Casual Games Association. http://casualconnect.org/research-reports.

Rideout, V., Foehr, U., & Roberts, D. (2010) *Generation M2: Media in the lives of 8–18 year olds.* Menlo Park, CA: Henry J. Kaiser Family Foundation.

Sesame Workshop (2013). *Best practices: Designing touch tablet experiences for preschoolers.* Retrieved from http://www.sesameworkshop.org/our-blog/2012/12/17/sesames-best-practices-guide-for-childrens-app-development/

Strayer, J. F. (2007). *The effects of the classroom flip on the learning environment: A comparison of learning activity in a traditional classroom and a flip classroom that used an intelligent tutoring system.* Dissertation. Ohio State University. http://etd.ohiolink.edu/view.cgi/Strayer%20Jeremy.pdf?osu1189523914.

Swap, S. (1987). *Enhancing parent involvement in schools.* New York: Teachers College Press.

Trumbull, E., Rothstein-Fisch, C., & Hernandez, E. (2003). Parent involvement—according to whose values? *School Community Journal, 13*(2), 45–72.

Tucker, B. (2012). The flipped classroom. *Education Next, 12*(1), 82–83. http://educationnext.org/the-flipped-classroom/

Wei, F., Wang, K., & Klausner, M. (2012) Rethinking college students' self-regulation and sustained attention: Does text messaging during class influence cognitive learning? *Communication Education, 61*(3), 185–204. doi: 10.1080/03634523.2012.672755

Williams, V. I., & Cartledge, G. (1997). Passing notes to parents. *Teaching Exceptional Children, 30*(1), 30–34.

Young, S., Kelsey, D., & Lancaster, A. (2011). Predicted outcome value of e-mail communication: Factors that foster professional relational development between students and teachers. *Communication Education, 60*(4), 371–388. doi: 10.1080/03634523.2011.563388

Part II

MEDIA AND RELATIONSHIPS

6

MEDIA AND SOCIAL GROUPS

Mary Beth Oliver, Jennifer Hoewe, Erin Ash,
Keunyeong Kim, Mun-Young Chung, and Drew D. Shade

The means by which we learn about other cultures, genders, races, and nationalities unquestionably reflects a host of variables, including direct experiences, peers, and educational influences. Yet books, films, music, television, and the Internet, among other media forms, undoubtedly play crucially important roles as well, providing us with particularly salient images of people and societies that we may never experience firsthand. Through the lens of media, we get glimpses of other cultures, we view models of how we should enact our own behaviors, we learn lessons of how others live in ways that are similar to or different from our own, and we come to form expectations regarding our anticipated or imagined interactions. In short, the media represent an important teacher in the understanding of ourselves and other social groups, and we—the viewers, readers, listeners, gamers, or creators—are the students of these cultural "lessons."

The goal of this chapter is to overview scholarship regarding the role of media in affecting and potentially shaping our perceptions of social groups and to suggest some potentially fruitful avenues for future study. We begin by providing a synthesis of research concerning media portrayals themselves, and then turn to theoretical perspectives regarding how we, as media consumers, may be affected by these recurrent themes. We also believe that great opportunities exist for using the media as a means for creating greater connectedness, and therefore we next reflect on the possibilities of prosocial media outcomes. Finally, we end our discussion by briefly considering the implications of changing technologies on intergroup perceptions.

Media Depictions of Social Groups

A voluminous body of scholarship in media psychology has documented the media's tendency to depict social groups in ways that sometimes mirror, but typically distort, social reality. Although research has tended to focus heavily on race and gender, in this section we expand our consideration to include social groups defined by sexual orientation and health-related issues.

Race and Ethnicity

Research focused on portrayals of race and ethnicity has examined a diversity of social groups, though the representation of African Americans has received the greatest amount of scholarly attention, perhaps because African Americans constitute the largest percentage of minority representation in U.S. media content (Mastro, 2009a). In this regard, research on news portrayals has generally indicated the continued association of African Americans with issues of crime and poverty. For example, Dixon and Linz's (2000a) analysis of local news coverage showed that Black individuals were overrepresented as the perpetrators of crimes and underrepresented as members of law enforcement (Dixon & Azocar, 2006; Dixon & Linz, 2000b). Likewise, Gilens' (1996) analysis of high-circulation newsmagazines demonstrated a strong tendency for news stories to overrepresent African Americans in photographs accompanying stories about poverty (see also Clawson & Trice, 2000; Gilens, 1996).

The media's coupling of African Americans with crime is a pattern replicated with depictions of Hispanics and Latinos. For example, in the aforementioned study, Dixon and Linz (2000a) reported that Latinos were also overrepresented as criminals and underrepresented as police officers in their sample of local television news. However, other research has reported Latinos to be underrepresented as the perpetrators of crimes (Dixon & Azocar, 2006; Dixon & Linz, 2000b). These findings may reflect the general underrepresentation of Latinos in comparison to Whites and African Americans in media. However, Mastro and Behm-Morawitz's (2005) analysis of primetime network television content showed that when Latino characters *were* featured, they were more provocatively dressed and had heavier accents than characters of other races and ethnicities (see also Monk-Turner, Heiserman, Johnson, Cotton, & Jackson, 2010).

Arabs and Muslims represent additional groups frequently depicted as the perpetrators of crimes. For example, Powell (2011) found national news coverage surrounding terrorism often focused on Muslims and Arabs—and particularly those not identified as Americans. Similarly, Shaheen's (2003) analysis of the portrayal of Middle Easterners in more than 900 films concluded that Muslims are frequently conflated with Arabs, and these individuals are represented as "insidious cultural 'others'" (p. 188). These media stereotypes are not new, however; research conducted prior to September 11, 2001, indicated Middle Easterners were often portrayed as being either oil suppliers or potential terrorists (Said, 1991).

To summarize, scholarship focused on representations of race and ethnicity has revealed recurrent media themes that likely serve to foster and sustain stereotypes, especially when it comes to criminal behavior. Of course, our review touches on only a small number of races and ethnicities, due in part to the general lack of media representation of groups such as Asian Americans and Native Americans. As the media landscape becomes increasingly diverse and begins to represent a greater number of racial and ethnic groups, we hope scholars will continue to expand the scope of this research.

Gender

Analyses of media portrayals of gender within television and film generally reflect two predominant themes (for recent overviews see Collins, 2011; Greenwood & Lippman, 2010). The first theme is the continued under-representation of female characters in speaking roles in comparison to male characters (Smith & Granados, 2009). The second theme involves the nature of gender portrayals, with female characters most commonly depicted as young, attractive, and sexualized (Lauzen & Dozier, 2005; Smith & Granados, 2009). Female characters are also more likely than male characters to be portrayed in domestic, caregiver roles, and less likely to be shown in occupational roles or as holding leadership positions in the workplace (Lauzen, Dozier, & Horan, 2008; Signorielli & Kahlenberg, 2001). In contrast, male characters are more frequently depicted in ways reflecting "hypermasculinity," including displays of aggression, toughness, and sexual callousness (Scharrer, 2001; Vokey, Tefft, & Tysiaczny, 2013).

As media landscapes evolve and more entertainment forms become available, one might hope for changes in the way that gender is depicted. Unfortunately, newer forms of entertainment such as video games continue to present stereotyped images of male and female characters. For example, content analyses report that female characters are typically underrepresented and are frequently depicted in hypersexualized ways compared to male characters (see, for example, Downs & Smith, 2010). We look forward to seeing whether gender portrayals will evolve, as women come to represent a larger percentage of gamers overall.

Sexual Orientation

The study of media portrayals of characters that are lesbian, gay, bisexual, transgendered, or queer/questioning (LGBTQ) is relatively new in the social-scientific community, which is likely a reflection of their infrequent media depictions until recently. Fortunately, research has indicated that LGBTQ characters are becoming more prevalent, with Wyatt's (2012) analysis of TV portrayals in English-speaking countries showing an increase from a mere 59 characters in the 1960s to 792 characters from 2001 to the present.

Despite the growing presence of LGBTQ characters, members of this group are still underrepresented compared to population estimates (Fouts & Inch, 2005; Klein & Shiffman, 2009; White, 2001). Further, stereotypes of the LGBTQ community persist, including caricatures of gay men as overly feminine (McCreary, 1994), an overemphasis on the sexual orientation of gay versus straight couples (Fouts & Inch, 2005), and a tendency for news stories to rely more heavily on heterosexual sources, even when discussing issues such as gay marriage (Moscowitz, 2010). With these stereotypes in mind, though, we find the popularity of celebrities such as Ellen Degeneres an optimistic sign that the media landscape may be changing and that viewers are becoming more accepting (e.g., Bonds-Raacke, Cady, Schlegel, Harris, & Firebaugh, 2007), though such interpretations clearly await future study.

Stigmatized Groups

The final set of portrayals that we touch on in this section pertains not to social groups defined by demographic or cultural characteristics, but rather by frequently stigmatized health conditions: obesity and mental illness. In terms of obesity, stereotypical portrayals of overweight or obese people can be seen throughout a diversity of media content, including news (McClure, Puhl, & Heuer, 2011), television programs (Greenberg, Eastin, Hofschire, Lachlan, & Brownell, 2003), and even video games (Latner, Rosewall, & Simmonds, 2007). Overweight or obese individuals are not only underrepresented overall compared to actual populations, but are also depicted as lazy, sloppy, uneducated, or physically unattractive (Greenberg et al., 2003).

Similarly, negative media depictions are associated with people who suffer from mental-health conditions. For example, media characters with mental illnesses often appear as significantly more violent than their real-world counterparts (Diefenbach, 1997). They are also frequently depicted as vulnerable, feeble, or generally incapable of regulating their own lives (Coverdale, Nairn, & Claasen, 2002).

As scholars continue to examine the influence of media on social cognition, we encourage a greater emphasis on groups that are frequently stigmatized in terms of variables such as health, sexual orientation, physical characteristics, and even behavioral characteristics (e.g., computer "geeks," vegans). Because such stereotypes are often widely shared and accepted, we believe viewers may be particularly vulnerable to negative depictions that may not be readily recognized as potentially objectionable.

Effects of Media Stereotyping

Given the prevalence of media stereotypes and their frequent negative characterizations of various social groups, research on the effects of such portrayals have frequently examined the possible harmful effects of media consumption on individuals' attitudes and beliefs. Within this large body of research, scholars have tended to examine how media can both prime or instigate existing stereotypes and how media may play a consequential role in stereotype formation.

Instigation of Existing Stereotypes

Research examining how media can serve to instigate stereotypes relies heavily on cognitive-association models of priming (see Roskos-Ewoldsen & Roskos-Ewoldsen, 2009, for a review). In brief, this perspective conceptualizes individuals' cognitions, feelings, and motor responses as nodes in a cognitive network, with semantically related nodes connected via associative pathways. When one node in a cognitive network is primed, this activation spreads out to associated nodes, making a constellation of related cognitive and affective elements accessible. As a result, during the time that a cognitive network has been primed, individuals will be likely to interpret ambiguous stimuli through the lens of the primed elements. For example, a given individual harboring stereotypical attitudes toward African Americans may possess a cognitive network that connects cognitions such as "lazy," "dangerous," or "criminal." For this individual then, should the media prime one of these elements (e.g., lazy), related elements will also be activated (e.g., fear, avoidance), with this activation having the potential to affect subsequent interpretations of stimuli (e.g., a Black teenager is perceived to be criminal) as long as the network is primed.

A host of studies have found support for the general idea that media portrayals can prime or activate social stereotypes, thereby influencing interpretations of and behavioral tendencies toward stereotyped targets (see Mastro, 2009b). For example, Johnson, Trawalter, and Dovidio (2000) found that exposure to music videos of violent rap music was related to subsequent judgments of African Americans as less intelligent (a stereotypical characteristic) but unrelated to judgments that were not stereotyped (e.g., spatial skills). Likewise, McKenzie-Mohr and Zanna (1990) reported that among gender-schematic males (i.e., those scoring high on masculinity and low on femininity), exposure to sexually explicit media portrayals not only resulted in greater attention to the physical appearance of a female encountered in a subsequent, unrelated task, but also in more frequent behaviors reflecting greater intimacy or sexual attraction (e.g., reducing special distance). Similar priming effects of sexual attitudes and perceptions have also been obtained for music videos (Aubrey, Hopper, & Mbure, 2011) and for video games (Yao, Mahood, & Linz, 2010).

One important implication of priming models is the assumption that cognitive networks need to be in place in order for spreading activation to occur. In other words, if a given person does *not* associate African Americans with criminality (for example), then the priming of this social group should not result in the activation of cognitions related to crime. However, in noting the importance of existing cognitive networks in the priming process, we are not suggesting that only those who consciously endorse stereotypes are susceptible. Rather, research on implicit attitudes suggests that many people are familiar with a variety of stereotypes via socially and culturally shared experiences, including the media (Verhaeghen, Aikman, & Van Gulick, 2011). As a result, stereotypical cognitions and associated affect can be primed for people who may be either low or high on measures of explicit prejudice. However, such activation should be less likely to influence behaviors when individuals are aware that activation has occurred and are motivated to control its effects on their behaviors (Fazio & Towles-Schwen, 1999). One implication of this reasoning is that media cues that may make individuals aware that stereotypes have been primed may ultimately diminish their influence among people who do not endorse stereotypical associations (e.g., Valentino, Hutchings, & White, 2002).

A second implication of priming on out-group perceptions concerns the anticipated duration of the effects of media exposure. In general, media priming of related cognitions is thought to be relatively short-lived (Arendt, 2013; Roskos-Ewoldsen & Roskos-Ewoldsen, 2009). With this in mind, though, this does not mean that priming cannot account for longer-term effects. Rather, Berkowitz, and Rogers (1986) argued that any given media portrayal (e.g., violence) can be associated with cues that, when encountered later in the environment, can prime or activate cognitions associated with the portrayal. For example, should media portrayals of Arab characters be repeatedly associated with terrorism, these two concepts may become linked in an associative network, with frequent exposure to such portrayals leading to a stronger association in memory. As a consequence, later exposure to one of these elements (e.g., an Arab individual) should prime thoughts of the other (e.g., terrorism). Consistent with this general argument, Mange, Chun, Sharvit, and Belanger (2012) reported that the participants in their sample (all White Americans) were quicker to fire at an ambiguous target in a shooting game when the category of Muslim/Arab had been primed than when it had not.

Formation of Stereotypes

In addition to priming existing cognitions of out-group members, media exposure is also thought to have the ability to influence the *creation, learning*, and/or *development* of perceptions and behaviors associated with social group membership. Indeed, the idea that media play a consequential role in the formation of stereotypes likely forms the basis of the greatest amount of research into media and social cognition—perhaps because it is generally thought to represent a wide-scale and long-lasting effect.

Cultivation theory is one of the most frequently studied perspectives on stereotype formation. This theory suggests that long-term, cumulative consumption of media content can lead to distorted perceptions of social reality that mirror the patterns of portrayals frequently featured in the media (Morgan, Shanahan, & Signorielli, 2012). This hypothesis has received support in a variety of contexts, including the role of media in cultivating perceptions of African Americans as criminals (Oliver & Armstrong, 1998), the effect of reality programming on heightened perceptions of the prevalence of teen pregnancies (Davis & Mares, 1998), and the importance of news consumption on perceived risk and fear of terrorism (Nellis & Savage, 2012).

More recent theorizing regarding the mechanisms explaining cultivation effects offers additional insights into when media may be most influential. Specifically, Shrum's (2008) heuristic model of cultivation processing points out that when making judgments or estimates (e.g., the percentage of African Americans on public assistance), people often base their judgments on examples that come to mind easily (including those from the media), and they frequently fail to carefully scrutinize the validity of these examples or the credibility of the source from which the example may have originated. As a result, these readily accessible examples serve to inflate perceptions of the prevalence of the phenomenon under consideration via the availability heuristic (Tversky & Kahneman, 1973). One implication of this line of research concerns the relative importance of information sources in social-reality judgments. Specifically, this model implies that media influence may be particularly influential when individuals lack direct contact with the target population under consideration, as under such circumstances media portrayals may serve as the only source of information available (Fujioka, 1999).

Whereas cultivation studies focus primarily on the effects of long-term media exposure on individuals' perceptions, exemplification theory experimentally demonstrates that brief exposure to media content can affect individuals' attitudes and beliefs, even when the exemplars are inconsistent with statistical base-rate information also presented (Brosius, 2003; Zillmann & Brosius, 2000). As a result, insofar as media examples frequently misrepresent information about social groups, individuals may be likely to develop inaccurate or distorted perceptions. Consistent with this reasoning, Gibson and Zillmann (2000) found that individuals' estimates of the prevalence of health-related concerns among different racial groups varied as a function of the race of individuals pictured in a news story about the issue. Although this study did not measure negative stereotypes specifically, it provides a strong rationale for suggesting that similar findings may be expected for issues such as poverty or crime that frequently employ racial minorities as exemplars.

Summary

Our overview of some of the most frequently employed theoretical approaches to understanding media's connection to perceptions of social groups is but a very brief treatment of the growing body of scholarship in this area. Additional topics include issues such as identity formation, social-cognitive effects, and schema development, as well as additional outcome variables such as political participation and public policy preferences. Further, given the potential influence that media may have on our perceptions, it is understandable that, in addition to looking at the harmful effects of media, scholars are also becoming increasingly interested in examining the ways in which media may be harnessed for purposes of social good—an issue we address in the next section of this chapter.

Using Media to Enhance Positive Intergroup Perceptions

Documenting the existence of harmful media outcomes on intergroup relations has occupied a much greater proportion of research attention among social scientists than has scholarship on the potential for positive outcomes. Perhaps this focus is a reflection of the pervasiveness and salience of negative portrayals. Nevertheless, there is an increasing momentum among media psychologists to also examine how media can be used for purposes of counter-stereotyping and for creating feelings or perceptions of greater connectedness between members of different social groups.

Counter-Stereotyping

The use of counter-stereotypes, or favorable exemplars, is arguably the most frequently studied means that researchers have employed to try to diminish or even reverse the effects of negative stereotyping and feelings of prejudice toward social groups frequently depicted in negative ways.

Early work in this area revealed promising results, with studies showing that exposure to favorable photographs of African Americans (and negative images of Whites) not only diminished self-reported racial prejudice among White participants, but also reduced negative implicit (or automatic) attitudes as assessed via the Implicit Association Test (e.g., Dasgupta & Greenwald, 2001). More recent research suggests that exposure to counter-stereotypical *media* depictions may reduce negative racial attitudes (e.g., Ramasubramanian & Oliver, 2007) and that recall of positive media depictions of homosexual media persona can heighten favorable attitudes toward gays and lesbians (Bonds-Raacke et al., 2007).

Although such findings present hopeful evidence that positive media exemplars may be an effective means of encouraging counter-stereotyping, caution is in order. For instance, Mastro and Tukachinsky (2011) pointed out that, under some circumstances, exposure to positive exemplars may result in individuals' subtyping the portrayal as an exception, ultimately retaining the overall, negative stereotype. As a consequence, these authors argued that the use of prototypes in which favorable portrayals are shown to be representative of the overarching social group may be more effective. Similar to this argument, additional scholarship suggests that exposure to neutral or even positive portrayals of race may actually serve to sustain negative stereotypes, as individuals appear to interpret or remember information that is consistent with prevailing stereotypes (Oliver & Fonash, 2002; Vidmar & Rokeach, 1974). Together, these results imply that efforts at using positive exemplars would most likely be successful when the exemplars are consistent, salient, and unambiguous.

Parasocial Contact

Allport's (1954) contact hypothesis generally suggests that one of the most effective means of reducing prejudice and conflict between groups is via interpersonal contact. Yet for many individuals, interpersonal contact with out-group members is largely, if not completely, non-existent. For example, many Americans may have never met an Arab individual, yet depictions of Arabs are frequent within their media diets. As a result of these considerations, a number of researchers have explored the idea that the media may provide a "proxy" for interpersonal interaction (Fujioka, 1999; for a recent review, see Park, 2012). Namely, the parasocial contact hypothesis posits that viewers' parasocial relationships with out-group members depicted in the media may function in ways that are similar to interpersonal interaction in facilitating more positive perceptions of out-group members (Schiappa, Gregg, & Hewes, 2005).

In one early test of the parasocial contact hypothesis, Schiappa and his colleagues (2005) obtained general support for the idea that exposure to and positive parasocial responses to media depictions of gay and transvestite characters were associated with more favorable impressions of these out-group members overall. Ortiz and Harwood (2007) reported similar findings for both gay–straight and Black–White relationships. At the same time, though, Park (2012) points to the need for a greater exploration of the specific processes by which parasocial contact may function, the importance of individuals' tendencies to selectively expose themselves to (or avoid) media portrayals featuring out-group members, and the mediating role that viewers' perceptions and affective/cognitive responses to out-group characters may have on subsequent perceptions of out-group members overall.

Affective Responses as a Means of Facilitating Positive Outcomes

The importance of viewer responses to out-group character portrayals has led some scholars to focus their attention specifically on affect as an important mediator in the creation of positive out-group perceptions. Overall, this research suggests several affective states that appear to play particularly important roles in this process.

Because media frequently feature negative portrayals of individuals who are often targets of prejudice, oppression, or even stigmatization, it is understandable that a number of scholars have examined how media messages can be used to enhance feelings of empathy, caring, or compassion for these victimized groups. Earlier work in this area showed that verbal instructions to increase perspective taking while listening to an interview/story were effective at increasing empathy not only toward the specific individual featured in the story, but to the stigmatized group overall (Batson et al., 1997). More recently, Oliver, Dillard, Bae, and Tamul (2012) extended this line of research to news media specifically, showing that narrative stories about stigmatized/oppressed groups (e.g., people in prison, immigrants) were effective at increasing positive attitudes and even behaviors toward these groups by means of heightening empathic responses to the individuals featured in the news stories.

Additional research also suggests that affect may play an important role in enhancing favorable intergroup feelings by inducing other-praising emotions. Recently, scholars have begun to examine the affective state of elevation—the feeling that accompanies witnessing extraordinarily virtuous acts such as generosity, love, and kindness (Algoe & Haidt, 2009)—and how this state may serve to encourage positive attitudes and behaviors toward others. For example, Freeman, Aquino, and McFerran (2009) found evidence that elevation can serve to diminish the negative impact of social-dominance on Whites' altruistic behaviors toward African-American charities. Although this study is encouraging and suggests that elevation may be a promising avenue for future research, we recognize that scholarship in this area is in its very early stages and, therefore, awaits additional investigation and critical examination. For instance, some studies have pointed to the idea that individual differences, such as moral identity or benevolence, may moderate the likelihood of experiencing elevation (Aquino, McFerran, & Laven, 2011). Furthermore, it is likely that different types of media portrayals may be more or less effective at eliciting elevation depending on the viewers' moral standards and concerns. Finally, some types of "elevating" entertainment such as "White-savior" narratives (e.g., *The Blind Side*) may be paternalistic or may erroneously imply that racism is no longer a wide-scale problem (Ash, 2013). Hence, we look forward to future scholarship that more fully develops the moderators and mediators that predict when and how elevation may serve to enhance positive intergroup relations.

Future Directions

In this chapter we have attempted to provide an overview of extant scholarship and what it implies about the role of media in affecting social group perceptions and interactions. However, this scholarship obviously emphasizes communication media that have enjoyed prominence over the last several decades and undoubtedly fails to fully reflect what recent and evolving technologies may imply, both for good and bad. In this final section, we suggest several possible directions that may represent fruitful avenues of scholarship.

First, we believe it is important to broaden media research with an even greater recognition of the changing entertainment landscape that now includes not only film and television narratives, but also focuses on more interactive experiences, such as video games (see Klimmt, this volume). Although a number of scholars have provided evidence that games frequently depict social groups in distorted and negative ways (Dill & Thill, 2007), we also maintain hope that video games can be harnessed for purposes of counter-stereotyping. For example, customizing and controlling game characters or empathic engagement with game characters of other races could serve to enhance understanding of and identification with characters in different social groups (Lankoski, 2011; Lehdonvirta, Lehdonvirta, & Baba, 2011). In addition, gamers playing Massively Multiple Online Role-Playing Games (MMORPGs) may have more opportunities for contact with gamers of different ages, genders, and races/ethnicities. Such dynamic interaction with other players in the gaming environment may serve as counter-stereotyping experiences and represent an important research area for understanding changing perceptions of other groups.

Likewise, we look forward to additional research that examines the effects of social media on group perceptions (see Quinn & Papacharisi, this volume, and Utz, this volume). We recognize that social networks are generally employed as a means of staying in contact with existing networks (Ellison, Steinfield, & Lampe, 2007; Zhang, Tang, & Leung, 2011) and may therefore operate to strengthen existing in-group ties. At the same time, however, we believe that a variety of technological functions built into social media may offer the potential for counter-stereotyping. For example, the widespread sharing of media content with large numbers of people may increase the chance of exposure to media content that belies or counters preexisting negative views of others. Moreover, users of social networking sites can easily distribute media encouraging others to join prosocial activities by simply uploading, posting, or forwarding existing messages.

Finally, we believe that user-generated content provides avenues for scholarship on the role of media in changing group perceptions. On the one hand, user-generated sites such as YouTube may serve to increase intergroup hostilities via the hosting of stereotypical content, as well as added opportunity for users to engage in heated and critical comments via the ubiquitous phenomenon of "flaming" (O'Sullivan & Flanagin, 2003). On the other hand, we also believe that these types of venues provide unique opportunities to enhance positive intergroup relations. First, user-generated sites and related technologies have the ability to demonstrate and display intricate human networks and to allow for collaborative creativity in ways that may illustrate and cultivate the experience of connectedness. Second, unlike traditional entertainment media such as television or film, user-generated content provides individuals the opportunity to present themselves in ways that are desired and perhaps more accurate. So, for example, rather than having the media industry design and depict social groups in ways that are frequently distorted and stereotypical, user-generated sites allow individuals to create their own depictions in ways that may ultimately serve to address rather than sustain social stereotypes. Of course, these possibilities are merely speculative at this point, but we believe the shifting landscape of media creation provides unique opportunities to examine how media messages can be crafted and distributed for purposes of social good.

Final Thoughts

Stereotypes and in-group favoritism based on characteristics such as gender, race/ethnicity, and sexual orientation are enduring aspects of human history. However, the wide-scale use of media as a primary means of learning about other groups is what makes scholarship in this area particularly important. We value continued research into how media are often harmful and inaccurate in their portrayals and what this may imply about social attitudes and social injustice. At the same time, we are encouraged by the increased emphasis on the potential for positive media outcomes. We hope that scholars continue to focus their energies on this challenging avenue of research, as we believe that evolving media technologies provide us with an unparalleled opportunity to create, enact, and perceive the experience of a flourishing state of human connectedness.

References

Algoe, S. B., & Haidt, J. (2009). Witnessing excellence in action: The "other-praising"emotions of elevation, gratitude, and admiration. *The Journal of Positive Psychology, 4*(2), 105–127. doi: 10.1080/17439760802650519

Allport, G. W. (1954). *The nature of prejudice.* Cambridge, MA: Perseus Books.

Aquino, K., McFerran, B., & Laven, M. (2011). Moral identity and the experience of moral elevation in response to acts of uncommon goodness. *Journal of Personality and Social Psychology, 100*(4), 703–718. doi: 10.1037/a0022540

Arendt, F. (2013). News stereotypes, time, and fading priming effects. *Journalism & Mass Communication Quarterly, 90*, 347–362. doi: 10.1177/107769901 3482907

Ash, E. (2013). *Emotional responses to savior films: Concealing privilege or appealing to our better selves?* Ph.D. Dissertation, Penn State University, University Park, PA.

Aubrey, J. S., Hopper, K. M., & Mbure, W. G. (2011). Check that body! The effects of sexually objectifying music videos on college men's sexual beliefs. *Journal of Broadcasting & Electronic Media, 55*(3), 360–379. doi: 10.1080/08838151.2011.597469

Batson, C. D., Polycarpou, M. P., HarmonJones, E., Imhoff, H. J., Mitchener, E. C., Bednar, L. L., Klein, T. R., & Highberger, L. (1997). Empathy and attitudes: Can feeling for a member of a stigmatized group improve feelings toward the group? *Journal of Personality and Social Psychology, 72*, 105–118. doi: 10.1037//0022-3514.72.1.105

Berkowitz, L., & Rogers, K. H. (1986). A priming effect analysis of media influences. In J. Bryant & D. Zillmann (Eds.), *Perspectives on media effects* (pp. 57–82). Hillsdale, NJ: Lawrence Erlbaum Associates.

Bonds-Raacke, J. M., Cady, E. T., Schlegel, R., Harris, R. J., & Firebaugh, L. (2007). Remembering Gay/Lesbian media characters: Can Ellen and Will improve attitudes toward homosexuals? *Journal of Homosexuality, 53*(3), 19–34. doi: 10.1300/J082v53n03_03

Brosius, H. B. (2003). Exemplars in the news: A theory of the effects of political communication. In J. Bryant, D. Roskos-Ewoldsen & J. Cantor (Eds.), *Communication and emotion: Essays in honor of Dolf Zillmann* (pp. 179–194). Mahwah, NJ: Lawrence Erlbaum Associates.

Clawson, R. A., & Trice, R. (2000). Poverty as we know it: Media portrayals of the poor. *Public Opinion Quarterly, 64*, 53–64.

Collins, R. L. (2011). Content analysis of gender roles in media: Where are we now and where should we go? *Sex Roles, 64*(3–4), 290–298. doi: 10.1007/ s11199-010-9929-5

Coverdale, J., Nairn, R., & Claasen, D. (2002). Depictions of mental illness in print media: A prospective national sample. *Australian and New Zealand Journal of Psychiatry, 36*(5), 697–700. doi: 10.1046/j.1440-1614.2002.00998.x

Dasgupta, N., & Greenwald, A. G. (2001). On the malleability of automatic attitudes: Combating automatic prejudice with images of admired and disliked individuals. *Journal of Personality and Social Psychology, 81*(5), 800–814. doi: 10.1037//0022-3514.81.5.800

Davis, S., & Mares, M. L. (1998). Effects of talk show viewing on adolescents. *Journal of Communication, 48*(3), 69–86. doi: 10.1093/joc/48.3.69

Diefenbach, D. L. (1997). The portrayal of mental illness on prime-time television. *Journal of Community Psychology, 25*(3), 289–302. doi: 10.1002/(SICI)1520-6629(199705)25:3<289::AID-JCOP5>3.0.CO;2-R

Dill, K. E., & Thill, K. P. (2007). Video game characters and the socialization of gender roles: Young people's perceptions mirror sexist media depictions. *Sex Roles, 57*, 851–864. doi: 10.1007/s11199-007-9278-1

Dixon, T. L., & Azocar, C. L. (2006). The representation of juvenile offenders by race on Los Angeles area television news. *Howard Journal of Communications, 17*(2), 143–161. doi: 10.1080/10646170600656896

Dixon, T. L., & Linz, D. (2000a). Overrepresentation and underrepresentation of African Americans and Latinos as lawbreakers on television news. *Journal of Communication, 50*(2), 131–154. doi: 10.1111/j.1460-2466.2000.tb02845.x

Dixon, T. L., & Linz, D. (2000b). Race and the misrepresentation of victimization on local television news. *Communication Research, 27*(5), 547–573. doi: 10.1177/009365000027005001

Downs, E., & Smith, S. L. (2010). Keeping abreast of hypersexuality: A video game character content analysis. *Sex Roles, 62*(11–12), 721–733. doi: 10.1007/s11199-009-9637-1

Ellison, N. B., Steinfield, C., & Lampe, C. (2007). The benefits of Facebook "friends": Social capital and college students' use of online social network sites. *Journal of Computer-Mediated Communication, 12*(4), 1143–1168. doi: 10.1111/j.1083-6101.2007.00367.x

Fazio, R. H., & Towles-Schwen, T. (1999). The MODE model of attitude-behavior processes. In S. Chaiken & Y. Trope (Eds.), *Dual-process theories in social psychology* (pp. 97–116). New York: Guilford Press.

Fouts, G., & Inch, R. (2005). Homosexuality in TV situation comedies: Characters and verbal comments. *Journal of Homosexuality, 49*(1), 35–45. doi: 10.1300/J082v49n01_02

Freeman, D., Aquino, K., & McFerran, B. (2009). Overcoming beneficiary race as an impediment to charitable donations: Social dominance orientation, the experience of moral elevation, and donation behavior. *Personality and Social Psychology Bulletin, 35*(1), 72–84. doi: 10.1177/0146167208325415

Fujioka, Y. (1999). Television portrayals and African American stereotypes: Examination of television effects when direct contact is lacking. *Journalism & Mass Communication Quarterly, 76*, 52–75. doi:10.1177/107769909907600105

Gibson, R., & Zillmann, D. (2000). Reading between the photographs: The influence of incidental pictorial information on issue perception. *Journalism & Mass Communication Quarterly, 77*, 355–366. doi: 10.1177/107769900007700209

Gilens, M. (1996). Race and poverty in America: Public misperceptions and the American news media. *Public Opinion Quarterly, 60*, 515–541.

Greenberg, B. S., Eastin, M., Hofschire, L., Lachlan, K., & Brownell, K. D. (2003). Portrayals of overweight and obese individuals on commercial television. *American Journal of Public Health, 93*(8), 1342–1348. doi: 10.2105/AJPH.93.8.1342

Greenwood, D. N., & Lippman, J. R. (2010). Gender and media: Content, uses, and impact. In J. C. Chrisler & D. R. McCreary (Eds.), *Handbook of gender research in psychology, Vol 2: Gender research in social and applied psychology* (pp. 643–669). New York: Springer.

Johnson, J. D., Trawalter, S., & Dovidio, J. F. (2000). Converging interracial consequences of exposure to violent rap music on stereotypical attributions of Blacks. *Journal of Experimental Social Psychology, 36,* 233–251. doi: 10.1006/jesp.1999.1404

Klein, H., & Shiffman, K. S. (2009). Underrepresentation and symbolic annihilation of socially disenfranchised groups ("out groups") in animated cartoons. *The Howard Journal of Communications, 20*(1), 55–72. doi: 10.1080/10646170802665208

Lankoski, P. (2011). Player character engagement in computer games. *Games and Culture, 6,* 291–311. doi: 10.1177/1555412010391088

Latner, J. D., Rosewall, J. K., & Simmonds, M. B. (2007). Childhood obesity stigma: Association with television, videogame, and magazine exposure. *Body Image, 4*(2), 147–155. doi: 10.1016/j.bodyim.2007.03.002

Lauzen, M. M., & Dozier, D. M. (2005). Maintaining the double standard: Portrayals of age and gender in popular films. *Sex Roles, 52*(7–8), 437–446. doi: 10.1007/s11199-005-3710-1

Lauzen, M. M., Dozier, D. M., & Horan, N. (2008). Constructing gender stereotypes through social roles in prime-time television. *Journal of Broadcasting & Electronic Media, 52*(2), 200–214. doi: 10.1080/08838150801991971

Lehdonvirta, M., Lehdonvirta, V., & Baba, A. (2011). Prosocial behaviour in avatar-mediated interaction: The influence of character gender on material versus emotional help-giving. *On the Horizon, 19,* 165–173. doi: 10.1108/10748121111163878

Mange, J., Chun, W. Y., Sharvit, K., & Belanger, J. J. (2012). Thinking about Arabs and Muslims makes Americans shoot faster: Effects of category accessibility on aggressive responses in a shooter paradigm. *European Journal of Social Psychology, 42*(5), 552–556. doi: 10.1002/ejsp.1883

Mastro, D. E. (2009a). Effects of racial and ethnic stereotyping. In J. Bryant & M. B. Oliver (Eds.), *Media effects: Advances in theory and research* (3rd ed., pp. 325–341). New York: Routledge.

Mastro, D. E. (2009b). Racial/ethnic stereotyping and the media. In R. L. Nabi & M. B. Oliver (Eds.), *The Sage handbook of media processes and effects* (pp. 377–392). Newbury Park, CA: Sage.

Mastro, D. E., & Behm-Morawitz, E. (2005). Latino representation on prime-time television. *Journalism and Mass Communication Quarterly, 82*(1), 110–130.

Mastro, D. E., & Tukachinsky, R. (2011). The influence of exemplar versus prototype-based media primes on racial/ethnic evaluations. *Journal of Communication, 61*(5), 916–937. doi: 10.1111/j.1460-2466.2011.01587.x

McClure, K. J., Puhl, R. M., & Heuer, C. A. (2011). Obesity in the news: Do photographic images of obese persons influence antifat attitudes? *Journal of Health Communication, 16*(4), 359–371. doi: 10.1080/10810730.2010.535108

McCreary, D. R. (1994). The male role and avoiding femininity. *Sex Roles,* *31*(9–10), 517–531. doi: 10.1007/BF01544277

McKenzie-Mohr, D., & Zanna, M. P. (1990). Treating women as sexual objects: Look to the (gender schematic) male who has viewed pornography. *Personality and Social Psychology Bulletin, 16,* 296–308. doi: 10.1177/0146167290162010

Monk-Turner, E., Heiserman, M., Johnson, C., Cotton, V., & Jackson, M. (2010). The portrayal of racial minorities on prime time television: A replication of Mastro and Greenberg study a decade later. *Studies in Popular Culture, 32*(2), 101–114.

Morgan, M., Shanahan, J., & Signorielli, N. (Eds.). (2012). *Living with television now: Advances in cultivation theory and research.* New York: Peter Lang.

Moscowitz, L. M. (2010). Gay marriage in television news: Voice and visual representation in the same-sex marriage debate. *Journal of Broadcasting & Electronic Media, 54*(1), 24–39. doi: 10.1080/08838150903550360

Nellis, A. M., & Savage, J. (2012). Does watching the news affect fear of terrorism? The importance of media exposure on terrorism fear. *Crime & Delinquency, 58*(5), 748–768. doi: 10.1177/0011128712452961

O'Sullivan, P., & Flanagin, A. (2003). Reconceptualizing "flaming" and other problematic messages. *New Media & Society, 5,* 69–94.

Oliver, M. B., & Armstrong, G. B. (1998). The color of crime: Perceptions of Caucasians' and African Americans' involvement in crime. In M. Fishman & G. Cavender (Eds.), *Entertaining crime: Television reality programs* (pp. 19–35). New York: Aldine de Gruyter.

Oliver, M. B., & Fonash, D. (2002). Race and crime in the news: Whites' identification and misidentification of violent and nonviolent criminal suspects. *Media Psychology, 4*(2), 137–156. doi: 10.1207/S1532785XMEP0402_02

Oliver, M. B., Dillard, J. P., Bae, K., & Tamul, D. J. (2012). The effect of narrative news format on empathy for stigmatized groups. *Journalism & Mass Communication Quarterly, 89,* 205–224. doi: 10.1177/1077699012439020

Ortiz, M., & Harwood, J. (2007). A social cognitive theory approach to the effects of mediated intergroup contact on intergroup attitudes. *Journal of Broadcasting & Electronic Media, 51*(4), 615–631. doi: 10.1080/08838150701626487

Park, S. Y. (2012). Mediated intergroup contact: Concept explication, synthesis, and application. *Mass Communication and Society, 15*(1), 136–159. doi: 10.1080/15205436.2011.558804

Powell, K. A. (2011). Framing Islam: An analysis of U.S. media coverage of terrorism since 9/11. *Communication Studies, 62*(1), 90–112. doi: 10.1080/10510974.2011.533599

Ramasubramanian, S., & Oliver, M. B. (2007). Activating and suppressing hostile and benevolent racism: Evidence for comparative media stereotyping. *Media Psychology, 9*(3), 623–646. doi: 10.1080/15213260701283244

Roskos-Ewoldsen, D. R., & Roskos-Ewoldsen, B. (2009). Current research in media priming. In R. L. Nabi & M. B. Oliver (Eds.), *The Sage handbook of media processes and effects* (pp. 177–192). Thousand Oaks, CA: Sage.

Said, E. W. (1991). *Covering Islam: How the media and the experts determine how we see the rest of the world.* New York: Vintage Books.

Scharrer, E. (2001). Tough guys: The portrayal of hypermasculinity and aggression in televised police dramas. *Journal of Broadcasting & Electronic Media, 45,* 615–634. doi: 10.1207/s15506878jobem4504_5

Schiappa, E., Gregg, P. B., & Hewes, D. E. (2005). The parasocial contact hypothesis. *Communication Monographs, 72*(1), 92–115. doi: 10.1080/0363775052000342544

Shaheen, J. G. (2003). Reel bad Arabs: How Hollywood vilifies a people. *Annals of American Acadamy of Political and Social Science, 588,* 171–193. doi: 10.1177/0002716203588001011

Shrum, L. J. (2008). Media consumption and perceptions of social reality: Effects and underlying processes. In J. Bryant & M. B. Oliver (Eds.), *Media effects: Advances in theory and research* (3rd ed., pp. 50–73). New York: Routledge.

Signorielli, N., & Kahlenberg, S. (2001). Television's world of work in the nineties. *Journal of Broadcasting & Electronic Media, 45,* 4–22.

Smith, S. L., & Granados, A. D. (2009). Content patterns and effects surrounding sex-role stereotyping on television and film. In J. Bryant & M. B. Oliver (Eds.), *Media effects: Advances in theory and research* (pp. 342–361). New York: Routledge.

Tversky, A., & Kahneman, D. (1973). Availability: A heuristic for judging. *Cognitive Psychology, 5,* 207–232. doi: 10.1016/0010-0285(73)90033-9

Valentino, N. A., Hutchings, V. L., & White, I. K. (2002). Cues that matter: How political ads prime racial attitudes during campaigns. *American Political Science Review, 96,* 75–90. doi: 10.1017/S0003055402004240

Verhaeghen, P., Aikman, S. N., & Van Gulick, A. E. (2011). Prime and prejudice: Co-occurrence in the culture as a source of automatic stereotype priming. *British Journal of Social Psychology, 50*(3), 501–518. doi: 10.1348/014466610X524254

Vidmar, N., & Rokeach, M. (1974). Archie Bunker's bigotry: A study in selective perception and exposure. *Journal of Communication, 24*(1), 36–47. doi: 10.1111/j.1460-2466.1974.tb00353.x

Vokey, M., Tefft, B., & Tysiaczny, C. (2013). An analysis of hyper-masculinity in magazine advertisements. *Sex Roles, 68*(9–10), 1–15. doi: 10.1007/s11199-013-0268-1

White, J. D. (2001). Bisexuals who kill: Hollywood's bisexual crimewave, 1985–1998. *Journal of Bisexuality, 2*(1), 39–54. doi: 10.1300/J159v02n01_04

Wyatt, D. A. (2012, September 12). *Gay/lesbian/bisexual television characters.* Retrieved from http://home.cc.umanitoba.ca/~wyatt/tv-characters.html

Yao, M. Z., Mahood, C., & Linz, D. (2010). Sexual priming, gender stereotyping, and likelihood to sexually harass: Examining the cognitive effects of playing a sexually-explicit video game. *Sex Roles, 62*(1–2), 77–88. doi: 10.1007/s11199-009-9695-4

Zhang, Y., Tang, L. S.-T., & Leung, L. (2011). Gratifications, collective self-esteem, online emotional openness, and traitlike communication apprehension as predictors of Facebook uses. *Cyberpsychology, Behavior, and Social Networking, 14*(12), 733–739. doi: 10.1089/cyber.2010.0042

Zillmann, D., & Brosius, H. B. (2000). *Exemplification in communication: The influence of case reports on the perception of issues.* Mahwah, NJ: Lawrence Erlbaum Associates.

7

THE DOMESTICATION OF MEDIA IN THE FAMILY

Marina Krcmar

With the introduction of each new communication technology that enters the home, zealots, critics, and pundits make claims, often extreme, about the likely effect the new technology will have on family life, the home, and relationships within its walls. As early as the introduction of the telephone at the end of the nineteenth century, it was argued that this technology allowed strangers into the home, uninvited. Concerns were expressed over the possibility that young women, in particular, might have relationships with men that could easily be kept a secret from parents and, thus, could become duly corrupted (Marvin, 1990). Similar patterns of concern can be seen with the rise of radio and its possible direct influence on listeners (Badenoch, 2005) and television with its introduction of moving images (Berger, 1995). Present arguments have emerged over the rise of the Internet and social media, with both utopian (Kahn & Kellner, 2004) and dystopian (Kraut et al., 1998) prophesies.

Wild claims aside, new communication technologies do appear to influence family life (Mesch, 2006) in ways that will be discussed in this chapter; however, it is not just *new* technologies that have done so. As Marvin (1990) argued, since the advent of the telegraph: "all the communication inventions in between have simply been elaborations on the telegraph's original work" (p. 3). For example, Lull (1980) conducted an early study on television and family life, finding that families use television both as a medium for entertainment and a vehicle for social connection. Although family members may watch particular content, how they watch, when they watch, and with whom they watch affects the social interaction in the family. Television can be used to minimize conflict on one hand or provide an opportunity for two or more members to share physical proximity and contact on the other. Television, Lull argued, is not merely a purveyor of entertainment, but a social actor in the family. It influences the family in terms of when and how members relate to one another.

It is neither surprising, then, nor trivial that the Internet and social media have generated similar concerns. Media do influence our social lives, in particular our families, because so much media is now available in the home. The Internet has quite literally brought media, writ large, into the living room. Like the telephone of 1900, which could allow a suitor, uninvited, into the home of a young woman, the Internet potentially allows an entire world into the home and family. We wonder, perhaps rightly, what influence that may have.

Technological Introductions and Domestication

The process by which new technologies become integrated into family life has been described as domestication: a "process in which new technologies and services, by definition to a significant degree unfamiliar, and therefore both exciting but possibly also threatening and perplexing, are brought (or not) under control by and on behalf of domestic users" (Silverstone & Haddon, 1996, p. 60). This domestication implies a transactional process where family members consume and interpret a given communication technology, and in the process, the family culture, patterns of interaction, and individual family members are affected. Similar to the process Lull (1980) proposed for television, domestication implies that a technology may be interpreted and used not just as intended (e.g., television as an entertainment medium), but may be utilized in any number of ways (e.g., television coviewing as a way of sharing space between family members). In turn, this influences how time is used and shared in the family. Thus, it is not owning the technology that makes a difference, but its use, integration, and influence in the family. Here, I will discuss the domestication of two communication technologies: television as an example of an older technology, and the Internet as a new, if not nascent one.

Domestication, Television, and Influence on the Family

The primary finding of research on television and time use is related to the displacement hypothesis: the more television is consumed, the less time family members spend in other activities; television displaces other activities. Although research on families, television, and time use does suggest a negative relationship between time spent watching television and time spent in other activities, namely reading and school work among children (Neuman, 1988), the idea that television displaces other activities is not fully supported (e.g., Valkenburg & Peter, 2007). For example, in my research on families who do not watch (or own) a television (Krcmar, 2009), which involved in-depth interviews and time-use diaries, I found that not only do nonviewing families spend more time in other leisure activities such as reading than viewing families do, but they engage in a greater variety of activities from housekeeping to civic activities. In addition to asking partici- pants about how they spent their time, I asked them what they wished they did differently. One key finding was that nonviewers as compared to viewers wished they had even more free time to spend with spouses, children, and parents, even though the free time they had was not spent watching television.

This finding was somewhat surprising given that I expected television viewers to wish they had more free time. This led me to conclude that the displacement hypothesis was not entirely accurate in its portrait of fami- lies. Instead of television displacing other activities for viewers, it seemed to occupy only truly unstructured free time. Nonviewers, on the other hand, displaced television because they wanted to spend their free time in other and more varied activities. Ultimately, families who watch television are doing less of other kinds of activities, but perhaps this is because the families themselves differ, in structure and family dynamics, as compared to families who watch less.

In addition to the obvious trade-off between television time and other activities, Lull (1980) argued that television in the home fulfills two kinds of functions: structural and relational. Structurally, television can affect talk patterns by influencing when talk occurs and how much is said. Family talk and family interaction can be punctuated and structured by television time. In addition to this structural function, Lull found that tel- evision is also used to fulfill relational functions by providing opportunity for family contact; by creating barriers, especially among family mem- bers in conflict; and by facilitating communication by providing topics. For example, Kubey (1990) found that during coviewing, family mem- bers talk about 20 percent of the time, lending further evidence to the notion that families may watch television together as a way to share time and space. However, Kubey also found that family viewing experiences were reported as being more passive than family activities generally, with heavy viewers reporting lower levels of activity even during non-TV fam- ily activities than did light viewers.

A majority of this research, however, worked under the assumption that families view together because a centralized television set, perhaps in the living room or kitchen, acted as the focal point of the home. However, the ways we are able to access television programs have pro- liferated and changed in the last decade. Nevertheless, there is still some assumption that families watch together at least some of the time. Do the data support this? Livingstone (2007) argues that since the late 1980s, media consumption in general has become an increasingly individual experience. She refers to this as a shift to "bedroom cultures." In the earliest days of this shift, it arose from trends in families to own multiple television sets, increased variability in program offerings catering to narrower demographics, and a gradual cultural shift toward separated living spaces for parents and children. The shift towards a bedroom culture can be seen even more at present due to changes in media delivery systems. In her ethnographic work, Livingstone has found that family viewing is less common than it once was. Instead, individual family members may retreat to a bedroom to watch television, surf the Internet on a laptop, or use Facebook on a smartphone.

Nevertheless, some family viewing is still likely given the fact that most living rooms host a television in a central and prominent location. Parents in particular may value family time spent in front of the screen as a way to bring family members together despite disparate interests and schedules (Kotler, Wright, & Huston, 2001). For example, in a more recent examination of family viewing, Lee (2010) conducted a large-scale survey and found links between the kinds of television services families purchased, and their use of television as either an individual or family enterprise. Specifically, the findings indicated that consumption of mass broadcast television was positively related to preference for family viewing (as opposed to individual viewing) and negatively related to perceptions that family members preferred different programs from one another. On the other hand, multichannel television service subscription was positively related to perceptions among family members that their program preferences were heterogeneous. In other words, the structure of media availability in the home was related to not only how families used television, but how they perceived each other as well (Lee, 2010). Therefore, in a wired, multichannel universe, media do influence family interactions, as Lull (1980) suggested, but the increased availability of media impacts family as well. This dynamic relationship between media structure and family interaction suggests that media continue to be an important element in family life but cannot be thought of as having a unidirectional effect, from television to family. The relationship is indeed more complex and transactional.

Overall, it appears that television allows an opportunity for families to spend time together, but that the rise of the bedroom culture may discourage television time as family time. In addition to the bedroom culture that Livingstone (2007) points to, television and the structure of service in the home may further influence whether time is spent together or separately as a result. Additional research has also shown that family television time may be less active and interactive than time spent in other activities; and lastly, families who voluntarily watch less television engage in a greater variety of activities, perhaps encouraging greater social interaction within and outside of the family.

Domesticating the Internet, Mobile Devices and Social Media

From its initial domestication in the early 1950s, television gained in importance in the family home, with parents and children spending an increasing amount of time watching it. By the early 1990s, children consumed approximately three hours of television per day (Comstock & Scharrer, 2012). However, with the introduction and domestication of the Internet, children and families now consume not only more hours of screen time, with some estimates as high as seven and a half hours for all entertainment media combined (Rideout, Foehr, & Roberts, 2010), but often may use several screens at once, combining computer use, television viewing, and smartphone use simultaneously (Rideout, Foehr, & Roberts, 2010). Based on the extant research, it is not entirely clear how families have domesticated the Internet. Of course, as has been argued repeatedly, any medium is only as good as its content and use. The Internet may have the potential to improve family life but may also harm it.

One theoretical perspective that presents neither a utopian or dystopian perspective has been forwarded by Mesch (2006). Mesch (2006) argued for a *family boundaries* approach, suggesting that the Internet allows for a break in the boundary of the home, allowing the Internet in, and thus having a potentially harmful influence on the family. Specifically, Mesch argues, family life is conducted "backstage" where families protect the home from scrutiny and criticism. Furthermore, family time is protected within the walls, again, by a focus on how time is spent and shared in the home with and between family members. Through these processes, family cohesion is increased. The introduction of the Internet poses a problem to family boundaries. On one hand, individual time on the Internet, work brought home via the Internet (Salaff, 2002), and additional options for individual entertainment may take time away from the family. On the other, the Internet may allow for greater family cohesion with increased use of e-mail, Skype, instant messaging, and texting. Family members may find it easier to keep in touch and be aware of others' activities (Turkle, 2011). Thus, Mesch (2006) suggests, it is unclear whether family boundaries are harmed or aided by the Internet.

Empirical evidence on families and the Internet present contradictory results about whether families who are connected to the Internet differ in their communication patterns from families who are not (Katz & Rice, 2002). On one hand, participation in online family discussions facilitates access to social networks that supply social support, advice, and guidance to families (Hughes & Hans, 2001). In addition, children might use the Internet to conduct school work and consequently do better in school, as children who have a home computer report higher scores in mathematics and reading tests, even after controlling for family income (Attewell, 2001; Attewell & Battle, 1999). Also, and perhaps most relevant to *family* outcomes, the Internet provides opportunities for family collaboration in terms of keeping in touch, daily communication, game play, and joint information-gathering (Kiesler, Zdaniuk, Lundmark, & Kraut, 2000; Orleans & Laney, 2000; Turkle, 2011). For example, Internet use is often a shared household activity. In one study, approximately half the parents said they spent time each week using the Internet jointly with other family members. In the same study, a majority of participants said they did not feel ignored because other family members used the Internet too much, and both Internet users and nonusers felt similarly in terms of how much they thought members of the family talked and listened to one another (Cole et al., 2000).

Lastly, although empirical research has not examined this per se, the Internet may allow families to spend more time together because activities that were previously external to the home (e.g., shopping, work) can now be done in the home. As I write this, my husband, who previously worked outside of the home fifty hours per week, sits in his home office and works from there, often spending lunch or some time in the afternoon with other family members. All of these utopian perspectives suggest that the Internet could strengthen ties and improve communication between family members.

Of course, the Internet may be neither harmful nor beneficial in and of itself, as demonstrated by dystopian perspectives that share an almost-equal amount of support. Like television, which researchers argued more than thirty years ago could both connect and divide families (Lull, 1980), the Internet's impact on families varies on how it is used. For example, the Internet has been argued to reduce the time parents and children spend together and thereby might create social distance between parents and children (Nie, Simpser, Stepanikova, & Zheng, 2004). The digital divide, or the inequality between adults and children that results from differences in access, use, and knowledge, has also been found to increase intergenerational conflict (Mesch, 2003; Tapscott, 1997). One possible reason for this is that parents and children may have different expectations regarding its use. Parents report buying a computer so that their children may have Internet access and benefit from its educational uses (Lenhart, Rainie, & Lewis, 2001; Livingstone & Bober, 2004; Turow & Nir, 2000), and they think that the Internet can help their children to do better at school (Livingstone & Bober, 2004). Unlike their parents, however, children tend to value the social and entertainment uses of the Internet (Lenhart, Madden, & Hitlin, 2005; Livingstone & Bober, 2004). It is likely that these differing perceptions lead to conflict about how—not *if*—the Internet should be used.

Another possible reason that Internet access may be associated with conflict in the family is that Internet use is negatively associated with family time. One recent time-use diary study offered support for this contention, finding that Internet use at home was negatively related to time spent with family (Nie et al., 2004). Furthermore, the reduction in family time was higher for the average Internet user than for the average TV watcher (Nie et al., 2004). Interestingly, survey research suggests that parents and adolescents may be aware of this displacement effect. They report worrying that Internet use might have a negative effect on family communication and closeness (Jackson et al., 2003; Turow & Nir, 2000). In one study, Lenhart, Rainie, and Lewis (2001) also found that adolescents felt that their own Internet use did not help them to improve their relationships with their parents and that the Internet consumes time they would spend with their families.

Ultimately, then, the dystopian perspective would suggest that Internet access can harm family closeness not only through conflict about its use and displacement of more interactive activities, but also through expectations of its effect. If parents and children expect Internet time to harm relationships or cause conflict, it may be that those expectations themselves have a negative effect beyond any influence that the Internet itself may have.

Like the Internet, the cell phone has demonstrated diverse impacts on the family. Research suggests that families who connect via cell phone use may benefit from the increased connectivity that it offers, or in turn, be harmed by the constancy of its use. In fact, Turkle (2011) argues that these technologies are new enough that families are still in a phase of social unease regarding their use. Further, I have argued (Krcmar, 2012) that adolescents, in particular, have no clear mental model for how to approach these technologies, and that this deficit may result in interpersonal and family difficulties. For example, cell phones are a constant for many middle-class American teenagers. In her ethnographic work with teenagers, Turkle (2011) has found that teenagers and their parents both express unease about the cell phone and the constant connection it offers. Turkle refers to these teens as "tethered," and states that this concern with being constantly connected—parent to child—is not simply a desire of teens to shed themselves of parent supervision. Rather, teens feel a need to be away from their parents, as is developmentally appropriate and normal in adolescence; but Turkle also found, somewhat unexpectedly, that teenagers rely on parents' constant availability to them via the cell phone. She argues that this may in fact hinder a certain amount of independence and growth in teenagers. Thus, teens feel ambivalent about their tethering, at once decrying yet relying on what the cell phone offers.

Similarly, conventional wisdom would suggest that parents might want to keep tabs on their adolescent children at all times, thus allowing them to monitor and protect them. Turkle did find that this was true to some extent, but parents' expressed their ambivalence too, wanting to free themselves from the constant monitoring that cell phones not only allow, but may begin to require. Thus, connection in the family, between parents and adolescent children in particular, seems to create an unease with the technology precisely because it offers connection—constantly. Both parents and adolescents indicated a desire to be alone and disconnected at times. Thus, what may seem to be the ultimate advantage to families—a device that offers near constant connection—may have some hidden drawbacks as family members attempt to carve out private spaces for themselves and as teenagers and parents struggle to develop a mental model that is appropriate for its use (Krcmar, 2012).

Integrating Technology Into the Family: A Systems Approach

Since the introduction of the telephone into the home, families have had to adapt to and integrate new technologies that have had both positive and negative effects on family communication, connectivity, and interpersonal dynamics. Just as there is no one correct interpretation of this impact, so too is there no one dimension through which to understand it. For this reason, a systems approach is useful in order to permit a more unified understanding of the impact of technology on the family.

Systems theory itself was originally applied to biological systems (Bertalanffy, 1972) in order to understand how a complex system might adapt to changing environments and to changes within the system. One of the most basic premises of systems theory is that in order to understand any system, the whole and not the individual parts must be examined. As the interactions of the family share characteristics with those of a biological system, the family provides an appropriate subject for the application of systems theory.

For example, in the broadest sense, systems theory is the study of the abstract organization of phenomena, independent of their substance. The phenomena or entities are related to one another through some regular interaction, such as parent–child or sibling interactions. The entities are interdependent and exhibit some coherent behavior as a result. A system is open to and interacts with its environments, as a family does in its immediate and far-reaching environment. This includes information in the environment, and the interaction can result in the acquisition of qualitatively new properties such as a new language or a new set of skills. Technology use in the family is one obvious example of this adaptive process. Therefore, in order to truly understand the system, no one part can be studied independently. Rather, systems theory focuses on the arrangement of and relations between the parts which connect them into a whole.

As systems theory began to be applied to social systems, rather than to exclusively biological systems, it became apparent that social-system analysis may benefit from its use (Bochner & Eisenberg, 1987). For example, in systems theory, input from the environment and subsequent adaptation by the system is a major component of the system. Within a family, adoption of the cell phone, for example, or the use of Facebook to connect might be one kind of input. When this new entity is taken into the family, whether the entity is a person, a belief, a normative way of being, or a technology, that entity then influences every aspect of the system. Connections and interconnections between dyads or triads are influenced, norms that guide behavior may change, and beliefs about the entity influence existing attitudes. Is it an overstatement, then, to say that a new way of interacting, via cell phone or Facebook, influences the family?

For example, recent research on Facebook use has found that parents use it to keep tabs on their children's behavior (McMillan, 2011). Whereas this may indeed be a valid use of the site, consider this from a systems approach. The behavior (i.e., a kind of electronic eavesdropping) must be incorporated into the family environment. Now, the family members are faced with potential knowledge gained from the electronic eavesdropping that may influence their own and others behavior within the system. Furthermore, the very behavior of eavesdropping itself is likely to have an effect on the relationship, apart from any information gained. Both the act of eavesdropping and any information gained through the process may then be used by the family to affect rules and norms in the family. In many ways, the relative accuracy of the information is irrelevant in its effect on family functioning. The electronic behavior may itself become the new entity in the system. Of course one could easily argue that parents have always had the ability to eavesdrop and, certainly, nothing there has changed. But like any new technology, as it enters the system, we adapt and adopt norms and guidelines for its use. Or we do not adopt norms, and tensions arise within the family due to differing expectations of its use (Mesch, 2003).

Conclusion

Media exist in almost every household. Bringing media under the control of the family and developing norms, rules, and guidelines for its use is a kind of domestication process (Silverstone & Haddon, 1996). Family members may either explicitly or implicitly decide how to use media in the home, and those norms in turn influence interactions between members, beliefs within the family, and behaviors of its members. Thus, domestication can be seen as the broad framework for considering media use, both old and new, within families. If we consider certain instances of media, we can begin to see how the process works for a given media (e.g., television), but it then may even duplicate itself when a new technology emerges (e.g., Internet and the ensuing social media enabled by it). For example, research on television has shown that while television content may indeed influence families (for example, by presenting sexual content to adolescents that could then spark conversations between parents and children about sexual risk-taking), television as a medium can structure family interactions (Lull, 1980). In this way, television becomes part of family life, a kind of pseudo-social family member (Krcmar, 2009).

Similarly, the introduction of the Internet and its accessibility in the home has offered both new content to family members and many new ways of interacting with members. Like an older screen already well-known in families, the computer screen can draw family members away from one another, provide them new topics to talk about, or offer a way for them to share time and space. For example, a parent may be able to work from home more readily due to Internet access, thus enabling her to share time and space with other members in the home. Thus, the Internet offers new content to family members, and new ways of interacting between members (e.g., via text messaging, or blogging), but in some ways provides many of the same outlets and constraints as the media that came before it.

Despite these very real similarities in terms of the effects of new media on the family, there are also some new options that provide new challenges. For example, it is now possible for family members to remain in near-constant connection. While this constant connectivity may offer benefits to planning, organizing, and perhaps even family cohesion, it also has drawbacks. Both adolescents and their parents feel that the technology comes with a kind of implied pressure to be constantly connected (Turkle, 2011). After all, adolescence is a time when children typically gain greater independence with both the benefits and responsibilities this entails. As Turkle (2011) has suggested, constant connectivity means parents and children can be in constant contact, but both parents and adolescent children may benefit from not being so. In her study, parents and children both stated that, at times, they wanted somewhat more freedom but that connectivity seems to disallow it.

These ideas fit well into the systems approach. Because family members are interdependent, exhibit somewhat coherent behavior, and are open to the environment, the use of cell phones as well as the Internet can become part of the family system. Once again, it is not the medium itself (e.g., the cell phone) that becomes solely part of the system. Rather, it is the meaning the family gives it and the way they use it that can influence family dynamics. One family may find constant texting pleasurable, another may find it an annoyance, and still another may opt not to do so. In addition, members within a family may differ in their attitudes about this behavior. These differing expectations, and not the behavior itself, then create tension in the system.

Thus, when we consider media, both older and new, it is important to realize that media in the home has, in some ways, expanded the home and allowed new information into it in ways not seen before. However, in other ways, the domestication of each new technology might well follow patterns that already exist in the family system. Family members who desire closeness are apt to find ways to achieve it; so are those who prefer greater distance. Media are used time and again to achieve those goals. As Marvin (1990, p. 3) argued,

> *New Technologies* is a historically relative term. We are not the first generation to wonder at the rapid and extraordinary shifts in the dimension of the world and the relationships it contains as a result of new forms of communication or to be surprised by the changes those shifts occasion in the regular pattern of our lives.

In terms of the domestication of media, then, family systems often look to them and use them in ways that fit into the existing patterns of their lives.

References

Attewell, P. (2001). The first and second digital divides. *Sociology of Education, 74*, 252–259.

Attewell, P., & Battle, J. (1999). Home computers and school performance. *The Information Society, 15*, 1–10.

Badenoch, A. (2005). Making Sunday what it actually should be: Sunday radio programming and the re-invention of tradition in occupied Germany 1945–1949. *Historical Journal of Film, Radio & Television, 25*, 577–598. doi: 10.1080/01439680500262975

Berger, A. A. (1995). *Essentials of mass communication theory.* London: SAGE Publications.

Bertalanffy, L. V. (1972). History and status of general systems theory. *The Academy of Management Journal, 15* (4), 407–426.

Bochner, A. P. & Eisenberg, E. M. (1987). Family process: System perspectives. In C. R. Berger & S. H. Chaffee (Eds.), *Handbook of communication science* (pp. 540–563). Newbury Park, CA: Sage Publications.

Cole, J. I., Suman, M., Schram, P., Van Bel, D., Lun, B., Maguirre, P., Hanson, K., Singh, R., & Aquino, J. S. (2000). *Surveying the digital future.* Los Angeles, CA: UCLA Center for Communication Policy. Retrieved August 12, 2010, from www.ccp.ucla.edu.

Comstock, G., & Scharrer, E. (2012). Use of television and other media. In D. G. Singer & J. L. Singer (Eds.), *Handbook of children and media* (2nd ed., pp. 13–44). Los Angeles, CA: Sage.

Hughes, R., & Hans, J. (2001). Computers, the Internet and families. *Journal of Family Issues, 22*, 776–790. doi: 10.1177/019251301022006006

Jackson, L. A., Von Eye, A., Barbatsis, G., Biocca, F., Zhao,Y., & Fitzgerald, H. E. (2003). Internet attitudes and Internet use: Some surprising findings from the HomeNetTOOproject. *International Journal of Human–Computer Studies, 59*, 355–382. doi: 10.1016/S1071-5819(03)00069-7

Kahn, R., & Kellner, D. (2004). New media and internet activism: From the 'Battle of Seattle' to blogging. *New Media & Society, 6*(1), 87–95.

Katz, J. E., & Rice, R. E. (2002). *Social consequences of Internet use.* Cambridge, MA: MIT Press.

Kiesler, S., Zdaniuk, B., Lundmark,V., & Kraut, R. (2000). Troubles with the Internet: The dynamics of help at home. *Human–Computer Interaction, 15,* 322–351.

Kotler, J. A., Wright, J. C. & Huston, A. C. (2001). Television use in families with children. In J. Bryant & J. A. Bryant (Eds.), *Television and the American family* (pp. 33–48), Mahwah, NJ: Earlbaum.

Kraut, R., Patterson, M., Lundmark, V., Kiesler, S., Mukopadhyay, T., & Scherlis, W. (1998). Internet paradox: A social technology that reduces social involvement and psychological well-being? *American Psychologist, 53*(9), 1017–1031.

Krcmar, M. (2009). *Living without the screen.* Routledge: New York.

Krcmar, M. (2012). The effect of media on children's moral reasoning. In R. Tamborinin (Ed.), *Media and the moral mind,* New York: Routledge.

Kubey, R. (1990). Television and the quality of family life. *Communication Quarterly, 38,* 312–324. doi: 10.1080/01463379009369769

Lee, F. L. F. (2010). The influence of family viewing preferences on television consumption in the era of multichannel services. *Asian Journal of Communication, 20,* 281–298. doi: 10.1080/01292981003802176

Lenhart, A., Rainie, L., & Lewis, O. (2001). *Teenage life online: The rise of the instant-message generation and the Internet's impact on friendships and family relationships.* Retrieved December 20, 2005, from www.pewinternet.org/report_display.asp?r=36 (available from Pewand American Life Project, 1100 Connecticut Ave., NW suite 710, Washington, DC 20036).

Lenhart, A., Madden, M., & Hitlin, P. (2005). *Teens and technology.* Washington, DC: Pew and American Life Project.

Livingstone, S. (2007). Strategies of parental regulation in the media-rich home. *Computers in Human Behavior, 23*(2), 920–941.

Livingstone, S., & Bober, M. (2004). *UK children go online.* London: London School of Economics.

Lull, J. (1980). The social uses of television. *Human Communication Research, 6*(3), 120–136.

Marvin, C. (1990). *When old technologies were new: Thinking about electric communication in the late nineteenth century.* London: Oxford University Press.

McMillan, G. (2011). More than 50% of parents use Facebook to spy on their kids, time techland. Retrieved October 15, 2012 from http://techland.time.com/2011/07/18/more-than-50-of-parents-use-facebook-to-spy-on-their-kids/. Read more: http://techland.time.com/2011/07/18/more-than-50-of-parents-use-facebook-to-spy-on-their-kids/#ixzz29NCp68FG

Mesch, G. S. (2003). Family boundaries and the Internet: Exploring a family boundaries approach. *The Journal of Family Communication, 6,* 119–138. doi: 10.1207/s15327698jfc0602_2

Mesch, G. S. (2006). Family characteristics and intergenerational conflicts over the Internet. *Information, Communication & Society, 9,* 281–302. doi: 10.1080/13691180600858705

Neuman, S. B. (1988). The displacement effect: Assessing the relation between television viewing and reading performance. *Reading Research Quarterly, 23*(4), 414–440.

Nie, N. H., Simpser, A., Stepanikova, I., & Zheng, L. (2004). *Ten years after the birth of the Internet, how do Americans use the Internet in their daily lives?* Stanford, CA: Stanford Center for the Quantitative Study of Society.

Orleans, M., & Laney, M. C. (2000). Early adolescent social networks and computer use. *Social Science Computer Review, 18,* 56–72. doi: 10.1177/0894 43930001800104

Rideout, V. J., Foehr, U. G., & Roberts, D. F. (2010). *Generation M2: Media in the lives of 8- to 18-year-olds.* Retrieved November 11, 2013, from www.kff.org/entmedia/8010.cfm

Salaff, J. W. (2002). Where home is the office: The new form of flexible work. In B. Wellman & C. Haythornthwaite (Eds.), *The Internet in everyday life* (pp. 464–495). Oxford, England: Blackwell.

Silverstone, R., & Haddon, L. (1996). Design and the domestication of information and communication technologies: Technical change and everyday life. In R. Silverstone & R. Mansell (Eds.), *Communication by design: The politics of information and communication technologies* (pp. 44–74). Oxford, England: Oxford University Press.

Tapscott, D. (1997). *Growing up digital: The rise of the Net generation.* New York: McGraw-Hill.

Turkle, S. (2011). *Alone together: Why we expect more from technology and less from each other.* New York: Basic Books, pp. 274–277.

Turow, J., & Nir, L. (2000). *The Internet and the family 2000: The view from the parents, the view from the kids.* Philadelphia, PA: Annenberg Public Policy Center, University of Pennsylvania. Retrieved September 30, 2010, from www.appcpenn.org/Internet/

Valkenburg, P. M. & Peter, J. (2007). Online communication and adolescent well-being: Testing the stimulation vs. displacement hypothesis. *Journal of Computer-Mediated Communication, 12*(4), 1169–1182. doi: 10.1111/j.1083-6101.2007.00368.x

8

MEDIA AND FRIENDSHIPS

Sonja Utz

In her book *Alone Together*, Turkle (2011) worries that social media and smartphones just give people the illusion of connection rather than provide actual, intimate friendships. Rainie and Wellman (2012) come to the opposite conclusion and argue that social media give people the opportunity to derive more social support than ever from their admittedly more loosely knit networks. It is not the first time that the question arises whether media hamper or foster the development of friendships—similar discussions rose from the introduction of the telephone and the rise of the Internet (see Wellman & Gulia, 1999). The pessimists always considered the mediated relationships as inferior to the face-to-face (FTF) relationships and feared that mediated relationships replace "real" relationships. The optimists focused on the opportunities new media brought to stay in touch with people (far) away and perceived mediated communication as a supplement or even enrichment of FTF relationships.

Although media have been used to maintain or build relationships for centuries (such as in written letters) or at least decades (phone, e-mail), one thing is indeed new since the widespread adoption of smartphones: the ubiquity of media and the integration of several media into one device (see Campbell, Ling, & Bayer, this volume). With a smartphone, one can, for instance, call a friend, send a text message to the friend, write an e-mail, post a public message on the Facebook wall of the friend, or use the chat function of Facebook. So the question of which medium people choose to maintain friendships gets more interesting because it is less constrained by technological options. Due to the ubiquity of media, almost no friendship is entirely based on FTF communication any longer.

The focus of this chapter is on the effects of the use of *communication* media on friendships, but not on topics such as watching TV or playing games as shared ritual or how watching movies affects (stereotypical) expectations on friendships. Within communication media, the main focus will be on online communication, covering the various forms ranging from asynchronous pseudonymous computer-mediated communication (CMC) to "nonymous" communication occurring on social network sites (SNS) such as Facebook (Zhao, Grasmuck, & Martin, 2008, p. 1816). Before I turn to the effects of media on friendships, I will start with a definition of friendships.

Friendships

Friendships are a specific form of interpersonal relationships. Beebe, Beebe, and Redmond (2011, p. 252) define interpersonal relationships as "a perception shared by two people of an ongoing interdependent connection that results in the development of relational expectations and varies in interpersonal intimacy." Interpersonal relationships can be classified on a continuum from stranger to acquaintance—casual friend—friend—close friend, to best friend/spouse. Friendships are thus interpersonal relationships characterized by a high degree of intimacy, interdependence, and relational expectations. An important characteristic is also the sharedness of the perception. Friends provide us with emotional support, and emotional support is an important buffer against stress and contributes to well-being (Abbey, Abramis, & Caplan, 1985; Albrecht & Goldsmith, 2003; Amichai-Hamburger, Kingsbury, & Schneider, 2013).

Media and Friendships

When it comes to the role of media, researchers have basically studied two important questions: (1) What is the role of communication media in building new friendships?; and (2) What is the role of communication media in maintaining friendships?

The first question became especially relevant with the rise of the Internet. People have used media to communicate with others for a long time; they have written letters to each other or used the phone. However, letters and phone media were rarely used to meet strangers. With the rise of the Internet, it has become much more common to meet strangers via media communication. Indeed, many of the early online communities were topic centered (e.g., Usenet newsgroups), and the opportunity to find like-minded individuals from all over the world was promoted as one of the biggest advantages of the Internet (McKenna & Bargh, 2000). Even nowadays, some online venues are explicitly designed to meet strangers, such as online dating sites.

The question of the role of media in *maintaining* relationships has received more attention recently because SNS are online venues specifically designed for keeping in touch with one's pre-existing network. The (semi) public nature of communication on SNS or subtle communication forms

112

such as the "like" button offer new ways of communicating. An analysis of the role of media in friendship formation and maintenance should therefore take a closer look at the characteristics of specific media.

Media Characteristics

The media landscape has changed rapidly within the last few decades and even more so within the last ten years when social media such as SNS and Twitter were developed. For a long time, letters and, later, phone calls were the primary communication media. Before the rise of web browsers, the Internet was characterized by separate services that had to be accessed via specific programs such as news readers to join the discussions in the Usenet environment, telnet to play multi-user-dungeon games (text-based adventure role-playing), or chat clients to participate in Internet Relay Chat (IRC) chats. Communication was usually anonymous or at least pseudonymous. Nowadays, SNS are the most popular online venues. SNS are "nonymous environments" in which people display their "anchored relationships" (Zhao et al., 2008, p. 1816). Because of the rapid development of online venues, it makes more sense to focus on specific media characteristics or affordances and to examine how these characteristics enable, facilitate, or hinder friendship formation and maintenance.

Some authors talk about constraints when characterizing media. For example, Clark and Brennan (1991) identify copresence, visibility, audibility, cotemporality, simultaneity, sequentiality, reviewability, and revisability as media characteristics. Many of these characteristics are confounded with the synchronicity of communication (requiring copresence, simultaneity, cotemporality) and the text-based (vs. audio- or videobased) nature of communication. These two dimensions are also most important for friendships because they refer to the ability to maintain a friendship over distances and the ability of the medium to transfer nonverbal and more intimate content.

Media richness approaches assume that people are rational actors and choose richer media when they want to build or maintain relationships (e.g., Daft & Lengel, 1986). However, empirical studies have shown that people do not always choose the most suited media, and that people also differ in their perceptions of media richness. Social norms within an environment or even a specific relationship also influence the choice of a medium (e.g., Fulk, Steinfield, Schmitz, & Power, 1987). Other authors, therefore, use Gibson's (1977) concept of "affordances" to characterize media. Affordances are built into a technology, but perceived differently by different persons and across different contexts (Hutchby, 2001).

When it comes to social media, Treem and Leonardi (2012) focus on visibility, editability, persistence, and association as the most important affordances. On social media, the boundaries between private and public communication are blurring; posts are often visible at least for all

113

"friends." Not only is the actual communication (e.g. a post or tweet) visible on social media, but other behaviors such as likes, views, or ratings are also displayed. Status updates or tweets can be edited before they are sent, but wikis or blog posts can be edited even after being posted. *Persistence* refers to the fact that many posts are archived, and *association* describes the fact that on social media, the associations between people (e.g., friends on Facebook, connections on LinkedIn) or the associations between people and their posts or other contributions are made explicit and visible.

The affordances of media influence whether the development and maintenance of friendships are hampered or supported. In the next section, I will review primary theories on relationship formation and relationship maintenance and discuss whether they also hold for mediated communication.

Primary Theories on Relationship Formation

Relationship formation is a process. As a first step, there has to be some attraction between two strangers so that they start to interact with each other. The second step is that the individuals get to know one other and to build up intimacy. Self-disclosure has been regarded as the most important underlying process leading to the development of a friendship.

Attraction

Classical factors predicting attraction to strangers are physical attractiveness, proximity (Festinger, Schachter, & Back, 1950), and attitude similarity (Byrne, 1969). We are more attracted to physically attractive others, partly because beautiful people are perceived as more familiar (Monin, 2003). Festinger et al. (1950) found that physical proximity increases the likelihood of friendships. Students were more likely to become friends with the students living in the next room than with students from a more distant room or even a different floor of the dorm building. Last but not least, we like people who are similar to us. The social psychologist Byrne (1969) demonstrated this for attitude similarity; sociologists often use the broader concept of *homophily* to refer also to similarity in demographics or culture.

The physical attractiveness of a person is often not visible in CMC. On newer venues, such as SNS, people display profile pictures and often hundreds of additional pictures, but in newsgroup groups, chats, and many forums or Multi-User Dungeons (MUDs), no information about attractiveness is available. Thus, physical attractiveness often plays a less important role when friendships are formed in anonymous or pseudonymous online communities (McKenna & Bargh, 2000), but it is still important in "nonymous" environments such as Facebook (Wang, Moon, Kwon, Evans, & Stefanone, 2010).

Proximity also plays a smaller role in CMC. Of course, there are language barriers and many virtual communities that are bound to a specific region, but the Internet has made it much more likely to meet a person from a different region, country, or continent than it has been in the very recent past.

Instead of physical attractiveness and proximity serving as the most important predictors of interpersonal attraction, attitude similarity has become a more prominent predictor in the online environment. In topic-centered virtual communities such as Usenet newsgroups, people with similar interests came together. According to the social identity and deindividuation (SIDE) model (Reicher, Spears, & Postmes, 1995), the anonymity and isolation of CMC even increased the salience of social identities, that is, memberships to specific groups. For example, people may enter a forum for horse lovers, expect all others to love horses as well, and because there are fewer nonverbal cues, they do not see differences between the group members. As a consequence, people overestimate the similarities and underestimate the differences to the other community members. Attitude or interest similarity is therefore a main driver of attraction in online communication characterized by low visibility/high anonymity.

Impression Formation via Computer-Mediated Communication

Because of the anonymity or at least pseudonymity of many online venues, research has often focused on the question whether it is possible to build a reliable (first) impression of another person online. Early CMC theories identified the reduced availability of social cues as the core characteristic of CMC. Examples are social presence theory (Short, Williams, & Christie, 1976) or the reduced social cues approach (Kiesler & McGuire, 1984; Sproull & Kiesler, 1986). According to these theories, impression formation on CMC is seriously hampered because not enough nonverbal cues are available. CMC was also described as task-oriented and rather impersonal by these approaches, noting that reports of flaming and hostile communication are common (see Lea & Spears, 1991, for a review). However, many of these findings are based on laboratory studies in which FTF and CMC groups had the same amount of time to solve a problem or make a decision. Because it takes longer to type than to talk, it is not surprising that CMC groups were more task-focused (Walther, 1992). Moreover, in many of these earlier studies, participants' interactions were studied in one-shot experiments where there was no anticipation of any future interaction.

In contrast, observations of virtual communities resulted in different findings, with people reporting to have made friends online. With the social information processing (SIP) perspective, Walther (1992) provided an explanation for this discrepancy. He argued that it is possible to form an impression of an interaction partner and to develop interpersonal relationships via CMC, but that it takes more time than in FTF communication. According to SIP, people are driven by affiliation motives and employ strategies to get to know their interaction partners. They also adapt to the reduction of social cues and learn to verbalize nonverbal contents.

Just a few years later, Walther (1996) developed the hyperpersonal model that argued that CMC could, under some circumstances, be even more social and interpersonal than FTF communication. This model noted that especially in asynchronous CMC situations, individuals can carefully think about their self-presentation. Further, most people tend to present themselves in an idealized way, and interaction partners frequently base their first impression on the few cues available in CMC environments. Consequently, if these cues are very positive, individuals are likely to form a positive first impression of other individuals and to treat them as very friendly. A self-fulfilling prophecy thus develops; both interaction partners engage in very friendly, "hyperpersonal" interactions.

Whereas early CMC has been described as reduced in social cues, many social media platforms now provide individuals with additional cues not available so easily in FTF communication. Tong, Van der Heide, Langwell, and Walther (2008) distinguish between self-generated, friends-generated, and system-generated cues. Self-generated cues comprise the information posted and the photos uploaded by the individual. Friends-generated information comes from the group of SNS friends, for example comments on status updates. System-generated information is automatically tracked and displayed by the system, such as the number of friends or the number of likes. According to the warranting principle (Walther & Parks, 2002), information that is more difficult to manipulate should be perceived as more reliable and therefore have a larger impact on impression formation.

In the context of SNS, this means that friends- and system-generated information should have more impact on the final impression than the self-generated information. Empirical support for this claim is mixed (see Utz, 2010), though clear evidence for warranting theory has been found in the domain of physical attractiveness (Walther, Van Der Heide, Hamel, & Shulman, 2009). Although friends- or system-generated information does not always have more impact than self-generated information, there is clear evidence that there are now even more cues available and that people can form reliable impressions based on Facebook profiles (Gosling, Gaddis, & Vazire, 2007).

Self-Disclosure

A central process in developing a relationship is self-disclosure—that is, the revealing of personal information (Collins & Miller, 1994). According to self-penetration theory (Altman & Taylor, 1973), self-disclosure fosters intimacy, at least in dyadic or small-group interactions. Self-disclosure can vary in depth and breadth. Breadth refers to the number of areas touched upon (e.g. work, family, political views), whereas depth characterizes the level of intimacy of the self-disclosure. When getting acquainted to someone, conversation is usually rather superficial (the weather, general information on occupations), but in close friendships people discuss intimate problems in various areas of life.

116

Research on CMC has often found that self-disclosure in CMC is higher than in FTF interactions. There have been three explanations for this phenomenon. First, the self-awareness explanation argues that sitting alone in front of a computer (versus being in the same room with an interaction partner) increases private self-awareness (awareness of one's feelings and inner thoughts), thus leading to increased self-disclosure (Matheson & Zanna, 1988). Another line of argumentation assumes that sitting alone in front of a computer reduces public self-awareness and fear of sanctions, and that this drives enhanced self-disclosure (Joinson, 2001). A third, more recent, explanation argues that the perceived higher intimacy in CMC is driven by misattributions; the same level of self-disclosure is attributed more to the interaction partner's concern for the relationship when communication is via CMC than FTF settings (Jiang, Bazarova, & Hancock, 2011)

Thus, self-disclosure is often higher in mediated communication, at least in anonymous and pseudonymous communication situations. In line with the self-disclosure intimacy hypothesis, Craig and Wright (2012) report that self-disclosure depth and breadth in the communication with a specific Facebook friend predicted relationship quality. Moreover, several studies which have compared the quality of online and offline friendships have reported that friendships formed online are not significantly less close than FTF friendships (Parks & Floyd, 1996; Parks & Roberts, 1998). Taken together, there is evidence that that friendship formation online is possible and at least partly driven by higher self-disclosure.

Relationship Maintenance

Many close friendships hold for years or even a lifetime, so people spend usually more time maintaining friendships than building new friendships. When relationship maintenance is the focus of attention, many researchers have studied which media people actually use to maintain relationships and which media are most suited for maintaining relationships. Most studies in this area have focused on media use in long-distance relationships, when communication has to be mediated at least partly.

Media Niches

According to the uses and gratifications approach, individuals select media based on their motivations and the gratifications provided by the respective medium (Katz, Blumler, & Gurevitch, 1974). Maintaining a friendship is an example of such a motivation (compared to other motivations such information, entertainment, etc.). Based on a unique set of gratifications, a medium might occupy a certain gratification niche and thereby outperform other media (Dimmick, Kline, & Stafford, 2000). For example, Dimmick et al. (2000) found that the phone was perceived as more suited for the maintenance of friendships than e-mail. Ramirez, Dimmick, Feaster, and Lin (2008) did a follow up study also including newer media such as the cell phone and instant messaging (IM). These authors found that the cell phone was now perceived as superior on many of the sociability gratifications (e.g., exchanging personal messages, express caring), followed by IM, whereas e-mail and the landline phone lost popularity.

When compared to Facebook, IM is perceived as more suited for maintaining relationships (Quan-Haase & Young, 2010). The gratifications of Facebook lie mainly in having fun and knowing about the activities in one's social network (Quan-Haase & Young, 2010). However, people are not always rational actors using richer media for more intimate communication. SNS are designed for maintaining friendships, and users value the efficient and convenient way of updating their whole network with one post (Urista, Dong, & Day, 2009). Numerous studies have shown that maintaining existing relationships is the main motivation for Facebook use according to the users (Ellison, Steinfield, & Lampe, 2011; Smock, Ellison, Lampe, & Wohn, 2011; Urista, Dong, & Day, 2009). Users perceive SNS useful in maintaining existing friendships (Craig & Wright, 2012), and SNS use indeed appears to increase bonding capital (Ellison, Steinfield, & Lampe, 2007).

Multiplexity

An often overlooked phenomenon when focusing on the suitability of a specific medium for the maintenance of friendships is multiplexity. People do usually not communicate via only one medium with friends, but rather engage in multiple activities and different contexts with their friends. Consequently, instead of focusing on the use of one specific medium, it may be more useful to look at the combined use of several media, as the closer the friendship, the more media are usually used (Haythornthwaite, 2000). For example, Utz (2007) found that closer friends had more contact via the phone and sent each other more e-mails than less close friends. Interestingly, the level of intimacy in the e-mails was uncorrelated to friendship strength; the content remained relatively superficial. However, phone calls were more intimate the stronger the bond between two individuals. These results suggest that some media are mainly used to keep friends updated about what's going on in one's life, but that synchronous media containing more nonverbal cues are used more for intimate communication. The same reasoning might hold for SNS, as the public self-disclosure on SNS is relatively superficial and mainly focused on positive aspects (Utz, 2012b).

Taken together, existing research demonstrates that media can play an important role in maintaining relationships, especially long-distance relationships. For the discussion of intimate topics, people still prefer synchronous media such as the cell phone or IM. However, SNS are a convenient tool for keeping others updated and receiving information about one's network.

Next Steps

As technology and scholarship continue to evolve in the area of media and friendships, the number of future research questions is potentially limitless. In this section I consider questions regarding implications of social media on the number and type of friendships that people may have, as well as the underlying processes involved in social media use and friendships.

Numbers and Types of Friendships

One interesting question for future research is whether social media, and especially SNS, enable us to maintain a higher number of close friendships. Dunbar (1995) assumed that we can only maintain networks of roughly 150 people due to cognitive constraints, but newer studies have come to the conclusion that we might be able to maintain networks of 400 people (Parks, 2010). These networks contain mostly weak or even absent ties, but Parks (2010) found that a surprisingly high proportion of Facebook friends were characterized as "close friends."

Related to this finding is the question of whether social media genuinely increase our social connectedness (Rainie & Wellman, 2012) or rather only provide us with an illusion of connection (Turkle, 2011). Consistent with this line of reasoning, perhaps it is apt to question whether relationships maintained or developed via social media might even be described as parasocial relationships. The concept of parasocial interaction and relationships was developed to describe relationships with fictional characters or media figures such as news anchors (Horton & Wohl, 1956). Parasocial friendships are not considered to be "real" friendships because the media figure does usually not share the perception of friendship (see definition earlier in this chapter). However, social media, especially such as Twitter that allow for asymmetric ties, appears to blur the distinction between "real" and "media" friendships. Celebrities cannot talk back to the viewers on TV, but they can respond on Twitter, or the follower might at least feel addressed by such tweets—even if the tweets go out to hundreds or thousands of others.

Underlying Processes

In addition to examining the effects of social media on the number and type of friendships, future research may also profitably consider the underlying processes that are involved with online friendship development and maintenance. For example, self-disclosure has been regarded as the central underlying process of friendship development. However, the self-disclosure intimacy hypothesis has been challenged by social media. Studies in FTF settings have found that the intimacy of self-disclosure decreases from dyads to three- or four-person groups; yet these theories are not able to explain why people post sensitive information on semi-public networks. Nevertheless, most self-disclosure on SNS remains relatively superficial; people talk mostly about positive experiences and report where they have been (Utz, 2012b). The primary function of self-disclosure on SNS seems to be entertainment and self-presentation (Utz, 2012a). However, this type of self-disclosure might change the ways good friends talk to each other in FTF contexts. Instead of reporting first what they have done and where they have been in the last week, they may immediately refer to the Facebook posts and pictures.

Thompson (2008) coined the term *ambient intimacy* to describe the phenomenon that people are able to distill quite accurate pictures of the lives of their friends by skimming the stream of status updates and tweets. However, these predictions have not been studied empirically so far. Consequently, ambient intimacy could be caused merely by simple exposure, but also the level of intimacy in the tweets and status updates. The symmetry of relationships—including at least occasional reactions (even as subtle as a like button)—might also play a role.

Summary

Media have changed the way we form and maintain friendships. Smartphones allow us to be always connected to our network. When it comes to meeting new people in anonymous or pseudonymous online environments, similarity in attitudes and interests is a stronger driver of initial attraction, and self-disclosure is still the central underlying process. When it comes to maintaining relationships, people perceive synchronous dyadic communication via the cell phone or IM as most appropriate, but use often SNS for reasons of convenience and efficiency of the communication. Whether social media really help us to maintain larger networks or whether some people get lost in the illusion of connection remains a question for further research.

References

Abbey, A., Abramis, D., & Caplan, R. (1985). Effects of different sources of social support and social conflict on emotional well-being. *Basic and Applied Social Psychology, 6*(2), 111–129. doi: 10.1207/s15324834basp0602_2

Albrecht, T. L., & Goldsmith, D. J. (2003). Social support, social networks, and health. In T. L. Thompson, A. M. Dorsey, K. I. Miller, & R. Parrott (Eds.), *Handbook of health communication* (pp. 263–284). Hillsdale, NJ: Lawrence Erlbaum.

Altman, I., & Taylor, D. (1973). *Social penetration: The development of interpersonal relationships.* New York: Holt, Rinehart, & Winston.

Amichai-Hamburger, Y., Kingsbury, M., & Schneider, B. H. (2013). Friendship: An old concept with a new meaning? *Computers in Human Behavior, 29*, 33–39. doi: 10.1016/j.chb.2012.05.025

Beebe, S. A., Beebe, S. J., & Redmond, M. V. (2011). *Interpersonal communication: Relating to others* (6th ed.). Boston, MA: Allyn & Bacon.

Byrne, D. (1969). Attitudes and attraction. In L. Berkowitz (Ed.), *Advances in experimental social psychology* (Vol. 4, pp. 35–89). New York: Academic Press.

Clark, H. H., & Brennan, S. E. (1991). Grounding in communication. In L. Resnick, J. Levine, & S. Teasley (Eds.), *Perspectives on socially shared cognition* (pp. 127–149). Hyattsville, MD: American Psychological Association.

Collins, N., & Miller, L. (1994). Self-disclosure and liking: A meta-analytic review. *Psychological Bulletin, 116*, 457–475. doi: 10.1037/0033-2909.116.3.457

Craig, E., & Wright, K. B. (2012). Computer-mediated relational development and maintenance on Facebook®. *Communication Research Reports, 29*(2), 119–129. doi: 10.1080/08824096.2012.667777

Daft, R. L., & Lengel, R. H. (1986). Organizational information requirements, media richness and structural design. *Management Science, 32*(5), 554–571. doi: 10.1287/mnsc.32.5.554

Dimmick, J., Kline, S., & Stafford, L. (2000). The gratification niches of personal e-mail and the telephone competition, displacement, and complementarity. *Communication Research, 27*(2), 227–248. doi: 10.1177/009365000027002005

Dunbar, R. I. M. (1995). Neocortex size and group size in primates: A test of the hypothesis. *Journal of Human Evolution, 28*(3), 287–296. doi: 10.1006/jhev.1995.1021

Ellison, N. B., Steinfield, C., & Lampe, C. (2007). The benefits of Facebook "friends": Social capital and college students' use of online social network sites. *Journal of Computer-Mediated Communication, 12*(4), 1143–1168. doi: 10.1111/j.1083-6101.2007.00367.x

Ellison, N. B., Steinfield, C., & Lampe, C. (2011). Connection strategies: Social capital implications of Facebook-enabled communication practices. *New Media & Society, 13*(6), 873–892. doi: 10.1177/1461444810385389

Festinger, L., Schachter, S., & Back, K. (1950). The spatial ecology of group formation. *Journal of Mammalogy, 86*, 141–161.

Fulk, J., Steinfield, C. W., Schmitz, J., & Power, J. G. (1987). A social information processing model of media use in organizations. *Communication Research, 14*(5), 529–552. doi: 10.1177/009365087014005005

Gibson, J. (1977). The concept of affordances. In R. E. Shaw & J. Bransford (Eds.), *Perceiving, acting, and knowing: Toward an ecological psychology* (pp. 67–82). Hillsdale, NJ: Lawrence Erlbaum.

Gosling, S. D., Gaddis, D., & Vazire, S. (2007). *Personality impressions based on Facebook profiles.* Paper presented at the ICWSM, Boulder, Colorado, USA.

Haythornthwaite, C. (2000). Online personal networks: Size, composition, and media use among distance learners. *New Media & Society, 2*(2), 195–226. doi: 10.1177/14614440022225779

Horton, D., & Wohl, R. R. (1956). Mass communication and para-social interaction: Observations on intimacy at a distance. *Psychiatry, 19*(3), 215–229.

Hutchby, I. (2001). Technologies, texts and affordances. *Sociology, 35*(2), 441–456. doi: 10.1177/S0038038501000219

Jiang, L. C., Bazarova, N. N., & Hancock, J. T. (2011). The disclosure–intimacy link in computer-mediated communication: An attributional extension of the hyperpersonal model. *Human Communication Research, 37*(1), 58–77. doi: 10.1111/j.1468-2958.2010.01393.x

Joinson, A. N. (2001). Self-disclosure in computer-mediated communication: The role of self-awareness and visual anonymity. *European Journal of Social Psychology, 31*(2), 177–192. doi: 10.1002/ejsp.36

Katz, E., Blumler, J. G., & Gurevitch, M. (1974). Utilization of mass communication by the individual. In J. G. Blumler & E. Katz (Eds.), *The uses of mass communications: Current perspectives on gratifications research* (pp. 19–32). Beverly Hills, CA: Sage.

Kiesler, S., & McGuire, T. W. (1984). Social psychological aspects of computer-mediated communication. *American Psychologist, 39,* 1123–1134. doi: 10.1037/0003-066X.39.10.1123

Lea, M., & Spears, R. (1991). Computer-mediated communication, deindividuation, and group decision-making. *International Journal of Man-Machine Studies, 34,* 283–301. doi: 10.1016/0020-7373(91)90045-9

Matheson, K., & Zanna, M. P. (1988). The impact of computer-mediated communication on self-awareness. *Computers in Human Behavior, 4*(3), 221–233. doi: 10.1016/0747-5632(88)90015-5

McKenna, K., & Bargh, J. (2000). Plan 9 from cyberspace: The implications of the Internet for personality and social psychology. *Personality and Social Psychology Review, 4*(1), 57. doi: 10.1207/S15327957PSPR0401_6

Monin, B. (2003). The warm glow heuristic: when liking leads to familiarity. *Journal of Personality and Social Psychology, 85*(6), 1035–1048. doi: 10.1037/0022-3514.85.6.1035

Parks, M. R. (2010, June). *Who are Facebook friends? Exploring the composition of Facebook friend networks.* Paper presented at the 60th Annual ICA conference, Singapore.

Parks, M. R., & Floyd, K. (1996). Making friends in cyberspace. *Journal of Computer Mediated Communication, 1*(4). doi: 10.1111/j.1083-6101.1996.tb00176.x

Parks, M. R., & Roberts, L. (1998). "Making MOOsic": The development of personal relationships on line and a comparison to their off-line counterparts. *Journal of Social and Personal Relationships, 15*(4), 517–537. doi: 10.1177/0265407598154005

Quan-Haase, A., & Young, A. L. (2010). Uses and gratifications of social media: A comparison of Facebook and instant messaging. *Bulletin of Science, Technology & Society, 30*(5), 350–361. doi: 10.1177/0270467610380009

Rainie, L., & Wellman, B. (2012). *Networked: The new social operating system.* Cambridge, MA: MIT Press.

Ramirez Jr, A., Dimmick, J., Feaster, J., & Lin, S. F. (2008). Revisiting interpersonal media competition the gratification niches of instant messaging, e-mail, and the telephone. *Communication Research, 35*(4), 529–547. doi: 10.1177/0093650208315979

Reicher, S. D., Spears, R., & Postmes, T. (1995). A social identity model of deindividuation phenomena. *European Review of Social Psychology, 6*(1), 161–198. doi: 10.1080/14792779443000049

Short, J., Williams, E., & Christie, B. (1976). *The social psychology of telecommunications.* Toronto, ON: Wiley.

Smock, A. D., Ellison, N. B., Lampe, C., & Wohn, D. Y. (2011). Facebook as a toolkit: A uses and gratification approach to unbundling feature use. *Computers in Human Behavior, 27*(6), 2322–2329. doi: 10.1016/j.chb.2011.07.011

Sproull, L., & Kiesler, S. (1986). Reducing social context cues: Electronic mail in organizational communication. *Management Science, 32,* 1492–1512. doi: 10.1287/mnsc.32.11.1492

Thompson, C. (2008). Brave new world of digital intimacy. *New York Times, 5.*

Tong, S. T., Van Der Heide, B., Langwell, L., & Walther, J. B. (2008). Too much of a good thing? The relationship between number of friends and interpersonal impressions on Facebook. *Journal of Computer-Mediated Communication, 13*(3), 531–549. doi: 10.1111/j.1083-6101.2008.00409.x

Treem, J., & Leonardi, P. (2012). Social media use in organizations: Exploring the affordances of visibility, editability, persistence, and association. *Communication Yearbook, 36,* 143–189.

Turkle, S. (2011). *Alone together: Why we expect more from technology and less from each other.* New York: Basic Books.

Urista, M., Dong, Q., & Day, K. (2009). Explaining why young adults use MySpace and Facebook through uses and gratifications theory. *Human Communication A Journal of the Pacific and Asian Communication Association, 12*(2), 215–230.

Utz, S. (2007). Media use in long-distance friendships. *Information, Communication & Society, 10*(5), 694–713. doi: 10.1080/13691180701658046

Utz, S. (2010). Show me your friends and I will tell you what type of person you are: How one's profile, number of friends, and type of friends influence impression formation on social network sites. *Journal of Computer-Mediated Communication, 15*(2), 314–335. doi: 10.1111/j.1083-6101.2010.01522.x

Utz, S. (2012a). Selbstoffenbarung und Selbstpräsentation [Self-disclosure and self-presentation]. In L. Reinecke & S. Trepte (Eds.), *Unterhaltung in neuen Medien [Entertainment in new media]* (pp. 140–157). Cologne: Halem.

Utz, S. (2012b). Social network site use among Dutch students: Effects of time and platform. In F. Comunello (Ed.), *Networked sociability and individualism: Technology for personal and professional relationships* (pp. 104–126). Hershey, PA: IGI Global.

Walther, J. B. (1992). Interpersonal effects in computer-mediated interaction: A relational perspective. *Communication Research, 19*(1), 52–90. doi: 10.1177/009365092019001003

Walther, J. B. (1996). Computer-mediated communication: Impersonal, interpersonal, and hyperpersonal interaction. *Communication Research, 23*(1), 3–43. doi: 10.1177/009365096023001001

Walther, J. B., & Parks, M. R. (2002). Cues filtered out, cues filtered in: Computer-mediated communication and relationships. In M. L. Knapp & J. A. Daly (Eds.), *Handbook of interpersonal communication* (3rd ed., pp. 529–563). Thousand Oaks, CA: Sage.

Walther, J. B., Van Der Heide, B., Hamel, L. M., & Shulman, H. C. (2009). Self-generated versus other-generated statements and impressions in computer-mediated communication: A test of warranting theory using facebook. *Communication Research, 36*(2), 229–253. doi: 10.1177/0093650208330251

Wang, S. S., Moon, S.-I., Kwon, K. H., Evans, C. A., & Stefanone, M. A. (2010). Face off: Implications of visual cues on initiating friendship on Facebook. *Computers in Human Behavior, 26*(2), 226–234. doi: 10.1016/j.chb.2009.10.001

Wellman, B., & Gulia, M. (1999). Net surfers don't ride alone: Virtual communities as communities. In M. A. Smith & P. Kollock (Eds.), *Communities in cyberspace* (pp. 167–194). London: Routledge.

Zhao, S., Grasmuck, S., & Martin, J. (2008). Identity construction on Facebook: Digital empowerment in anchored relationships. *Computers in Human Behavior, 24*(5), 1816–1836. doi: 10.1016/j.chb.2008.02.012

9

SEX, ROMANCE, AND MEDIA

Taking Stock of Two Research Literatures

Jennifer Stevens Aubrey and Hilary Gamble

Given concerns about the distorted representations of romance and sexuality in the media, media effects researchers have given a substantial and growing amount of attention to two related research areas. One literature has examined the role of the media in shaping young people's sexual socialization, whereas a separate literature has focused on the effects of popular media exposure on attitudes and beliefs about romantic relationships. Additionally, a small number of studies have examined media effects on the intersections of sexuality- and romance-related outcomes. In this chapter, we unite and summarize evidence indicating a link between media use and young people's attitudes about romance and sexuality.

Focusing on entertainment media, which encompasses television, magazines, and films, we examine the findings of dozens of studies compiled using both electronic and ancestral search mechanisms that were as exhaustive as possible. We divided the findings into content analyses, correlational survey research, and experimental studies.

Media and Sexuality: Messages and Effects on Sexual Beliefs, Attitudes, and Behaviors

The research on media and sexuality has examined whether media use encourages distorted sexual beliefs and expectations, stereotypical attitudes toward sexual relationships, and permissive sexual behaviors. In the following, our discussion is organized by the type of study and the type of sexual outcome in question: beliefs, attitudes, and behaviors.

124

Content Analyses

Content analyses of sex on television have examined the frequency and explicitness of sexual behavior and dialogue (Franzblau, Sprafkin, & Rubinstein, 1977; Kunkel et al., 2003). Sexual information is plentiful in the media, especially in television popular among young people. Content analyses have estimated that approximately two-thirds of television programs contained sexual messages with an average of just over four scenes per hour (Kunkel et al., 2003). At the same time, sexual risk and responsibility themes are remarkably sparse (Eyal & Finnerty, 2009).

Moreover, content analytic evidence points to gender differences in line with the sexual double standard, a pervasive cultural norm whereby it is more acceptable for boys to accumulate sexual experience than it is for girls. Male characters are more likely to initiate sexual behaviors than female characters (Aubrey, 2004; Kunkel et al., 2003). Although negative consequences of sexuality are rare, female characters are more likely to experience sexual consequences than male characters (Eyal & Finnerty, 2009), and they are more likely to result when female characters rather than male characters initiate sexual activities (Aubrey, 2004).

Other content analyses have attempted to measure gender-role-based sexual scripts on mainstream television. Ward's (1995) content analysis examined sexual talk and found that most dialogue focused on masculine sexual themes. The most frequent message was that men value women based on their physical appearance, and the second most frequent message was that being sexual is a defining characteristic of masculinity. Fewer verbal interactions focused on the female sexual role, but of these messages, the most common was that women are only attracted to certain types of men, who have financial or social resources. Inspired by Ward's (1995) study, Kim et al.'s (2007) content analysis focused on the "heterosexual script," a dominant script in western culture that defines what is considered appropriate relational and sexual behavior for men and women. Kim et al. found evidence for three major elements of the heterosexual script in popular television programs: (1) the sexual double standard; (2) courtship strategies, whereby men use active and powerful ways to attract women, and women use submissive and alluring ways to attract men; and (3) attitudes toward commitment, suggesting that men avoid and women seek commitment in romantic and sexual relationships.

Similarly, content analyses of women's and teen-girl lifestyle magazines have shown that the coverage of sexual topics foregrounds male sexuality and supports the sexual double standard (Durham, 1998). Girls are encouraged to cast themselves as sexualized objects of male desire by using myriad beauty and cosmetic products advertised in the magazines; on the other hand, the underlying sexual advice of the magazines discourages females from acknowledging their sexuality (Duffy & Gotcher, 1996).

Also, for girls, magazines emphasize the relational contexts of sex; the most prevalent theme in *Seventeen* magazines from 1974 to 1994 was the script that valued sex in committed relationships (Carpenter, 1998). According to Garner, Sterk, and Adams (1998), boys in teen magazines are portrayed as users and controllers of sex, whereas girls are characterized as needing to negotiate boys' desire to use them sexually. In magazines targeting adult women, Gill (2009) found that a dominant script was that women should become sexually adventurous in order to keep men interested in them.

Lad magazines are the male version of lifestyle magazines such as *Seventeen* and *Cosmopolitan*. They focus heavily on sex and feature numerous photos of provocatively posed, scantily clad women. Taylor's (2005) content analysis of lad magazines (*Maxim*, *FHM*, and *Stuff*) showed that although 41 percent of the articles about sex had "how to pleasure women" as their primary theme, closer inspection of the articles revealed that the underling motivation for pleasuring women was to receive sexual pleasure in return.

Correlational Studies

The earliest work in assessing the impact of media exposure on young people's sexuality took the form of correlational studies, asking the question: "Does self-reported regular exposure to media's frequent portrayals of sex encourage viewers to adopt distorted and permissive perspectives of sexuality?" Although the effect sizes are typically small, the answer is mostly, yes, there is a link.

Sexual Attitudes

First, exposure to sexually oriented television genres is linked to recreational and permissive attitudes about sexuality (e.g., Strouse & Buerkel-Rothfuss, 1987; Ward & Friedman, 2006; Ward & Rivadeneyra, 1999). Likewise, involvement with the TV watching experience (e.g., identification with television characters, motivation to learn from TV) also predicts stereotypical sexual attitudes, such as the endorsement of the beliefs that sex is recreational, that men are sex-driven, and that women are sex objects (Ward, 2002; Ward & Friedman, 2006; Ward & Rivadeneyra, 1999).

Sexual Beliefs

Another question that research has attempted to answer is: "To what extent does media exposure shape viewers' estimates of the frequency of sex occurring among their peers?" The research on this question has reported consistently strong correlations, such that greater exposure to sexually oriented media is linked to viewers' assumption about the prevalence of sex (Ward, 2002; Ward & Rivadeneyra, 1999). For this reason, entertainment media, particularly narratives that feature adolescents, teens, and young adults engaging in casual sexual experiences, have been described as a "super peer" (Brown, Halpern, & L'Engle, 2005; Strasburger, 1995), applying pressure on young viewers to engage in similar behaviors.

Correlational studies have also demonstrated that television exposure can be linked to one's sexual self-image. For instance, three studies conducted by Stanley Baran and his colleagues in the 1970s examined the sexual self-image as an outcome of television exposure. Baran (1976a, 1976b) found a positive relationship between perceived reality of sex on television and dissatisfaction with one's own sex life among high school and college students. Courtright and Baran (1980) also found a relationship between heavy television viewing and negative attitudes about remaining a virgin. More current research found that among college women, general television viewing, exposure to soap operas, and exposure to prime-time dramas was negatively correlated with their sexual self-concept, operationally defined as sexual esteem, sexual assertiveness, sexual interest, sexual anxiety (reverse-coded), and body-image self-consciousness during physical intimacy (Aubrey, 2007). Similarly, Tolman, Kim, Schooler, and Sorsoli (2007) found that exposure to media scripts that emphasized sexual objectification of women and men's avoidance of relational commitment negatively predicted adolescent girls' sexual agency.

To examine the impact of popular magazines, Kim and Ward (2004) found that college women who frequently read adult-oriented (e.g., *Cosmopolitan*) contemporary women's magazines reported more support for sexual assertiveness in women and more agreement with recreational sexual attitudes, but less support of a view that equated sex with risk and danger. On the other hand, women who regularly read teen-oriented women's magazines (e.g., *Seventeen*) were more likely to report support of stereotypical male sexual roles and the belief that women should be submissive and alluring to attract men's interest.

Sexual Behavior

Correlational analyses have also explored the link between general television viewing and sexual behaviors, though the results of the early studies on this topic were inconsistent (Brown & Newcomer, 1991; Peterson, Moore, & Furstenberg, 1991). Recent work has shown that more consistent results emerge when exposure to specific sexually oriented media use is examined. Pardun, L'Engle, and Brown (2005) found that exposure to sexual content in television predicted intentions to have sex (also L'Engle, Brown, & Kenneavy, 2006), whereas viewing sexually oriented movies positively predicted sexual activities. Similarly, Fisher et al. (2009)

demonstrated that exposure to sexually oriented cable television was associated with increased likelihood of having oral sex and sexual intercourse, and greater intentions of engaging in sexual behaviors in the next year.

Recent longitudinal research has also made a compelling case for media exposure influencing the initiation of sexual intercourse among adolescents (Brown et al., 2006; Collins et al., 2004; L'Engle & Jackson, 2008). Looking across four media that weighted frequency of use by the frequency of sexual content in each medium, Brown et al. (2006) found that a "sexy media diet" predicted sexual activity and risk of earlier initiation of sexual intercourse, especially for White adolescents. Further, Bleakly, Hennessy, Fishbein, and Jordan (2008) argued that the relationship between these variables is reciprocal. Their study showed evidence that teens who exposed themselves to sexual content were more likely to be sexually active and that sexually active teens were more likely to expose themselves to sexual content.

Experiments

Experimental studies have examined the impact of sexual content on television on sexuality-related outcomes. Bryant and Rockwell (1994) found that teens who viewed television content portraying pre-, extra-, or nonmarital sexual relations regarded such acts as less morally reprehensible than teens who viewed sexual relations between married partners or nonsexual relations between adults. Similarly, Eyal and Kunkel (2008) found that the valence of the consequence (positive vs. negative) in portrayals of sexuality in teen dramas explained differences in college students' attitudes toward premarital intercourse and moral judgments of characters engaging in sex. Participants who were assigned to view negative consequences had more negative attitudes and more negative moral judgments than those assigned to positive consequences.

Also, experimental research has examined the impact of exposure to sexual content on sexual attitudes. For instance, Ward (2002) found that female participants who were exposed to a sexual stereotype, such as sex as a game, women as sexual objects, or men as sex-driven creatures, were more likely to endorse that stereotype than those who viewed a clip not featuring the stereotype. Ward and Friedman (2006) replicated this study with high school students and found similar results.

Taken together, the literature on sex and media has grown from the central question on whether sexual media exposure is linked to sexual permissiveness, especially among adolescents, to more recent work that examines additional outcomes focused on facets of young people's self-concepts, distorted expectations about sexual relationship, and the development and activation of sexual stereotypes.

Media and Romance: Messages and Effects
on Romantic Beliefs, Attitudes, and Behaviors

Romantic relationships in the media have consistently been portrayed as effortless and idealistic (de Souza & Sherry, 2006; Johnson & Holmes, 2009; Signorielli, 1982), themes that match young adults' personal romantic narratives (Bachen & Illouz, 1996). Thus, researchers have questioned whether viewers develop unrealistic attitudes and beliefs about romantic relationships from media (e.g., Eggermont, 2004; Segrin & Nabi, 2002, Signorielli, 1991).

Content Analyses

Content analyses of romantic relationships in magazines, television, and films have found little variety in how romantic relationships are portrayed. Most romantic relationships portrayed on television and films are between White, adult, heterosexual men and women (de Souza & Sherry, 2006; Signorielli, 1982). Their relationships are uncomplicated, easy to manage without much effort, and highly romantic. The couples argue, but conflict does not have a lasting impact (de Souza & Sherry, 2006; Johnson & Holmes, 2009; Pardun, 2002). In fact, most of their arguments could be resolved through a romantic gesture that reaffirmed their idealistic love (Hefner, 2011). These findings tell a story about how relationships work, but they do not prepare viewers for the ups and downs of romantic relationships. When romantic relationships inevitably fail to meet the idealized expectations presented in the media, teen magazines for girls, including *Seventeen* and (the now defunct) *CosmoGirl*, do not offer much solace; rather, they place additional pressure on girls by encouraging them to take responsibility for the initiation and upkeep of their romantic relationships (Firminger, 2006).

Correlational Studies

Much of the research on media and romance has taken the form of correlational analyses. Of these studies, television is the primary medium under investigation.

Signorielli's (1991) flagship study found that heavy television exposure was correlated with the belief that happy marriages were rare, but more recent correlational studies have found television viewing is related to unrealistic, often idealistic, relationship beliefs (e.g., Haferkamp, 1999; Holmes, 2007; Holmes & Johnson, 2009; Rehkoff, 2005; Shapiro & Kroeger, 1991). Television use was also correlated with the beliefs that "the sexes are different," that "sexual perfectionism is expected," and "mind reading is expected" (Haferkamp, 1999; Holmes, 2007; Holmes

& Johnson, 2009; Shapiro & Kroeger, 1991). In turn, these studies found those who endorsed these unrealistic relationship beliefs were less satisfied in their romantic relationships (Holmes & Johnson, 2009; Rehkoff, 2005; Shapiro & Kroeger, 1991).

Interestingly, those who were less satisfied in their relationships and who endorsed unrealistic relationship beliefs were the most likely to create and maintain parasocial relationships with media characters (Rehkoff, 2005). That is, those who watched television may develop unrealistic relationship beliefs, which lead them to be less satisfied in their relationships; so, they turned to parasocial relationships to satisfy their need for romance. Recent work by Aubrey, Click, and Behm-Morawitz (2013) supports these findings, within the context of the *Twilight* fandom. Their results demonstrated that among fans of the *Twilight* series, relational dissatisfaction predicted parasocial interaction with the main romantic characters of the series. Thus, both studies suggest that parasocial interaction might offer a refuge when there are deficits in real-life romantic relationships.

Television viewing has also been found to correlate with relationship expectations. Signorielli's (1991) study found that television viewing predicted future marital-related behaviors. Similarly, Segrin and Nabi (2002) found that college-aged participants who reported watching more romantic media were more likely to have unrealistic marriage expectations and were more likely to say they intended to get married. Rivadeneyra and Lebo (2008) also found a positive relationship between romantic television viewing and endorsement of traditional dating roles. Eggermont (2004) reported positive correlations between total television viewing and romantic expectations.

Only a couple of correlational studies have attempted to determine what behavioral responses media may inspire. First, Rivadeneyra and Lebo (2008) found those who watch more television, especially soap operas, were more likely to begin dating earlier and to have more dating partners. Second, Fallis, Fitzpatrick, and Friestad (1985) found that marital couples who vacillate between conventional and non-conventional relational ideologies, defined as "separates," were likely to discuss relationship-relevant issues following television viewing.

Experiments

The number of studies experimentally testing hypotheses involving the effects of romantic media use on romantic attitudes, beliefs, and behaviors is relatively small. First, Taylor (2012) found media representations of partner scarcity or abundance changes women's preference for the type of partner they would want in a short-term or long-term relationship. Second, Holmes and Johnson (2009) found people in relationships reported being more satisfied in their relationships after viewing a romantic film, whereas those not in a relationship reported being much less satisfied with their most recent romantic relationship after watching the romantic film.

Taken together, these studies demonstrate heavier media consumption, especially romantic media, could result in inflated attitudes and beliefs about relationships that disappoint when reality is not congruent with a romantic partner's expectations.

Studies Examining Media's Influence on the Intersections of Both Romance and Sex

A small number of studies have examined media effects on the intersection of sexuality and romance. These studies recognize that many of the messages in the media, as well as the beliefs that audiences develop based on them, rest on the notion that sexual behaviors typically occur in the context of romantic relationships.

Given that the messages regarding sexuality are highly intertwined with messages about romance, it is not surprising, then, that when research examines the influence of media on viewers' beliefs and attitudes, romance and sexuality are intertwined as well. For example, Aubrey, Harrison, Kramer, and Yellin (2003) found that for men, exposure to sexually oriented television was related to expectations about having a greater variety of sexual acts in a romantic relationship, and for women, exposure to sexually oriented television predicted expectations about earlier sex in a relationship. This finding supports the "heterosexual script," whereby "good girls" set sexual limits, and "real men" pursue sex (Kim et al., 2007).

Zurbriggen and Morgan's (2006) study on reality dating television shows also highlights the intertwining of dating and sexuality in television. According to the authors, reality dating shows, such as *The Bachelor* and *Blind Date*, are "derived from gender stereotypical concepts of sexuality and dating" (p. 2). Not surprisingly, then, their results showed that for both men and women, exposure to reality dating programs was correlated with adversarial sexual beliefs, endorsement of the sexual double standard, the belief that men are sex-driven, the belief that appearance is important in dating, and that dating is a game. Vandenbosch and Eggermont's (2011) study on romantically themed reality shows likewise found a positive correlation between exposure to such shows and adolescents' estimates of their peers who are sexually active.

Finally, Eggermont (2006), in a three-year panel study of early and middle adolescents in Belgium, had his participants rate the effectiveness of both a romantic and a sexual approach in dating situations. He found that among early adolescents, TV viewing predicted a weakening belief in the romantic approach, and among middle adolescents, TV viewing strengthened beliefs in both the romantic and sexual approaches.

This small number of studies demonstrates that exposure to romantic themes in the media can impact young people's sexual beliefs and attitudes, and likewise, exposure to sexual narratives can impact young people's beliefs and attitudes about romance and romantic relationships. In this way, then, these studies recognize the interconnection between romance and sexuality in the schema of young audiences.

Dominant Theories Advancing Research on Media, Sex, Romance

Within these two literatures, three main theories have been used to study media effects on romance and sexuality. We briefly outline these below.

Social Cognitive Theory

According to social cognitive theory (SCT), human knowledge and behavior acquisition can occur via observation of media models, a process called vicarious learning (Bandura, 2009). Bandura suggested four stages that occur during the social learning process: attention, retention, production, and motivation. First, attention to models and their behaviors is affected by source and contextual features. Second, retention processes focus on the ability to symbolically represent the behavior that was modeled. Third, the production stage occurs when viewers translate symbolic representations into action. Finally, motivational processes influence whether symbolically represented behaviors are enacted based on whether the viewer perceives negative or positive consequences for the behavior.

Applied to media contexts, SCT suggests that audiences will be likely to model behaviors if they see that behavior as reinforced through the display of positive outcomes (Bandura, 2009). Additionally, viewers can learn from observing others' mistakes and can alter their own actions to avoid receiving similar negative consequences (Moyer-Gusé & Nabi, 2010). Moreover, modeling will occur more readily when the model is perceived as attractive and similar, and when the modeled behavior is possible, salient, simple, prevalent, and has functional value (Bandura, 2009). Thus, SCT predicts that people who attend to media content that includes depictions of attractive characters who enjoy having sexual intercourse and rarely suffer any negative consequences will be more likely to imitate the behavior. On the other hand, if the goal is to prevent or discourage sexual behaviors, or at least irresponsible ones, television characters are unlikely to serve as powerful behavioral models, as they are not likely to experience enduring negative consequences for their risky behavior (Nabi & Clark, 2008). Eyal and Kunkel's (2008) experiment, which manipulated the consequences associated with sexual activity as either positive or negative, is a clear example of testing this core principle of SCT.

Scripts-Based Theories

Research on media and sex, in particular, has utilized scripts-based theories, borrowing ideas about sexual scripts (Gagnon & Simon, 1973) and ideas about the processing and storage of scripts from the cognitive information processing model (Huesmann, 1997). According to Gagnon and Simon (1973), sexual scripts define who does what, with whom, when, how, and what it means. Mediated portrayals of sexuality, in particular, provide scripts at the cultural level, and they suggest what events are to happen in certain contexts, how the person should behave in response to these events, and what likely outcomes of those behaviors would be.

The cognitive information-processing model (Huesmann, 1997) suggests that people, through observational learning, create and store in their memories programs, that is, "scripts," to guide social behavior. Once scripts are firmly established, they may be automatically executed.

The process of observational learning proceeds through three main steps. First, the viewer attends to and interprets the behavior (Huesmann, 1997). Second, the script is retrieved from memory and evaluated to determine if it is appropriate to the situation. Finally, the viewer anticipates and evaluates society's responses to the behavior. Encoding of scripts will occur if they are salient to the viewer, the observed consequences are desirable, and the model of the behavior is attractive to the viewer. Continued use of the script depends on the extent to which the retrieved script produces a desirable outcome.

Further, the cognitive information-processing model recognizes that scripts differ according to the individual. According to the theory, viewers observe and acquire knowledge of sexuality from myriad televised verbal and visual examples of dating, intimacy, sex, and relationships, and develop models of behavior and values that are appropriate to their identity. One aspect of identity that has been investigated is gender. For example, Aubrey et al. (2003) argued that men and women encode differing scripts from sexually oriented media because there are different rules and norms governing sexual scripts for men and women (Aubrey, 2004; Kim et al., 2007; Ward, 1995), thus, they are likely to be especially receptive to the scripts that are appropriate for their gender.

Cultivation Theory

Given the emphasis of the two literatures on television portrayals, it is not surprising that much of the research in these areas is based on cultivation theory (Morgan, Shanahan, & Signorielli, 2009). Cultivation theory provides a framework for studying the long-term, cumulative effects of television on viewers' social realities, defined as individuals' pictures of what exists, what is important, what is related to what, and what is right

(Gerbner & Gross, 1976). The central hypothesis is that compared to light television viewers, heavy television viewers are more likely to perceive the real world in ways that reflect the most common and recurrent messages of the television world (Shanahan & Morgan, 1999).

Although some research has reported that frequency of viewing impacts adolescents' romantic expectations of their partners (Eggermont, 2004; Haferkamp, 1999), most studies have concluded that content-specific television has a stronger effect on sexual outcomes than general television exposure (Aubrey et al., 2003; Brown & Newcomer, 1991; Strouse & Buerkel-Rothfuss, 1987; Strouse et al., 1995; Ward & Rivadeneyra, 1999). Additionally, based on cultivation theory, studies demonstrate a correlation between exposure to romantically themed television and unhealthy relationship beliefs or expectations in its viewers (Haferkamp, 1999; Holmes, 2007; Holmes & Johnson, 2009; Rehkoff, 2005; Rivadeneyra & Lebo, 2008; Shapiro & Kroeger, 1991; Signorielli, 1991).

Suggestions for Future Directions

Looking over the scope of research on media and sexuality and romance, it is useful to reflect on the most important next steps for scholars to consider, based on limitations in existing research and evolving findings in these literatures. First, we will consider the limitations in existing research. Both the sexuality and romance literature suffer from a lack of experimental studies, at least compared to correlational studies. Moreover, there are even fewer experimental studies that examine the impact of media messages on adolescents in particular, a critical developmental period for these questions because puberty and new experiences with romance and sex make such media messages particularly salient. One explanation for this lack of experimental work is the difficulty in obtaining access to adolescent samples in public school districts for ostensible ethical reasons (Strasburger, 1995). Researchers, thus, might think of more creative ways to obtain access to adolescents, for example, by utilizing after-school programs, summer camps, or online networks to recruit adolescent participants. Moreover, oftentimes when adolescents are studied, they are examined in a monolithic fashion, without attention to the finer distinctions between stages of adolescence. Steele and Brown's (1995) study on "room culture" clearly illustrates the importance of considering developmental stage. While early adolescent girls were largely turned off by romantic and sexual media texts, post-pubertal, middle adolescent girls were interested in media texts regarding sexuality and romance, and they wrestled with the contradictions within media messages targeting them.

Limitations in measurement of key variables constitute a methodological concern for both the romance and sex literatures. For example, in the romance literature in particular, the measurement of romantic ideals is

134

rather inconsistent, making it difficult to make comparisons across studies or to understand what ideals are most clearly being communicated in entertainment media. Relationship status is only measured in about one-half of the studies on media effects on romance-related outcomes. And while studies have considered the role of individuals' viewing involvement, such as identification with main characters (Ward, 2002; Ward & Friedman, 2006; Ward & Rivadeneyra, 1999), a systematic understanding of motives for viewing sexually and romantically themed media is as yet unexamined.

Next, we will consider how evolving research findings inspire new research on the topics of romance and sex. Thanks to the contribution of important studies demonstrating a longitudinal link between exposure to sexual media and behavioral outcomes, such as age at first intercourse and the initiation of first intercourse (e.g., Brown et al., 2006; Collins et al., 2004), it is empirically clear that exposure to sexual media is predictive of sexual behaviors. An examination of just those variables, however, seems to "medicalize" the issue, making the focus primarily on health behaviors. Some of the broader issues are more social in nature. How do these behaviors make young people feel? Do they feel ready to be sexual? Are they making the decisions that are right for them? These questions related to the media's influence on young people's romantic and sexual self-concept remain open for further examination.

In 2007, the American Psychological Association released a task force report on the sexualization of women and girls in the media, documenting the insidious media practice of sexualizing females and detailing the numerous negative effects associated with this practice (American Psychological Association, 2007). In study after study, content analytic findings have indicated that women more often than men are portrayed in a sexualized and objectified manner. The report calls for more research attention to the way that the media encourage women and girls, in particular, to engage in self-sexualization and its impact for their mental and physical well-being. We also underscore the importance of research on this topic and suggest that the emphasis on sexualization might serve to degrade young people's idealistic expectations about romance.

The intersections between sexuality and new technologies also promise to provoke fruitful research inquiries as well. Advances in technology, in particular mobile media devices and social networking, mean that audiences have more opportunities to "try out" and rehearse their beliefs and understandings of romance and sexuality that they learn, in part, from entertainment mass media. Sexualized self-presentations on Facebook are one example of this rehearsal (Rill & Aubrey, 2012). Young people are aware that others in their social networks are observing their self-presentations, thus, there is oftentimes a struggle between presenting the "true self" and presenting the self as sexually desirable, resulting in the presentation of an "ideal self" (Ellison, Heino, & Gibbs, 2006). Researchers cannot ignore the performative nature of online self-presentations, be it on a social networking profile, an avatar in a virtual world, or a client on a dating website, and clearly, there are implications here for how people define themselves sexually and romantically.

"Sexting," sharing sexual content and images via mobile phones, is clearly an additional way for adolescents and young people to "perform" their sexual identity, as learned, at least in part, through the mass media. Qualitative research on the sexual dimensions and dynamics of mobile media demonstrates that these technologies are integral to youth sexual identities, relationships, hazards, and pleasures (Ringrose et al., 2012). From a social perspective, the concern is that sexting occurs within a sexualized, "pornified" mainstream culture (Levy, 2005), in which young people might feel pressure to conform to highly sexualized standards and perform them via sexting. Certainly, this is a fruitful avenue for further research.

Conclusion

At the same time that media use is correlated with casual and recreational attitudes, beliefs, and behaviors related to sexuality, magazines, television shows, and films also encourage idealistic and unrealistic beliefs and attitudes about romance. Thus, expectations regarding sexuality are lowered, whereas expectations about romance are heightened. Taken together, the media messages and lessons create a distorted and contradictory outlook on these two important aspects of young people.

References

American Psychological Association. (2007). *Report of the APA Task Force on the sexualization of girls*. Retrieved from http://www.apa.org/pi/women/programs/girls/report-full.pdf

Aubrey, J. S. (2004). Sex and punishment: An examination of sexual consequences and the sexual double standard in teen programming. *Sex Roles, 50,* 505–514. doi: 10.1023/B:SERS.0000023070.87195.07

Aubrey, J. S. (2007). Does television exposure influence college-aged women's sexual self-concept? *Media Psychology, 10,* 157–181. doi:10.1080/152132607013 75561

Aubrey, J. S., Click, M., & Behm-Morawitz, E. (2013). *The Twilight of youth: Understanding the roles of transportation and parasocial interaction in Twilight fans' connection to the young-adult vampire series*. Paper presented at the 2013 National Communication Association, Washington, DC.

Aubrey, J. S., Harrison, K., Kramer, L., & Yellin, J. (2003). Variety versus timing: Gender differences in college students' sexual expectations as predicted by exposure to sexually oriented television. *Communication Research, 30,* 432–460. doi: 10.1177/0093650203253365

Bachen, C. M., & Illouz, E. (1996). Imagining romance: Young people's cultural models of romance and love. *Critical Studies in Mass Communication, 13,* 279. doi: 10.1080/15295039609366983

Bandura, A. (2009). Social cognitive theory of mass communication (3rd ed.). In J. Bryant & D. Zillmann (Eds.), *Media effects: Advances in theory and research* (pp. 94–124). Mahwah, NJ: Lawrence Erlbaum Associates.

Baran, S. J. (1976a). How TV and film portrayals affect sexual satisfaction in college students. *Journalism Quarterly, 53*(3), 468–473.

Baran, S. J. (1976b). Sex on TV and adolescent sexual self-image. *Journal of Broadcasting, 20*(1), 61–68.

Bleakly, A., Hennessy, M., Fishbein, M., & Jordan, A. (2008). It works both ways: The relationship between exposure to sexual content in the media and adolescent sexual behavior. *Media Psychology, 11,* 443–461. doi: 10.1080/152132 60802491986

Brown, J. D., & Newcomer, S. F. (1991). Television viewing and adolescents' sexual behavior. *Journal of Homosexuality, 21,* 77–91. doi: 10.1300/J082v21n01_07

Brown, J. D., Halpern, C. T., & L'Engle, K. L. (2005). Mass media as a sexual super peer for early maturing girls. *Journal of Adolescent Health, 36,* 420–427. doi: 10.1016/j.jadohealth.2004.06.003

Brown, J. D., L'Engle, K. L., Pardun, C. J., Guo, G., Kenneavy, K., & Jackson, C. (2006). Sexy media matter: Exposure to sexual content in music, movies, television and magazines predicts black and white adolescents' sexual behavior, *Pediatrics, 117,* 1018–1027. doi: 10.1016/j.jadohealth.2004.06.003

Bryant, J., & Rockwell, S. C. (1994). Effects of massive exposure to sexually oriented prime-time television programming on adolescents' moral judgment. In D. Zillman, J. Bryant, & A. C. Huston (Eds.), *Media, children, and the family* (pp. 177–195). Cresskill, NJ: Hampton Press.

Carpenter, L. M. (1998). From girls into women: Scripts for sexuality and romance in *Seventeen* magazine, 1974–1994. *Journal of Sex Research, 35,* 158–168. Retrieved from: http://www.jstor.org/stable/3813668

Collins, R. L., Elliott, M. N., Berry, S. H., Kanouse, D. E., Kunkel, D., Hunter, S. B., & Miu, A. (2004). Watching sex on television predicts adolescent initiation of sexual behavior. *Pediatrics, 114*(3), 843.

Courtright, J. A., & Baran, S. J. (1980). The acquisition of sexual information by young people. *Journalism Quarterly, 57*(1), 107–114. doi: 10.1177/107769908005700116

de Souza, R., & Sherry, J. L. (2006). Portrayals of romantic relationships on adolescent television: A content analysis. *Media Report to Women, 34,* 13–21. Retrieved from http://search.proquest.com/docview/210172726?accountid=14576

Duffy, M., & Gotcher, J. M. (1996). Crucial advice on how to get the guy: The rhetorical vision of power and seduction in the teen magazine YM. *Journal of Communication Inquiry, 20*(1), 32–48.

Durham, M. G. (1998). Dilemmas of desire: Representations of adolescent sexuality in two teen magazines. *Youth and Society, 29,* 369–389. doi: 10.1177/0044118X98029003005

Eggermont, S. (2004). Television viewing, perceived similarity, and adolescents' expectations of a romantic partner. *Journal of Broadcasting & Electronic Media, 48,* 244–265. doi: 10.1207/s15506878jobem4802_5

Eggermont, S. (2006). Television viewing and adolescents' judgment of sexual request scripts: A latent growth curve analysis in early and middle adolescence. *Sex Roles, 55,* 457–468. doi: 10.1007/s11199-006-9099-7

Ellison, N., Heino, R., & Gibbs, J. (2006). Managing impressions online: Self-presentation processes in the online dating environment. *Journal of Computer-Mediated Communication, 11,* 415–441. doi: 10.1111/j.1083-6101.2006.00020.x

Eyal, K., & Finnerty, K. (2009). The portrayal of sexual intercourse on television: How, who, and with what consequence? *Mass Communication and Society, 12,* 143–169. doi: 10.1080/15205430802136713

Eyal, K., & Kunkel, D. (2008). The effects of sex in television drama shows on emerging adults' sexual attitudes and moral judgments. *Journal of Broadcasting and Electronic Media, 52,* 161–181. doi: 10.1080/08838150801991757

Fallis, S., Fitzpatrick, M. A., & Friestad, M. (1985). Spouses' discussion of television portrayals of close relationships. *Communication Research, 12,* 59–81.

Firminger, K. B. (2006). Is he boyfriend material? Representation of males in teenage girls' magazines. *Men and Masculinities, 8,* 298–308. doi: 10.1177/00936 5085012001003

Fisher, D. A., Hill, D. L., Grube, J. W., Bersamin, M. M., Walker, S., & Gruber, E. L. (2009). Televised sexual content and parental mediation: Influences on adolescent sexuality. *Media Psychology, 12,* 121–147. doi: 10.1080/15213260902849901

Franzblau, S., Sprafkin, J. N., & Rubinstein, E. A. (1977). Sex on TV: A content analysis. *Journal of Communication, 27,* 164–170. doi: 10.1111/j.1460-2466.1977.tb01844.x

Gagnon, J., & Simon, W. (1973). *Sexual conduct: The social sources of human sexuality.* Chicago, IL: Aldine.

Garner, A., Sterk, H. M., & Adams, S. (1998). Narrative analysis of sexual etiquette in teenage magazines. *Journal of Communication, 48,* 59–78. doi: 10.1111/j.1460-2466.1998.tb02770.x

Gerbner, G., & Gross, L. (1976). Living with television: The violence profile. *Journal of Communication, 26,* 172–194. doi: 10.1111/j.1460-2466.1976.tb01397.x

Gill, R. (2009). Mediated intimacy and postfeminism: A discourse analytic examination of sex and relationships advice in a women's magazine. *Discourse and Communication, 3,* 345–369. doi: 10.1177/1750481309343870

Haferkamp, C. J. (1999). Beliefs about relationships in relation to television viewing, soap opera viewing, and self-monitoring. *Current Psychology, 18,* 193–204. doi: 10.1007/s12144-999-1028-9

Hefner, V. (2011). *From love at first sight to soul mate: Romantic ideals in popular films and their association with young people's beliefs about relationships.* Dissertation, University of Illinois at Urbana-Champaign. Retrieved from ProQuest (3479093).

Holmes, B. M. (2007). In search of my "one-and-only": Romance-oriented media and beliefs in romantic relationship destiny. *Electronic Journal of Communication, 17*(3 & 4). Retrieved from http://www.cios.org.proxy.mul.missouri.edu/EJCPUBLIC/017/3/01735.HTML

Holmes, B. M., & Johnson, K. R. (2009). Where fantasy meets reality: Media exposure, relationship beliefs and standards, and the moderating effect of a current relationship. In E. P. Lamont (Ed.), *Social psychology: New research* (pp. 117–134). Hauppauge, NY: Nova Science.

Huesmann, L. R. (1997). Observational learning of violent behavior: Social and biosocial processes. In A. Raine (Ed.), *Biosocial bases of violence* (pp. 69–88). New York: Plenum Press.

Johnson, K. R., & Holmes, B. M. (2009). Contradictory messages: A content analysis of Hollywood-produced romantic comedy feature films. *Communication Quarterly, 57*, 352–373. doi: 10.1080/01463370903113632

Kim, J. L., & Ward, L. M. (2004). Pleasure reading: Associations between young women's sexual attitudes and their reading of contemporary women's magazines. *Psychology of Women Quarterly, 28*, 48–58. doi: 10.1111/j.1471-6402.2004.00122.x

Kim, J. L., Sorsoli, J. L., Collins, K., Zylbergold, B. A., Schooler, D., & Tolman, D. L. (2007). From sex to sexuality: Exposing the heterosexual script on primetime network television. *Journal of Sex Research, 44, 2*, 145–157. doi: 10.1080/00224490701263660

Kunkel, D., Biely, E., Eyal, K., Cope-Farrar, K., Donnerstein, E., & Fandrich, R. (2003). *Sex on TV: A biennial report to the Kaiser Family Foundation*. Menlo Park, CA: Kaiser Family Foundation.

L'Engle, K. L., & Jackson, C. (2008). Socialization influences on early adolescents' cognitive susceptibility and transition to sexual intercourse. *Journal of Research on Adolescence, 18*, 353–378. Available from: http://dx.doi.org/10.1016/j.jadohealth.2005.03.020

L'Engle, K. L., Brown, J. D., & Kenneavy, K. (2006). The mass media are an important context for adolescents' sexual behavior. *Journal of Adolescent Health, 38*, 186–192. doi: 10.1016/j.jadohealth.2005.03.020

Levy, A. (2005). *Female chauvinist pigs: Women and the rise of raunch culture*. New York: Free Press.

Morgan, M., Shanahan, J., & Signorielli, N. (2009). Growing up with television: Cultivation processes. In J. Bryant and M. B. Oliver (Eds.), *Media effects: Advances in theory and research* (3rd ed., pp. 34–49). New York: Routledge.

Moyer-Gusé, E., & Nabi, R. L. (2010). Explaining the effects of narrative in an entertainment television program: Overcoming resistance to persuasion. *Human Communication Research, 36*, 26–52. doi: 10.1111/j.1468-2958.2009.01367.x

Nabi, R. L., & Clark, S. (2008). Exploring the limits of social cognitive theory: Why negatively reinforced behaviors on TV may be modeled anyway. *Journal of Communication, 58*, 407–427. doi: 10.1111/j.1460-2466.2008.00392.x

Pardun, C. J. (2002). Romancing the script: Identifying the romantic agenda in top-grossing movies. In J. D. Brown, J. R. Steele, & K. Walsh-Childers (Eds.), *Sexual teens, sexual media: Investigating media's influence on adolescent sexuality* (pp. 211–226). Mahwah, NJ: Lawrence Erlbaum Associates.

Pardun, C. J., L'Engle, K. L., & Brown, J. D. (2005). Linking exposure to outcomes: Early adolescents' consumption of sexual content in six media. *Mass Communication & Society, 8*, 75–92. doi: 10.1207/s15327825mcs0802_1

Peterson, J. L., Moore, K. A., & Furstenberg, F. F. (1991). Television viewing and early initiation of sexual intercourse: Is there a link? *Journal of Homosexuality, 21*, 77–91. doi: 10.1300/J082v21n01_08

Rehkoff, R. (2005). *Romantic TV and emotional satisfaction: Do romantic beliefs moderate the relationship between satisfaction and parasocial relationship strength?* Presented at the International Communication Association, New York. Retrieved from http://www.allacademic.com/meta/p14533_index.html

Rill, L., & Aubrey, J. S. (2012). *"How do I look?": College students' use of self-objectification in Facebook profile photos and its links to the internalization of media ideals and social comparison.* Unpublished manuscript.

Ringrose, J., Gill, R., Livingstone S. et al. (2012). *A qualitative study of children, young people and 'sexting': A report prepared for the NSPCC.* London: National Society for the Prevention of Cruelty to Children.

Rivadeneyra, R., & Lebo, M. J. (2008). The association between television-viewing behaviors and adolescent dating role attitudes and behaviors. *Journal of Adolescence, 31*, 291–305. doi: 10.1016/j.adolescence.2007.06.001

Segrin, C., & Nabi, R. L. (2002). Does television viewing cultivate unrealistic expectations about marriage? *Journal of Communication, 52*, 247–263. doi: 10.1111/j.1460-2466.2002.tb02543.x

Shanahan, J., & Morgan, M. (1999). *Television and its viewers: Cultivation theory and research.* Cambridge, United Kingdom: Cambridge University Press.

Shapiro, J., & Kroeger, L. (1991). Is life just a romantic novel? The relationship between attitudes about intimate relationships and the popular media. *The American Journal of Family Therapy, 19*, 226–236. doi: 10.1080/01926189108250854

Signorielli, N. (1982). Marital status in television drama: A case of reduced options. *Journal of Broadcasting & Electronic Media, 26*, 585–597. doi: 10.1080/08838158209364027

Signorielli, N. (1991). Adolescents and ambivalence toward marriage: A cultivation analysis. *Youth & Society, 23*, 121–149. doi: 10.1177/0044118X91023001006

Steele, J. R., & Brown, J. D. (1995). Adolescent room culture: Studying media in the context of everyday life. *Journal of Youth and Adolescence, 24*(5), 551–567. doi: 10.1007/BF01537056

Strasburger, V. C. (1995). *Adolescents and the media: Medical and psychological impact.* Thousand Oaks, CA: Sage.

Strouse, J. S., & Buerkel-Rothfuss, N. L. (1987). Media exposure and the sexual attitudes and behaviors of college students. *Journal of Sex Education and Therapy, 13*, 43–51.

Strouse, J. S., Buerkel-Rothfuss, N. L., & Long, E. C. (1995). Gender and family as moderators of the relationship between music video exposure and adolescent sexual permissiveness. *Adolescence, 30*(119), 505–521.

Taylor, L. D. (2005). All for him: Articles about sex in American lad magazines. *Sex Roles, 52*, 153–163. doi: 10.1007/s11199-005-1291-7

Taylor, L. D. (2012). Cads and dads on screen: Do media representations of partner scarcity affect partner preferences among college-aged women? *Communication Research, 39*, 523–542. doi: 10.1177/0093650211405647

Tolman, D. L., Kim, J. L., Schooler, D., & Sorsoli, C. L. (2007). Rethinking the associations between television viewing and adolescent sexuality development: Bringing gender into focus. *Journal of Adolescent Health, 1*, 84.e9-84.e16. Retrieved from: http://dx.doi.org/10.1016/j.jadohealth.2006.08.002

Vandenbosch, L., & Eggermont, S. (2011). *Temptation Island, The Bachelor, Joe Millionaire*: A prospective cohort study on the role of romantically themed reality television in adolescents' sexual development. *Journal of Broadcasting and Electronic Media, 4*, 563–580. doi: 10.1080/08838151.2011.620663

Ward, L. M. (1995). Talking about sex: Common themes about sexuality in prime-time television programs children and adolescents view most. *Journal of Youth and Adolescence, 24*(5), 595–615. doi: 10.1007/BF01537058

Ward, L. M. (2002). Does television exposure affect emerging adults' attitudes and assumptions about sexual relationships? Correlational and experimental confirmation. *Journal of Youth and Adolescence, 31*, 1–15. doi: 10.1023/A:1014068031532

Ward, L. M., & Friedman, K. (2006). Using TV as a guide: Associations between television viewing and adolescents' sexual attitudes and behavior. *Journal of Research on Adolescence, 16*,(1), 133–156. doi: 10.1111/j.1532-7795.2006.00118.x.

Ward, L. M., & Rivadeneyra, R. (1999). Contributions of entertainment television to adolescents' sexual attitudes and expectations: The role of viewing amount versus viewer involvement. *The Journal of Sex Research, 36*, 237–249. Retrieved from: http://www.jstor.org/stable/3813435

Zurbriggen, E. L., & Morgan, E. (2006). Who wants to marry a millionaire? Reality dating television programs, attitudes toward sex, and sexual behaviors. *Sex Roles, 54*, 1–17. doi: 10.1007/s11199-005-8865-2

10

MEDIATED RELATIONSHIPS AND SOCIAL LIFE

Current Research on Fandom, Parasocial Relationships, and Identification

Jonathan Cohen

Relationships make up an important part of social life. As we go through our day, our relationships at work, with family members, and with friends occupy our thoughts and evoke emotional responses. But beyond the limited scope of relationships we have with people with whom we interact physically, our life is inhabited by relationships with people we have never actually met. We know them only through their media presence, but they have an important role in our life. Some of these mediated relationship partners may be completely fictional such as Captain Ahab who may have taught us a life lesson about single-mindedness and perseverance; some may be historical figures, such as Napoleon, who were in fact quite real but that we could have never actually met but only read and learned about. Still others may be celebrities or politicians who we know to exist in reality but whom we have never met (e.g., Mitt Romney). Some such people (e.g., Oprah), we may have seen or heard for many years through media and feel that we know quite well and understand. Regardless of how fictional or real these people or characters may be, our relationships with them are meaningful to us and in that sense they are very real, even if they are mediated.

We may have strong attitudes, and know quite a bit, about such mediated relational partners, but we also suspect that what we know about them is highly selective and contrived. Toward all these types of personas we can develop strong feelings and a sense of intimate acquaintance without ever meeting them. Such relationships are considered mediated relationships because no direct contact occurs between the two interactants and they are based solely on communication through mass media. It is worth noting that relationships are not either mediated or direct but rather that mediation in relationships is a matter of degree. No matter how close we may be, we can never fully and thoroughly know even our closest friends or family members (Buber, 1970), and may always be surprised by something new we learn about them. But even if all relationships may be somewhat mediated (e.g., by culture or language), research has shown that technological mediation of personal relationships has specific effects. For example, mediated relationships tend to be more unidirectional and imbalanced than social relationships; media can also extend the scope of our relationships and usually lowers their intensity (Eyal & Cohen, 2006); but in some ways mediated relationship are also similar to social relationships.

Like the variation of social relationships, our mediated relationships also vary greatly. They may be short-lived or last for years; they may be important to us or rather casual; they may evoke strong emotional responses or affect us mildly. But unlike social relationships, mediated relationships reside mostly in our imagination because they are one-way relationships. So, for example, while I may feel I know a lot about Patriots quarterback Tom Brady, seek information about what happens to him on or off the field, and can be emotionally involved in his daily life, he is very unlikely to care about my personal life or even know who I am. In some ways, this makes the relationship safe (i.e., I am very unlikely to insult or disappoint him, nor will he pick a fight with me) but also perhaps less satisfying. Though many of the studies reported below show that mediated relationships are similar to social relationships, the unidirectional nature of mediated relationships should not be overlooked.

Forms of Mediated Relationships

Fandom

Mediated relationships come in various forms. Fandom, or in the extreme, worship, occurs when a media persona seems larger than life and the fan is in awe of the persona and wishes to emulate him or her (McCutcheon, Lange, & Houran, 2002; but see also Stever, 2011). This form of relationship is often developed with athletes, musicians, or others who are seen as having a special talent or skill that is especially valued in one's culture. What is unique about fandom is that the distance between fan and hero is perceived as especially great and that the hero is an object of emulation rather than of intimate interaction. It is the "larger than life" quality of celebrities one worships that makes them appealing, and the constant desire, never really fulfilled, to get close to them that makes such fandom rewarding.

Parasocial Interaction

Parasocial interaction (PSI) occurs between audience members and media personae and is generally characterized by a feeling of closeness between the audience member and the character who is presented as "down to earth" and rather normal. Horton and Wohl (1956) originally defined the essence of PSI as "intimacy at a distance" suggesting a sense of intimacy together with the one-sided and mediated nature of PSI. PSI occurs when an audience member responds in some way to a mediated performance by speaking back to a screen or book, laughing, or feeling suspense or fear. Repeated PSI over time constitutes a parasocial relationship (PSR) that extends beyond exposure to the character and includes a desire to find out more about the persona and possibly reach out to the persona in some way. Hartmann and Goldhoorn (2011) argued that PSI is based on automatic mind reading by audiences and re-conceptualized PSI as a user experience rather than a relationship. In doing so, Hartmann and Goldhoorn (2011) further strengthen the distinction between PSI as an online response and PSR as an ongoing relationship.

Talk show hosts, newscasters, or stand-up comedians are prototypical of the kind of personae with which it is easy to develop PSI. Because they appear as themselves rather than in a role, address the audience directly, and appear repeatedly and regularly in the same situation and surroundings, audiences are most likely to create relationships with such personae. The informal nature of the setting of many talk shows and news sets also seems to invite audience members to feel comfortable and familiar with the persona, and the regular and repeated exposure creates the illusion of intimacy (Horton & Wohl, 1956). Feeling like we know a persona well, enjoying watching or listening to them, feeling like we are with a friend when we do, and missing them when they are gone are typical indicators of PSI. PSRs continue on a daily basis between exposures and can involve activities such as thinking or talking about the persona, reading about the persona, looking at websites, or following the persona on Facebook or Twitter.

Identification

A third form of mediated relationships is more temporary but also quite intense. Identification is defined through the psychological merging of character and audience member. While reading a book or watching TV or a film, for example, a viewer or reader adopts the character's identity and takes on the character's point of view, feelings, thoughts, and motives (Cohen, 2001, 2006, 2009). Identification is not an interactive form of relationship in that it does not occur between the viewer and character, but rather involves the merging of the two in a viewer or reader's mind. It can create strong emotional reactions (e.g., fear in a horror film; sadness in drama), but lasts for the duration of the exposure. It could be argued that because identification consists of a merging of identities, identification is not strictly a relational construct. However, because this merging includes bringing one's own identity, knowledge, beliefs, and attitude to the identification, it is beneficial to view it as a relationship. Identification is a routine source of learning by vicariously undergoing novel experiences, taking on new roles, and adopting new perspectives.

In the area of video games, Klimmt, Hefner, and Vorderer (2009) argued that identification involves an alteration of self-perception such that a player's understanding of his or herself becomes temporarily closer to that of the character he or she is identifying with. Traits that are associated with the character and game are activated, thereby becoming stronger and more salient, and traits that are usually important to the self but are irrelevant to the game become less important. Identification is medium dependent, and the interactivity of certain media may intensify identification. In interactive media, audiences are actively playing a role and have some control over the character and thus may become more strongly engaged and feel more connection to characters than in more passive media. Partial support for this hypothesis was reported by Williams (2010) who found that skinning a character—the ability to design the physical characteristics of the character—to resemble the player increased identification.

Fandom, PSRs, and identification may not be the only ways we connect to people in the media, but they are three of the most researched and distinct forms of mediated relationships. Despite their differences, all three concepts describe ways in which audience members develop strong emotional ties to characters and through which these characters become part of their lives. As media make up a larger part of social lives and take up more of our time, we need to better understand the important role that they play in many people's lives.

Recent and Current Trends in Research Into Mediated Relationships

Mediated and Social Relationships

In the past two decades or so, the majority of research on mediated relationships has focused on sketching the similarities between mediated and social relationships and on uncovering the effects of mediated relationships on attitudes, behaviors, and the self. Many studies have used theories developed in the context of interpersonal or social interaction and tested them successfully within PSRs (e.g., Eyal & Dailey, 2012; Gardner & Knowles, 2008; Schiappa, Gregg, & Hewes, 2005). Much of the recent research has focused on one type of mediated relationship or another, rather than on the more general phenomena of mediated relationships, reflecting increased conceptual clarity.

Studies find that what draws audiences to characters is similar to what draws them to other people in social situations (Hoffner, 1996; Hoffner & Cantor, 1991; Turner, 1993). Furthermore, people who tend to develop intense social relationships, such as those with anxious attachment styles, also tend to develop intense PSRs (Cohen, 1997; Cole & Leets, 1999). Like with social relationships, as PSRs last longer, audience members feel they know the persona better and have less uncertainty about their behavior (Rubin & McHugh, 1987). A recent study (Eyal & Dailey, 2012) compared the processes that explain both interpersonal friendships and PSRs, and found that commitment, network inclusion, and identification predicted both friendships and PSR. When personae discontinue their regular appearances, audiences miss them and feel sad losing them (Eyal & Cohen, 2006; Lather & Moyer-Gusé, 2011). Several studies have attempted to gauge the intensity of PSRs as compared to social relationships and have found that strong PSRs are akin to friendships or good neighbors (Gleich, 1997), but weaker than relationships with close friends, family, or romantic relationships (Eyal & Cohen, 2006; Eyal & Dailey, 2012). Koenig and Lessan (1985) report that favorite television personalities were rated as further from the self than close friends, but closer to the self than acquaintances. As Giles (2002) suggested and Eyal and Dailey (2012) demonstrated, PSRs do not compete with social relationships, but rather one of the draws of developing a relationship with a persona is that this relationships can be shared with family and friends.

Similarity and Mediated Relationships

Do we develop relationships with characters and persona that are more similar to us, or do characters and personae that we idolize and with whom we identify or develop PSRs only *seem* to be more similar to us? Though similarity has long been assumed to act as a basis for mediated relationships (e.g., Hoffner & Cantor, 1991; Maccoby & Wilson, 1957), very little evidence, experimental or otherwise, exists that can determine the casual order. Indeed, a recent experiment (Cohen & Weimann-Saks, 2012) found evidence that perceived similarity of readers with a character in a story was associated with identification, but that actual similarity in college majors (i.e., experimentally manipulated similarity) was not, even when this similarity was relevant to the message. Furthermore, there is little agreement about what similarity means in this context. Is similarity a demographic construct? Is it a similarity in a characteristic that is relevant to the specific context or show? Is it similarity in personality traits or in attitudes that matters?

It is unclear to what extent the similarity of characters to audience members is necessary for the development of a mediated relationship. Some evidence exists that suggests that we become attached not to characters that are similar to us but rather to those characters that represent what we desire to be like. Maccoby and Wilson (1957) found that children identified more with children not from their own social class but rather from the social class to which they aspired. One factor that is often seen to have an effect on mediated relationships is gender (Cohen & Weimann-Saks, 2012; Hoffner & Buchanan, 2005), but other studies have failed to find such a gender effect (Tian & Hoffner, 2010). Some studies have found that men tend to prefer male characters but that women are less affected by gender similarity (Cohen, 1999; Hoffner, 1996). Eyal and Rubin (2003) also found that aggressive children had stronger identification with aggressive characters than non-aggressive children, suggesting that similarity in trait aggressiveness was related to stronger relationships. In sum, the importance of character similarity remains an open question, but the success of animated media content as well as fantasy genres clearly demonstrates that even if similarity helps audiences develop PSRs or identification with characters, similarity is by no means a necessary condition for creating mediated relationships.

A recent experiment (Hartmann & Goldhoorn, 2011) has shown that direct address, where the performer faces the camera, created stronger mediated relationships than messages delivered by the same performer who was shown not facing the camera (a sideways view). Several explanations can be provided for these results, but they clearly show that production features matter. In addition, this study also confirmed earlier findings (e.g., Tsao, 1996) suggesting that personality factors such as perspective taking predict mediated relationships. Finally, the perceived attractiveness of the performer is correlated with the intensity of mediated relationships, though the causal order of this relationship is also in question.

Clarifying Conceptual Distinctions

Another issue that has continued to engage scholars is refining the distinctions between the concepts used to describe types of mediated relationships and issues of measurement. For example, McCutcheon, Lange, and Houran (2002) developed the Celebrity Worship Scale as a unidimensional measure to identify individuals who are overly involved with celebrities; but Stever (2011) has argued that it does not measure fandom which is a multidimensional construct. Giles (2002) offers a detailed conceptualization of PSRs with the aim of placing these relationships within the framework of social relationships. Klimmt, Hartmann, and Schramm (2006) stressed the distinction between PSI and PSR, and Schramm and Hartmann (2008) developed a measure for PSI that is multidimensional and focused on PSI as a mode of information processing. Cohen (2001) offered a four-component model of identification that was meant to distinguish identification from fandom and PSI. Though this conceptualization has been used extensively to measure identification, measures of PSI and fandom often include components that overlap with identification, and this remains a problem.

Social Media

A final issue that has been explored in recent years is the role of social media in mediated relationships. If the advent of the Internet and the creation of fan sites afforded audiences more ways of learning about celebrities, the use of social media has fundamentally changed the nature of mediated relationships in allowing celebrities easy and constant access to communicating with fans who became "friends" and "followers." Sweetser and Lariscy (2008) found that Facebook was used by U.S. political candidates, but mostly for one-way communication. Though supporters responded to these messages, candidates did not go further in communicating. Although not much published research is yet available on this topic, it seems highly likely that social media will change the nature of mediated relationships.

Theories Used in the Study of Mediated Relationships

An important feature of the study of mediated relationships is that it brings together the study of interpersonal communication and the study of mass communication. An early example of such research conceptualized PSRs as a functional equivalent to interpersonal relationships (Rosengren & Windahl, 1972), arguing that such relationships serve similar functions to social relationships. Later studies sought to show that loneliness was a predictor of PSRs (e.g., Rubin, Perse, & Powell, 1985), though these attempts did not provide general support for this hypothesis. In later research, mediated relationships were compared to interpersonal relationships, and theories and models explaining interpersonal relationships were used to explore the origin and effects of mediated relationships.

One group of studies explored how the dynamics of mediated relationships is similar and different from the dynamics of interpersonal relationships. Hoffner (1996) reported that children found television characters attractive based on characteristics that make social relational partners attractive (e.g., task attraction, humor, strength). Cohen (1999) found that when judging television drama characters, teens used social gender stereotypes. Perse and Rubin (1989) argued that like in interpersonal relationships, as media relationships endure, attributional confidence increases, and uncertainty decreases. Cohen (2010) used expectancy violation theory to suggest that like in social relationships, expectancy violations were expected to reduce closeness in PSRs. Using attachment theory, Cole and Leets (1999) found that PSRs were predicted by mental models of attachment which are known to be the basis for both parental and romantic relationships. Finally, the responses to the end of PSRs are similar to those evoked by the end of social relationships (Eyal & Cohen, 2006; Lather & Moyer-Gusé, 2011). Thus, applying interpersonal relationship theories to the study of mediated relationships has been a fruitful approach and has demonstrated the ways PSRs are similar to other types of relationships.

Another group of studies has explored the effects of mediated relationships following social-psychological theories of interpersonal and small group contact. This research has shown that mediated relationships are not only a way to powerfully deliver messages (e.g., celebrity endorsements), but they can serve as messages in and of themselves. In this vein, Schiappa, Gregg, and Hewes (2005, 2006) found that developing a mediated relationship with a minority character decreased prejudiced attitudes, especially among viewers who had limited direct contact with minority members. Importantly, exposure alone did not predict attitude change, but developing PSRs did (Davis, 2008). This effect is known as the parasocial contact hypothesis, following research pioneered by Allport (1954) showing that under the right condition, inter-group contact reduces prejudice.

The use of mediated relationships, and especially PSRs to educate, has been researched in the tradition of entertainment-education. A prominent example of this research is the study of the impact celebrities have on health attitudes. Thus, Brown and Basil (1995) showed that having a mediated relationship with Magic Johnson was related to increased concern about AIDS and intention to reduce risky sexual behaviors, whereas simply knowing about Johnson did not. Basil (1996) as well as Sood and Rogers (2000) also demonstrated the importance of mediated relationships in creating entertainment messages that affect health and development attitudes.

A relatively new area of research known as narrative persuasion looks into the power of exposure to narratives as opposed to informational messages to change attitudes. A central feature of this theory and a repeated finding of empirical work is that identification with narrative characters is a key to persuasive effects (Busselle & Bilandzic, 2008; Moyer-Gusé, 2008; Tukachinsky, 2011). Social cognitive theory (Bandura, 1996) suggests that identification creates modeling and increases self-efficacy. Moyer-Gusé and Nabi (2010) show that identification can also increase perceived vulnerability, which in turn makes risky behaviors seem riskier and less appealing. Identification is also a key component of becoming engaged in narratives which reduces one's desire and capacity for counter-arguing (Slater & Rouner, 2002).

In sum, the study of mediated relationships in their various forms has played an important role in developing many theoretical traditions of communication research. In turn, our understanding of mediated relationships, how they develop, and their effects on numerous attitudes and behaviors, have benefitted from diverse theoretical perspectives. The study of fandom, PSRs, and identification is an area of research that brings together not only various theoretical perspectives but also a variety of research approaches ranging from ethnographies (e.g., Jenkins, 1992) through in-depth interviews (e.g., Stever, 2011), survey research (e.g., Perse & Rubin, 1989) to experiments (e.g., Tal-Or & Cohen, 2010). The myriad theories and methods used to study mediated relationships is a promising feature of such research and makes it more likely that this area of scholarship will continue to be innovative and fruitful.

Future Directions

It is always foolhardy to anticipate where research will venture next when exploring a phenomenon. As theories develop, as new methods become available, new technologies are launched and the media ecology changes. Thus, predicting where scholars will look for answers is made all the more difficult. However, at present, several questions and challenges seem especially interesting and likely (or at least, hopefully) to draw scholars' attention in the near future.

Methodological Advances

One direction for future scholars focuses on question pertaining to methodology. The vast majority of knowledge we have about the role of mediated relationships in everyday life was collected through surveys, interviews, and observations. Much was learned in these ways, but as theories become more defined and more complex it seems that experimental work is necessary to test hypotheses. Because much of what is interesting about mediated relationships regards perceptions and emotions, it is often hard to distinguish cause from effect and often difficult to avoid potential spuriousness. As mentioned above, the issue of whether similarity precedes PSRs and identification or whether mediated relationships create a sense of similarity requires experimental validation. Similarly, whether identification is a vehicle to narrative engagement or a consequence of engagement remains to be seen (see Murphy, Frank, Moran, & Patnoe-Woodley, 2011). Another interesting issue that remains open is the extent to which mediated relationships tend to focus on fictional characters or on the actors who play them. Further experimental research is necessary, and is likely to emerge, in order to further explore these and other questions that are crucial to our understanding of mediated relationships.

New Genres

Cohen (2001) suggested that different types of relationships are encouraged by different genres. While sport, music, science fiction and superheroes tend to evoke intense fandom, news, and talk shows cultivate PSRs, and more realistic fictional drama and serial comedies generate identification. Though this hypothesis has never really been tested, it seems that the hypothesis itself may no longer be relevant as new genres emerge and new writing styles take hold. For example, starting in the 1990s many of the new comedy shows (e.g., *Seinfeld*) featured characters that were clearly meant to discourage any attempt to identify with them. Their humor was perhaps the basis of a strong PSR but the audience was clearly meant to see the characters from the outside rather than to develop empathy. Similarly, newer shows (e.g., *The Big Bang Theory*) seem designed around characters that viewers would be hard-pressed to find appealing or realistic. Regardless of which genres emerge and which old ones evolve in the coming years, understanding the association of different types of mediated relationships and genres seems important to our ability to understand their sources and impacts.

Another genre that challenges scholars of mediated relationships is reality TV (Nabi, Stitt, Halford, & Finnerty, 2006). Though programs within the genre differ greatly, the prototypical reality shows (e.g., *Survivor*, *Big Brother*, *Amazing Race*) have features designed to develop PSR (direct address monologues, interaction among characters and sometimes direct audience participation), they are also built around narratives, display a lot of emotions which seem to invite empathy and identification, and also often display the characters' skills so as to develop fandom. Ratings and audience responses provide strong evidence that reality shows create significant mediated relationships, but future inquiries should examine the nature of these relationships. Is a new kind of mediated relationship evolving or do these relationships conform to existing patterns?

Technological Changes

Finally, new technological developments raise new questions about mediated relationships. As mentioned above, there is some evidence that interactive video games intensify engagement with game characters. Control over how the character appears and some of its traits may increase similarity or attractiveness and in turn the character's appeal. Indeed, even if players do not design characters to look or behave like themselves, the sense of control over characters and how they look and behave may produce a sense of ownership that can increase identification. Furthermore, the experience of playing a video game in which the player activates a character and acts on the game through that character may make the connection to that character stronger (Klimmt, Hefner, & Vorderer, 2009) by making this connection transcend imagination (Cohen, 2001) to include action. Thus, identification in some video games may be characterized by acting from within the character rather than imagining being the character.

The rise of social media and their impact on our mediated relationships also require further study. As mentioned above, social media have opened up channels through which celebrities can and do communicate with their followers on a regular basis, making mediated relationships seem less unidirectional and perhaps more satisfying and intense. Another role that social media may play in mediated relationships is that they can more easily connect followers of certain celebrities with each other. Jenkins (1992) has already exposed the social and creative nature of fandom, but social media has made fan communication easier and more frequent. Rather than weekend conventions that require time off and expensive travel or fanzine sites that require long periods of writing and extensive readings of others' work, social networks allow fans to create groups and be in constant contact with each other. How this will affect fandom and PSRs and whether social media have made mediated relationships more a part of everyday life remain open, and very interesting, questions.

Another technological development that raises new questions about identification are new forms of media delivery. More and more content is being divorced from specific platforms, and media content is available in more places and times (Eveland, 2003). This could portend an increase in the role of mediated relationships in social lives, as our meetings with our mediated friends are no longer limited to specific times and places. Receiving status updates and tweets from our favorite actors, singers, and athletes throughout the day or watching and sharing clips of our favorite TV characters online may make them more a part of our daily routine. When our media outlets rest in our pockets and sleep in our beds (Perlow, 2012), our mediated friends are never too far away. Will this mean that they become more important? Will we spend more time and effort on cultivating these relationships? And will this mean that we will be less dependent on social relationships? So many predictions about the effects of new media have proven useless and simply wrong that it would be foolish to predict or speculate on the answers to these and related questions. All one can say is that these questions are likely going to continue being of interest to scholars in coming years.

Conclusion

Only two decades ago the notion of mediated relationships was treated among media scholars as no more than a curiosity. The role of PSI was known from the earliest days of communication research, but its study was not generally considered an important part of mass communication research. It is not surprising then, that in the thirty-four years since its publication, from 1956 to 1999, Horton and Wohl's (1956) seminal article on PSI was cited only 309 times, and in the twelve years since over a thousand. Advances in research on entertainment-education, the importance of mediated relationships to the processes of narrative persuasion (Moyer-Gusé, 2008), and the parasocial contact hypothesis have drastically increased the interest in this area. Advances in social cognitive theory (Bandura, 2001), and ethnographic work revealing the creative and social nature of fandom (Jenkins, 1992) have also contributed to the increase in interest about mediated relationships.

Burgeoning research has brought with it more conceptual clarity and new insights but also new challenges. In this chapter, I have tried to define and delineate the differences between three types of mediated relationships. The importance of each of them to individuals and society was surveyed using current research. As in much media effects research, new genres, platforms, and media forms challenge existing media use patterns and their effects and thus require new thinking. I have tried to lay out some theoretical principles suggesting how new developments may impact mediated relationships. These include more immediate and frequent exposure to mediated relationship partners, new ways to connect with them and with others who share these relationships, and new media forms that may create new types of relationships. There can be little doubt that such development coupled with new theory and methodologies will impact how we study mediated relationships in coming years. There is much to be excited about for scholars, new and old, who have found interest in understanding the role of mediated relationships in everyday life.

References

Allport, G. W. (1954). *The nature of prejudice*. Reading, MA: Addison-Wesley.

Bandura, A. (1996). *Self-efficacy: The exercise of self-control*. New York: Henry Holt and Company.

Bandura, A. (2001). Social cognitive theory of mass communication. *Media Psychology, 3*(3), 265–299. doi: 10.1207/S1532785XMEP0303_03

Basil, M. D. (1996). Identification as a mediator of celebrity effects. *Journal of Broadcasting & Electronic Media, 40*(4), 478–495. doi: 10.1080/08838159 609364370

Brown, W. J., & Basil, M. D. (1995). Media celebrities and public health: Responses to "Magic" Johnson's HIV disclosure and its impact on AIDS risk and high-risk behaviors. *Health Communication, 7*(4), 345–370. doi: 10.1207/ s15327027hc0704_4

Buber, M. (1970). *I and Thou*. Trans. Walter Kaufman. New York: Touchstone. Originally published in 1923.

Busselle, R., & Bilandzic, H. (2008). Fictionality and perceived realism in experiencing stories: A model of narrative comprehension and engagement. *Communication Theory, 18*(2), 255–280. doi: 10.1111/j.1468-2885.2008.00322.x

Cohen, E. L. (2010). Expectancy violations in relationships with friends and media figures. *Communication Research Reports, 27*(2), 97–111. doi: 10.1080/ 08824091003737836

Cohen, J. (1997). Parasocial relations and romantic attraction: Gender and dating status differences. *Journal of Broadcasting & Electronic Media, 41*(4), 516–529.

Cohen, J. (1999). Favorite characters of teenage viewers of Israeli serials. *Journal of Broadcasting & Electronic Media, 43*(3), 327–345. doi: 10.1080/0883 8159909364495

Cohen, J. (2001). Defining identification: A theoretical look at the identification of audiences with media characters. *Mass Communication & Society, 4*(3), 245–264. doi: 10.1207/S15327825MCS0403_01

Cohen, J. (2006). Audience identification with media characters. In J. Bryant & P. Vorderer (Eds), *Psychology of entertainment* (pp. 183–197). Mahwah, NJ: Lawrence Erlbaum.

Cohen, J. (2009). Mediated relationships and media effects: Parasocial interaction and identification. In R. Nabi & M. B. Oliver (Eds.), *The Sage handbook of media processes and effects* (pp. 223–236). Thousand Oaks, CA: Sage.

Cohen, J. & Weimann-Saks, D. (2012, May). *Exploring the similarity-identification hypothesis: The role of perceived similarity.* Paper presented at the annual meeting of the mass Communication Division of the International Communication Association. Phoenix, AZ.

Cole, T., & Leets, L. (1999). Attachment styles and intimate television viewing: Insecurely forming relationships in a parasocial way. *Journal of Social and Personal Relationships, 16*(4), 495–511. doi: 10.1177/0265407599164005

Davis, Y. A. (2008). *The parasocial contact hypothesis: Implications for changing racial attitudes.* Doctoral dissertation, The Ohio State University.

Eveland, Jr., W. P. (2003). A "mix of attributes" approach to the study of media effects and new communication technologies. *Journal of Communication, 53*(3), 395–410. doi: 10.1111/j.1460-2466.2003.tb02598.x

Eyal, K., & Cohen, J. (2006). When good friends say goodbye: A parasocial breakup study. *Journal of Broadcasting & Electronic Media, 50*(3), 502–523. doi: 10.1207/s15506878jobem5003_9

Eyal, K., & Dailey, R. M. (2012). Examining relational maintenance in parasocial relationships. *Mass Communication and Society, 15*(5), 758–781. doi: 10.1080/15205436.2011.616276

Eyal, K., & Rubin, A. M. (2003). Viewer aggression and homophily, identification, and parasocial relationships with television characters. *Journal of Broadcasting & Electronic Media, 47*(1), 77–98. doi: 10.1207/s15506878jobem4701_5

Gardner, W. L., & Knowles, M. L. (2008). Love makes you real: Favorite television characters are perceived as "real" in a social facilitation paradigm. *Social Cognition, 26*(2), 156–168. doi: 10.1521/soco.2008.26.2.156

Giles, D. C. (2002). Parasocial interaction: A review of the literature and a model for future research. *Media Psychology, 4*(3), 279–305. doi: 10.1207/S1532785XMEP0403_04

Gleich, U. (1997). Parasocial interaction with people on the screen. In P. Winterhoff-Spurk & T. H. A. van der Voort (Eds.), *New horizons in media psychology: Research cooperation and projects in Europe* (pp. 35–55). Wiesbaden, Germany: Westdeutscher Verlag.

Hartmann, T., & Goldhoorn, C. (2011). Horton and Wohl revisited: Exploring viewers' experience of parasocial interaction. *Journal of Communication, 61*(6), 1104–1121. doi: 10.1111/j.1460-2466.2011.01595.x

Hoffner, C. (1996). Children's wishful identification and parasocial interaction with favorite television characters. *Journal of Broadcasting & Electronic Media, 40*(3), 389–402. doi: 10.1080/08838159609364360

Hoffner, C., & Buchanan, M. (2005). Young adults' wishful identification with television characters: The role of perceived similarity and character attributes. *Media Psychology, 7*(4), 325–351. doi: 10.1207/S1532785XMEP0704_2

Hoffner, C., & Cantor, J. (1991). Perceiving and responding to mass media characters. In J. Bryant & D. Zillmann (Eds.), *Responding to the screen: Reception and reaction processes* (pp. 63–101). Hillsdale, NJ: Lawrence Erlbaum.

Horton, D., & Wohl, R. R. (1956). Mass communication and para-social interaction: Observations on intimacy at a distance. *Psychiatry, 19*(3), 215–229.

Jenkins, H. (1992). *Textual poachers: Television fans and participatory culture.* New York: Routledge.

Klimmt, C., Hartmann, T., & Schramm, H. (2006). Parasocial interactions and relationships. In J. Bryant & P. Vorderer (Eds.), *Psychology of entertainment* (pp. 291–313). Mahwah, NJ: Lawrence Erlbaum.

Klimmt, C., Hefner, D., & Vorderer, P. (2009). The video game experience as "true" identification: A theory of enjoyable alterations of players' self-perception. *Communication Theory, 19*(4), 351–373.

Koenig, F., & Lessan, G. (1985). Viewers' relationship to television personalities. *Psychological Reports, 57*(1), 263–266. doi: 10.2466/pr0.1985.57.1.263

Lather, J., & Moyer-Gusé, E. (2011). How do we react when our favorite characters are taken away? An examination of a temporary parasocial breakup. *Mass Communication and Society, 14*(2), 196–215. doi: 10.1080/15205431003668603

Leets, L. (1999). Attachment styles and intimate television viewing: Insecurely forming relationships in a parasocial way. *Journal of Social and Personal Relationships, 16*(4), 495–511.

Maccoby, E. E., & Wilson, W. C. (1957). Identification and observational learning from films. *The Journal of Abnormal and Social Psychology, 55*(1), 76. doi: 10.1037/h0043015

McCutcheon, L. E., Lange, R., & Houran, J. (2002). Conceptualization and measurement of celebrity worship. *British Journal of Psychology, 93*(1), 67–87. doi: 10.1348/000712602162454

Moyer-Gusé, E. (2008). Toward a theory of entertainment persuasion: Explaining the persuasive effects of entertainment-education messages. *Communication Theory, 18*(3), 407–425. doi: 10.1111/j.1468-2885.2008.00328.x

Moyer-Gusé, E., & Nabi, R. L. (2010). Explaining the effects of narrative in an entertainment television program: Overcoming resistance to persuasion. *Human Communication Research, 36*(1), 26–52. doi: 10.1111/j.1468-2958.2009.01367.x

Murphy, S. T., Frank, L. B., Moran, M. B., & Patnoe-Woodley, P. (2011). Involved, transported, or emotional? Exploring the determinants of change in knowledge, attitudes, and behavior in entertainment-education. *Journal of Communication, 61*(3), 407–431. doi: 10.1111/j.1460-2466.2011.01554.x

Nabi, R. L., Stitt, C. R., Halford, J., & Finnerty, K. L. (2006). Emotional and cognitive predictors of the enjoyment of reality-based and fictional television programming: An elaboration of the uses and gratifications perspective. *Media Psychology, 8*(4), 421–447. doi: 10.1207/s1532785xmep0804_5

Perlow, L. A. (2012). *Sleeping with your Blackberry: How to break the 24/7 habit and change the way You work.* Watertown, MA: Harvard Business Press.

Perse, E. M., & Rubin, R. B. (1989). Attribution in social and parasocial relationships. *Communication Research, 16*(1), 59–77. doi: 10.1177/009365089 016001003

Rosengren, K. E. and Windahl, S. (1972). Mass media consumption as a functional alternative. In D. McQuail (Ed.), *Sociology of mass communications* (pp. 166–194). Harmondsworth, England: Penguin.

Rubin, A. M., Perse, E. M., & Powell, R. A. (1985). Loneliness, parasocial interaction, and local television news viewing. *Human Communication Research, 12*(2), 155–180. doi: 10.1111/j.1468-2958.1985.tb00071.x

Rubin, R. B., & McHugh, M. P. (1987). Development of parasocial interaction relationships. *Journal of Broadcasting & Electronic Media, 31*(3), 279–292. doi: 10.1080/08838158709386664

Schiappa, E., Gregg, P. B., & Hewes, D. E. (2005). The parasocial contact hypothesis. *Communication Monographs, 72*(1), 92–115. doi: 10.1080/0363775052000342544

Schiappa, E., Gregg, P. B., & Hewes, D. E. (2006). Can one TV show make a difference? *Will & Grace* and the parasocial contact hypothesis. *Journal of Homosexuality, 51*(4), 15–37. doi: 10.1300/J082v51n04_02

Schramm, H., & Hartmann, T. (2008). The PSI-Process Scales. A new measure to assess the intensity and breadth of parasocial processes. *Communications, 33*(4), 385–401. doi: 10.1515/COMM.2008.025

Slater, M. D., & Rouner, D. (2002). Entertainment—education and elaboration likelihood: Understanding the processing of narrative persuasion. *Communication Theory, 12*(2), 173–191. doi: 10.1111/j.1468-2885.2002.tb00265.x

Sood, S., & Rogers, E. M. (2000). Dimensions of parasocial interaction by letter-writers to a popular entertainment-education soap opera in India. *Journal of Broadcasting & Electronic Media, 44*(3), 386–414. doi: 10.1207/s15506878jobem4403_4

Stever, G. S. (2011). Celebrity worship: Critiquing a construct. *Journal of Applied Social Psychology, 41*(6), 1356–1370. doi: 10.1111/j.1559-1816.2011.00765.x

Sweetser, K. D., & Lariscy, R. W. (2008). Candidates make good friends: An analysis of candidates' uses of Facebook. *International Journal of Strategic Communication, 2*(3), 175–198. doi: 10.1080/15531180802178687

Tal-Or, N., & Cohen, J. (2010). Understanding audience involvement: Conceptualizing and manipulating identification and transportation. *Poetics, 38*(4), 402–418. doi: 10.1016/j.poetic.2010.05.004

Tian, Q., & Hoffner, C. A. (2010). Parasocial interaction with liked, neutral, and disliked characters on a popular TV series. *Mass Communication and Society, 13*(3), 250–269. doi: 10.1080/15205430903296051

Tsao, J. (1996). Compensatory media use: An exploration of two paradigms. *Communication Studies, 47*(1–2), 89–109. doi: 10.1080/10510979609368466

Tukachinsky, R. (2011, May). *A meta-analytic review of effects of involvement with entertainment media.* Paper presented at the annual meeting of the Mass Communication Division of the International Communication Association. Boston, MA.

Turner, J. R. (1993). Interpersonal and psychological predictors of parasocial interaction with different television performers. *Communication Quarterly, 41*(4), 443–453. doi: 10.1080/01463379309369904

Williams, K. D. (2010). The effects of homophily, identification, and violent video games on players. *Mass Communication and Society, 14*(1), 3–24. doi: 10.1080/15205430903359701

Part III

EMERGING MEDIA
AND SOCIAL LIFE

11

VIDEO GAMES AND SOCIAL LIFE

Christoph Klimmt

Among the so-called new media, video games certainly occupy a special and prominent position. Much earlier than "the Internet" and other interactive communication services, video games have reached mass audiences and allowed the establishment of a new, profitable industry branch (Poole, 2000). Many scholars view video games as a truly distinct type of medium that deserves researchers' attention in its own right just as television and "the Internet" do (e.g., Vorderer & Bryant, 2006; Wolf & Perron, 2003). A considerable portion of the public debates on the chances, and, more saliently, on the risks of new media addressed video games and their players. When it comes to the implications of video games for social life, the debate in education, regulation, and the news media has so far mostly been driven by concerns about the detrimental impact of games on players and their social behavior (e.g., Anderson & Bushman, 2001).

In contrast, the present chapter attempts to draw a more complete picture of the indeed profound implications of video games on contemporary social life. It does justice to the critical issues raised by media effects research, but will also emphasize the positive role that gaming can play in the social lives of children, adolescents, and adults. The first step of analysis, however, focuses on the nature of the medium itself: How could game technology and game use affect social relationships and behavior?

The Evolution of Video Games and Their Social Relevance

The development of video games from their early beginnings as relatively simple arcade machines (e.g., "Packman") to the diversity of current systems and media platforms is remarkable (Lowood, 2006; Poole, 2000;

Social Outreach

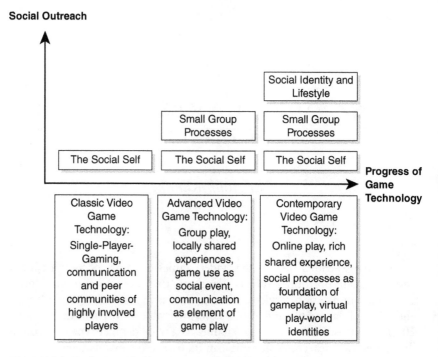

Figure 11.1 Evolution of video games and their social outreach

Wolf & Perron, 2003). With the progress of technical capabilities, video games have continuously expanded their relevance for social life. For the purpose of analytic simplicity, I propose a three-step account of video games' evolution as a social medium (Figure 11.1).

Level 1: Single Player Gaming and Players' Social Self

The initial stage is characterized by classic video game technology, as manifest in arcade game machines, many early computer games and console systems (e.g., the "Nintendo Entertainment System", NES), and the first decade of PC games (with classic games such as "Elite" or "Wing Commander"). These games were surprisingly diverse with regard to game play, genre, and audiovisual presentation, in spite of the constraints imposed by early computer technology. However, virtually all of these manifestations of video games shared the attribute of *single player* gaming. One individual sat or stood in front of the screen and played her/his game. The game system was only capable of processing inputs from one player, and interaction was thus limited to one human and one machine. This initial mode of video gaming could thus be understood as "non-social."

However, the great entertainment capacities and the innovativeness of the new medium rapidly attracted fans who engaged in frequent and intensive communication about their favorite pastime. Locations dedicated to gaming ("arcades") provided the spatial environment to facilitate both single-player gaming and communication among players (Selnow, 1984). Thus, the social relevance of early gaming (and thus, of single-player gaming, which is still an important mode of game use today) emerged from the (local) communities of players who met at dedicated places and talked about their experiences. As a consequence, the social implications of classic single-player gaming mainly related to users' *social self*, that is, their self-concept and its connections to their immediate environment of, for instance, similarly involved fans of video games.

Two examples shall serve to illustrate the impact of single-player games on the social self. One is the social-like experience of game play, which often transports the player into an imaginary world such as a space war, a medieval fantasy realm with heroes and sorcerers, or a professional sports context. By interacting with the game world and the simulated social entities in it (e.g., aliens, knights, or soccer stars), video game play facilitates shifts in players' self-imagination. Playing a war video game is likely to generate the illusion of being a war hero, and of being more brave, powerful, and assertive than one would actually experience oneself in real-world interactions. Various concepts and studies have addressed this phenomenon of altered self-perception in video game players. They have recurred on concepts such as identification (Klimmt, Hefner, & Vorderer, 2009a), wishful identification (Konijn, Bijvank, & Bushman, 2007), presence (Tamborini & Skalski, 2006), character attachment (Lewis, Weber, & Bowman, 2008), or enactment (Peng, 2008). The desirable (and, by the same token, entertaining) aspect of such self-illusions during game play is that players can feel closer to their ideal self, and to their desired kind of personality and social self (Bessière, Seay, & Kiesler, 2007; Jin & Park, 2009). Single-player video gaming can thus affect the social self by allowing altered experiences of one's identity, and by reducing perceived self-discrepancies (Klimmt et al., 2009a).

The other example of the social impact of single-player gaming addresses the role of interpersonal communication about games within (local) player communities. In the older times of games, meeting friends at arcades was a common mode of spending leisure time (e.g., Wigand, Borstelmann, & Boster, 1985). Similarly, owners of the same video game system and PC gamers often formed friend networks in which communication about games was essential; software piracy may also have played a relevant part in forming such game-based peer groups. In general, involvement with and communication about single-player games were drivers of friendship networks and peer group cohesion (Panelas, 1983), and they continue to be until today, albeit under very different social–technological circumstances

(Bryce & Rutter, 2003; see below). So the classic single-player gaming could and can affect players' social self via peer group dynamics: Individual players can, for instance, exploit their skill and experience with certain games as social resource and accumulate reputation among their friends by giving advice or demonstrating superiority in high score lists. The great capacity of video games to involve players thus creates social impact around the actual game play, while classic game play per se is more or less non-social.

Level 2: Co-Located Gaming and Small Group Processes

The second stage of the proposed model refers to advanced video game technology, which involves more sophisticated systems with better sound and graphics, more complex game designs, richer game narratives, and, most importantly, the capability to arrange synchronous game interaction of several players with one machine. Various early arcade machines already enabled co-play of two users, either in a competitive setting ("Barbarian") or in a collaborative arrangement (e.g., "Lost Vikings"). In this sense, those early game systems would already count as "advanced." While the classic PC games of the pre-Internet era never qualified as a multiplayer system, many video game consoles for home use did. Machines such as the Nintendo Super Entertainment System (SNES) or the first Sony PlayStation (in 1990) could connect to several input devices and display game events from different players' perspectives simultaneously via "split screen." Such games transformed play into a fundamentally social experience: The co-player was a core element of game play, communication with her/him was possible, could contribute to game enjoyment, and was of central importance, particularly in collaborative game settings. Groups of friends could gather in front of the television set and enjoy social processes of playful interaction, such as competitions.

With the emergence of this essentially social game technology, video game play turned into a family activity (e.g., Mitchell, 1985). The time spent together and the shared living room made families find many occasions for joint video game play (Chambers, 2012). However, peer groups and other social formations could and can also benefit from split-screen or otherwise co-located gaming, as social interaction is enabled or integral to game play, and the game experience is not only a topic to talk about, but is essentially shared in real-time. A large-scale variant of co-located game play in the living room emerged with the so-called local area network (LAN) parties, where many players gather at one location, but use individual, interconnected computers for social game play (Jansz & Martens, 2005).

Similarly to single-player gaming, advanced video game technology can thus affect players' social self. However, conceptually, co-located multiplayer gaming can be expected to have a more profound social impact on players, as *group processes* are intertwined with game use and play experiences. While peer communication was also important for conventional single-player gaming (see above), the new element of peer communication during game play enlarges the social relevance of game use beyond the social self to the dimension of interpersonal relationships. Game experiences shared by members of a small group (or family) contribute to the overall pool of collective memory and perceived commonalities.

Level 3: Online Gaming and Social-Virtual Identities

In recent years, gaming has been observed as one of the most popular ways to make use of broadband Internet communication. Early online games were mere extensions of offline games and initially served as a replacement for co-located gaming: Two people or small groups of players connect to the same server and interact in a virtual environment (e.g., Pena & Hancock, 2006). More recent developments in online games brought about persistent online game worlds, such as Massively Multiplayer Online Role Playing Games (MMOs; cf. Yee, 2006). These virtual game worlds exist independently from the presence and activity of single players and provide the means for large-scale social interaction among many players as well as small group processes (Williams et al., 2006). "World of Warcraft," launched in 2004, is still one of the most popular online games with a persistent game world and is known to attract millions of users worldwide on a regular basis. Many other MMOs and other virtual multiplayer worlds have been released since the late 1990s. For games researchers, these virtual playgrounds opened a universe of new questions, particularly on player motivation (e.g., Chan & Vorderer, 2006; Yee, 2006) and the social implications of spending (much) time and (much) thinking on social-virtual game worlds (e.g., Williams et al., 2006).

Indeed, with persistent online game worlds, the social implications of video games seem to become most salient. Just as single-player gaming and co-located gaming, online gaming can serve individual enjoyment and affect the social self. Similarly to co-located gaming, online gaming certainly affects relationships within small groups. However, the accessibility of game worlds via the Internet and the opportunity to maintain social contact with masses (or a few selected players) at any time and from any place provides yet another new dimension of sociality in game play. First of all, the possibility of sharing joyful experiences of joint game play is nowadays not restricted to co-located players. Users can participate in team gaming and even large-scale mass game competitions with remarkable flexibility. Mobile gaming hardware and seamless transitions from one device (e.g., the home console) to another (e.g., the smartphone) during game play further increase the availability of social gaming opportunities in contemporary everyday live (e.g., Klimmt & Hartmann, 2008).

Persistent online game worlds with their broad variety of user–game interaction and user–user interaction have not only revolutionized once more the qualities of game play and enjoyment, they have also massively extended the social relevance of gaming, as (frequent) players make use of the social features of such game worlds far beyond actual joint play. Meeting "in World of Warcraft" has become a standard mode of social contact, and players communicate about off-game topics on a regular basis (Steinkuehler & Williams, 2006). Friend networks organize parts of their shared activities by interacting via their game avatars. In turn, online games offer a rich variety of tools to support intensive social exchange among players, such as voice communication (Voice over Internet Protocol; e.g., Williams, Caplan, & Xiong, 2007).

For peer groups of frequent players, some of which are scattered around the globe, the social platform that game worlds provide still include a playful frame, however. For instance, customization of game avatars has been observed as a popular way of expressing self-related information, and many games offer diverse virtual accessories to individualize avatars for the purposes of players' social self-expression (Trepte, Reinecke, & Behr, 2009). Wright, Boria, and Breidenbach (2002) noted that some player groups reframe the rules and settings of their favorite online game to enable new, creative, and surprising group experiences that differ significantly from the game companies' original intentions. Anecdotes of rituals such as within-game marriages of two avatars, with many friend avatars attending the ceremony (which typically takes place at a scenic spot of the game's virtual landscape, with a romantic virtual sunset in the background), have also been reported. These examples suggest that contemporary online gaming provides the means for a virtualized lifestyle with modes of inventing and expressing a game-based social identity and/or incorporating elements of game involvement in one's offline identity. A manifestation of such social transfer to the offline world are so-called "cos-players" who love to masquerade so as to look like a (or "their") video-game character. In sum, contemporary video gaming has acquired a remarkable social outreach and, for many users, a fundamental social relevance. Compared to earlier stages of gaming culture, one could conclude that, today, games are not making use of the Internet any more, but rather, the social web takes advantage of video gaming (e.g., Kolo & Baur, 2004).

Video Games as Poison for Social Life: Research on Aggression and Game Addiction

Video Game Violence

The development of the medium of the video game has expanded games' social relevance exponentially. Today, the number of people playing video games on a regular basis is impressive, particularly in parts of Asia and in western countries. Players attend to the different modes of social opportunities, from the traditional single-player games to highly inclusive, group-based social lives in virtual game worlds. Because of the remarkably explicit violence depicted in some very successful games (e.g., Smith, Lachlan, & Tamborini, 2003), the social implications of video games have so far mostly been discussed with regard to undesirable effects of video games on social life. Driven by this public concern, much of the past social-scientific research on video games was dedicated to studying the poisonous social impact of video games, that is, the consequences of exposure to "video game violence" for aggression.

A substantial number of experimental and longitudinal media effects studies have been conducted in this area over the past decades, with contributions from communication, media psychology, and social psychology. Reviews and meta-analyses of this work suggest that there is indeed a relevant influence of (frequent) exposure to violent content of video games on aggression, particularly cognitive processes involved in aggressive behavior, such as hostile expectation and attribution biases (e.g., Anderson, 2004; Anderson et al., 2010; Sherry, 2001). The General Aggression Model (GAM; Bushman & Anderson, 2002) has been widely recognized as a theoretical framework that organizes the processes and origins of such aggression-promoting impact of video games.

Only a few contributions have explicitly reflected on the fact that (male) players seem to hold a stable interest in violent games, and that game play is voluntary and may thus serve particular needs—for instance, the need to form a masculine self-concept (Jansz, 2005; Kirsh, 2003) or to rebel against parental rules by breaking age restrictions (Nikken & Jansz, 2007). A conceptually realistic view of the impact of video game violence should combine selection preferences of players (e.g., young males) and classic effects perspectives (direct game effects and interactions of game x person x situation variables) in order to do justice both to variance in players' susceptibility to negative social consequences and to the intrapersonal dynamics of video game impact. The downward spiral model proposed by Slater and colleagues (Slater, 2007; Slater, Henry, Swaim, & Anderson, 2003) is particularly well-suited to provide such an integrated perspective of selection and exposure effects. A compact summary of the research on video game violence thus reads that (a) the average effect of exposure to game violence is significant, yet rather weak (e.g., Anderson, 2004). However, (b) some player segments, particularly those with a high burden of social-risk factors (e.g., family problems, school underperformance, peer rejection), must be considered as strongly susceptible to effects of increased aggression and to undergo substantial shifts in aggressive personality if they frequently consume violent games over long periods of (adolescent) development. In this sense, for some at-risk segments of the gamer audience, video game violence can indeed be seen as poison for social life, particularly because this poison is mixed with other poisons (risk factors) to synergistically create an adverse impact on personality development and behavior.

More recent research has investigated the effects of social play of violent gaming. The technological evolution of video games has certainly affected the ways in which war and combat games are being used, and network or online shooter games such as "Counterstrike" have inspired the game industry to invent entirely new modes of (non-violent) social gaming. The available studies on the effects of multiplayer game violence converge with previous research on single-player games: Playing violent social games is likely to induce higher levels of hostility and aggressive affect (e.g., Eastin, 2007). New psychological mechanisms of aggression induction have been assumed in violent social game play, particularly with regard to the fact that players *compete* in violent game contexts (Eastin & Griffiths, 2009; Williams & Clippinger, 2002). The frustration of losing competition, but also the rewards of making progress by doing harm to competitors seem to play a role in the aggression-related outcomes of game play. So the fact that online combat games enable collective violence (e.g., well-planned, strategic virtual killing by organized groups of players) seems to suggest that the poisonous effect of game violence on social life is likely to enlarge with the technological evolution of gaming towards a popular multi-user activity ("level 3," see above).

This concerned view of how the social impact of violent video games will evolve is in need of some additional perspectives, however. One is that there is also evidence for more positive consequences of social violent video game play. Pena and Hancock (2006) analyzed the text-based inter-personal communication among players of a violent online video game, "Jedi Knight 2," in which groups of players conduct virtual light sabre duels. They reported an overwhelming majority of positive and friendly commentaries and very little evidence for hostility among players; the communication frame that emerged rather mirrored a sports contest than an angry group fight. Of course, one could derive even more concern from the fact that gamers seem to frame virtual violence in a sports-like fashion and even make fun of their virtual kills. On the other hand, it seems worthwhile to consider the perspective that even violent co-play may serve positive social functions such as maintaining friendships and group-level mood regulation.

The more important perspective that is needed when discussing the poisonous effects of video games on social life is, however, that there are so many video games that are free of violent content. The evolution of video games, particularly in recent years, served industry intentions to reach out to new audience segments that are decidedly not attracted by violent genres such as shooters or war strategy games (Juul, 2010). Highly successful genres such as party and karaoke games ("Singstar") or social network games (e.g., "Farmville," which attracts millions of Facebook users) or browser games ("Travian") involve millions of players on a regular basis and create intense social experiences, either locally (by facilitating a karaoke party in the living room, for example) or online (e.g., Klimmt, Schmid, & Orthmann, 2009b). So a more realistic view of the toxic effects of video games on social life should mirror the insight from past research on conventional media such as television: Parts of games content will have negative effects on the social lives of parts of the gamer audience, and this is a true social problem; however, many other parts of video games will not have any toxic impact on many (if not all) segments of the player audience; for them, just the opposite, that is, positive effects, are much more likely.

Excessive Game Play and Collapse of Social Life

The rising popularity of "level 3" game technology, that is, games with permanent online functionality, huge interacting groups of players, and profound impacts on social life, has shifted public concern about video games in recent years. Clearly, the discourse on video game violence is continuing, cyclically fueled by the advent of ever-more violent games ("Call of Duty") or by public debates on connections between game violence and rampage shootings (Ferguson, 2008). However, MMOs and other social online games are being accused for causing excessive use, for seducing players to spend way too much time and energy on playing, and to neglect jobs, school, social relationships, family, sleep needs, and even food and liquid consumption. Interestingly, the concern of "video game addiction" has motivated research activities in disciplines that were formerly not involved with video game research, particularly in the psychiatric field of addiction studies (e.g., Thalemann, Wölfling, & Grüsser, 2007). Various university hospitals have opened ambulatory treatment services for excessive players, and reports on severe cases of complete breakdown in life management due to excessive online gaming can be found in the psychiatry literature. Parents can seek advice in book stores on how to prevent or counteract their children's (mostly sons') excessive game use (e.g., Bruner & Bruner, 2006).

The assumption behind the existence of a "problem" or a "disorder" (excessive game use is being discussed as to whether it should receive the status of a distinct diagnosis in future manuals of psychological disorders) is that modern video games can be so absorbing and motivating that individual players cannot resist their temptations. They lose control over the time spent playing, which then causes severe problems with daily routines, job demands, education goals, and so on. Because online game worlds such as "World of Warcraft" are permanently available and always offer new areas to visit and new things to do, they are blamed for fostering excessive consumption. A major consequence (and indicator of severe problems with video game play) is the collapse of social life—excessive players tend to conceal their addiction, to terminate contact with parents and friends, and to solely focus their social life within their online game world. Excessive game play is therefore being debated as the new toxic effect of video games on social life.

The research evidence on excessive video games once again suggests drawing a more fine-grained picture. First, survey-based research does not find a mass trend towards excessive game use. Prevalence rates obtained from methodologically sound studies converge with findings from other research areas on the portion of the general population with psychological problems or disorders. Lemmens, Valkenburg, and Peter (2009) report that only a very small fraction of Dutch adolescent players should be classified as "addicted" in a strict sense. But even the best-designed studies that rely on self-reports are facing several methodological problems: First, truly addicted respondents may want to conceal their addiction when asked, which would imply an underestimation of the actual prevalence of game addiction. But second, particularly younger gamers may mistake questions about severe problems with excessive games for measures of strong dedication to their beloved hobby—Amazon.com is selling a button that displays the wearer's self-description "Video Game Addict." Such misunderstandings of "I am addicted" as "I love games" would cause an overestimation of addiction rates. Separating frenetic involvement from addiction as a disorder is thus quite challenging in games research (Charlton & Danforth, 2007; Wood, 2008).

Another important issue in research in excessive game use is comorbidity. Psychiatrists who are treating clients for excessive game use typically report that game obsession is not the only and not the primary psychological problem of their cases. Other, more genuine psychological disorders are common among the (limited) number of individuals who are receiving therapy for excessive playing. Most importantly, depression and social anxieties seem to play a role: Individuals who are facing difficulties with self-regulation (e.g., due to depression) seem to lack motivational resources that could serve to control gaming time and resist the temptation of continued playing (cf. LaRose, Lin, & Eastin, 2003). From this perspective, the (relatively few) gamers who are drifting into excessive game use are suffering from fundamental psychological disorders, which merely become visible or are intensified by online games (e.g., Kim et al., 2006). A synergistic interaction of person variables (e.g., depressive symptoms) and the motivational power of online games thus seems to drive excessive game use, which in turn implies that mostly such players are at risk who are in need of psychological treatment for fundamental problems anyway. While this perspective does not free the online games industry from the responsibility to care about the problem of "too much time spent playing," it certainly contradicts public concerns that masses of players are in danger of ruining their social lives because they cannot quit playing their favorite online game.

Video Games as Glue for Social Life: Research on Communication, Group, and Family Cohesion

Similar to television's research history, communication studies have been, for quite some time, primarily interested in the potentially harmful effects of video games and have therefore discovered perspectives on possible positive impacts rather late. Today, research lines have been established that address the use and uses of video games with regard to, for instance, learning, social change ("serious games"), recreation, and health outcomes (e.g., Ritterfeld, Cody, & Vorderer, 2009). With regard to social life, the benign consequences of playing video games have not received much attention so far. This is interesting, given that there is a tradition of research on television and social life in the field (e.g., with a focus on families: Bryant & Bryant, 2001).

One reason for the reluctance in research and society to acknowledge positive social effects of video games might be that particularly in "level 3" gaming, sociality does not come with face-to-face contact. Players mostly reside physically separated from each other and maintain social contact by interaction in the virtual world by chatting or using voice communication. And even in "level 2" gaming, where players at least share a physical location, casual observation of players mostly detects silence—players are focused on their match and do not waste their time and attention on talking with each other. Can such artificial sociality really breed positive effects?

Benign social consequences of joint game play have in fact been observed in various studies, primarily because they have examined subjective experiences of social interaction among players instead of testing a prescribed disadvantage of technically mediated social contact (Klimmt & Hartmann, 2008). The key finding of thematic studies is that players indeed experience social interaction with other players, who are often "offline friends" anyway, as emotionally positive, trustful, enriching, and creating pleasantly intense social bonds (e.g., Cole & Griffiths, 2007; Smyth, 2007; Williams et al., 2007). At the same time, some of the very same surveys also find that the social magnetism of multiplayer gaming can cause (transient) neglect of offline social interaction (Smyth, 2007; Williams, 2006). The empirical evidence thus does certainly not justify replacing a universally negative judgment on interplayer sociality with an entirely positive assessment. Rather, joint game play should be considered as a social resource for players with great potential for improving social life that can, if their social life becomes focused too much on gaming, turn into a social problem as well (Jordan, in press). Balancing the network and frequencies of in-game and off-game sociality therefore emerges as the key challenge in gaining the best out of games' and other domains' social advantages.

Aside from online gaming, which mostly involves peers, co-located gaming seems to facilitate positive social consequences particularly among core family members. While early video game technology was difficult to handle, more recent systems such as the "Nintendo Wii," "Microsoft X-Box Kinect," or "Sony PlayStation Move" render games more accessible and usable for older players as well, such as parents or grandparents (Chambers, 2012). As a consequence, family video gaming emerges as a joint social activity with communication patterns and capabilities—similar to board games. Aarsand (2007) argues that joint video gaming holds a unique potential to particularly strengthen intergenerational bonds within families. Parents and grandparents gain access to children's preferred leisure time activity, serve as beatable competitors, and join in communication about game contents, technology, and playing strategies. While empirical evidence is limited, families emerge as one important structure for which contemporary video gaming can have very positive effects on social life.

Although some empirical studies indicate that video games can serve as glue for social life, further reasoning is needed to understand the causes and mechanisms of such positive functions. Research on video game enjoyment (e.g., Vorderer & Bryant, 2006; Yee, 2006) suggests that it is the *shared experience* of demanding, successful, suspenseful, funny, or otherwise outstanding game play that creates feelings of belongingness, friendship, and unity. Players conduct joint *actions* instead of merely talking with each other. They team up to resolve challenges and generate "big" stories. Sons who virtually save the world together with their fathers, friends who spend exhausting hours to win a player-versus-player competition online, and strangers who happen to virtually meet in front of a huge digital monster go through intense social and active experiences that they share and memorize easily. Video games serve as a virtual stage on which players can dramatize their social bonds: Mastering difficult situations together, helping and receiving help in critical instances, or reaching victory due to superior team spirit and collaboration are inherently social and outstanding experiences that contribute to the foundation of social relationships. It is this mechanism of shared, meaningful, and memorable experiences that seems to fuel the bonding power of social video game play.

Outlook: The Gamified Social Life of the Future

Because the evolution of video games to the mass entertainment medium is still ongoing, the current review of the social impact of video games cannot offer definite conclusions. For the time being, there are sound arguments and empirical evidence for both problematic and benign effects that game play can have on social life. While public discourse and past research have clearly prioritized negative over positive effects, the desirable social outcomes that are coming with the games' mass movement are clearly gaining relevance in game studies and public debates. Given the tremendous dynamics in the games industry and rapid technological progress, we should expect even more fundamental shifts in the sociality of video games in the future.

From recent industry innovations, some assumptions on the social life of future game players can be derived. Returning to the introductory description of video games' evolution toward a social medium, the "level 4" of gaming will clearly be driven by the mobility and pervasiveness of games. Multiplayer gaming is becoming accessible from mobile devices that are improving their multimedia capabilities constantly. Innovative game concepts actively include users' local environments (augmented reality, location-based game tasks, physical movement as part of the playing activity) and take advantage of mobile network connections among players who are permanently online. Playing video games is about to turn into a fun activity that is available to groups of users anywhere and anytime. Invitations to join a game will reach us during business meetings, on the bus, and during holidays. Continuing a paused game session will be possible for player teams even when a physical gathering is over.

In other words, video gaming that involves others (familiar people or strangers, by plan or by incidental encounter) will be with us as a second mode of everyday social behavior. This industry trend is likely to breed new ways of utilizing games, for instance, in public diplomacy (playing together to overcome stereotypes and nationalist sentiments), in politics (massively multiplayer worlds as arenas of public discourse), or art. In this sense, the future of video games will emerge as one key manifestation of macro-level changes that we can observe in contemporary societies: The growing importance of youth lifestyle, the adoption of leisure time activities that were formerly reserved for children or the uneducated masses, and the normative value of individuality and spontaneous behavior (e.g., Beck & Beck-Gernsheim, 2002). The remarkable evolution of video games will continue and bring about amazing innovations for social life—some of them will enrich and inspire us, and others will demand our attention to recognize and minimize the social risks that might be involved.

References

Aarsand, P. A. (2007). Computer and video games in family life: The digital divide as a resource in intergenerational interactions. *Childhood, 14*(2), 235–256. doi: 10.1177/0907568207078330

Anderson, C. A. (2004). An update on the effects of playing violent video games. *Journal of Adolescence, 27*(1), 113–122. doi: 10.1016/j.adolescence.2003.10.009

Anderson, C. A., & Bushman, B. J. (2001). Effects of violent video games on aggressive behavior, aggressive cognition, aggressive affect, physiological arousal, and prosocial behavior: A meta-analytic review of the scientific literature. *Psychological Science, 12*(5), 353–359. doi: 10.1111/1467-9280.00366

Anderson, C. A., Shibuya, A., Ihori, N., Swing, E. L., Bushman, B. J., Sakamoto, A., Rothstein, H. R., & Saleem, M. (2010). Violent video game effects on aggression, empathy, and prosocial behavior in Eastern and Western countries: A meta-analytic review. *Psychological Bulletin, 136*(2), 151–173. doi: 10.1037/a0018251

Beck, U., & Beck-Gernsheim, E. (2002). *Individualization*. London: Sage.

Bessière, K., Seay, A. F., & Kiesler, S. (2007). The ideal elf: Identity exploration in World of Warcraft. *CyberPsychology & Behavior, 10*(4), 530–535. doi: 10.1089/cpb.2007.9994

Bruner, O., & Bruner, K. (2006). *Playstation nation: Protect your child from video game addiction*. New York: Center Street Hachette Book Group.

Bryant, J., & Bryant, A. (Eds.). (2001). *Television and the American family* (2nd edition). Mahwah, NJ: Lawrence Erlbaum Associates.

Bryce, J., & Rutter, J. (2003). Gender dynamics and the social and spatial organization of computer gaming. *Leisure Studies, 22*, 1–15. doi: 10.1080/0261436030306571

Bushman, B. J., & Anderson, C. A. (2002). Violent video games and hostile expectations: A test of the general aggression model. *Personality and Social Psychology Bulletin, 28*(12), 1679–1686. doi: 10.1177/014616702237649

Chambers, D. (2012). "Wii play as a family": The rise in family-centred video gaming. *Leisure Studies, 31*(1), 69–82. doi: 10.1080/02614367.2011.568065

Chan, E., & Vorderer, P. (2006). Massively multiplayer online games. In P. Vorderer, & J. Bryant (Eds.), *Playing video games: Motives, responses, and consequences* (pp. 77–90). Mahwah, NJ: Lawrence Erlbaum Associates.

Charlton J. P., & Danforth, I. D. (2007). Distinguishing addiction and high engagement in the context of online game playing. *Computers in Human Behavior, 23*(3), 1531–1548. doi: 10.1016/j.chb.2005.07.002

Cole, H., & Griffiths, M. (2007). Social interactions in massively multiplayer online role-playing games. *CyberPsychology & Behavior, 10*(4), 575–583. doi: 10.1089/cpb.2007.9988

Eastin, M. (2007). The influence of competitive and cooperative group game play on state hostility. *Human Communication Research, 33*, 450–466. doi: 10.1111/j.1468-2958.2007.00307.x

Eastin, M., & Griffiths, R. (2009). Unreal: Hostile expectations from social gameplay. *New Media & Society, 11*(4), 509–531. doi: 10.1177/1461444809102958

Ferguson, C. J. (2008). The school shooting/violent video game link: Causal relationship or moral panic? *Journal of Investigative Psychology and Offender Profiling, 5*, 25–37. doi: 10.1002/jip.76

Jansz, J. (2005). The emotional appeal of violent video games for adolescent males. *Communication Theory, 15*(3), 219–241. doi: 10.1093/ct/15.3.219

Jansz, J., & Martens, L. (2005). Gaming at a LAN event: The social context of playing video games. *New Media & Society, 7*(3), 333–355. doi: 10.1177/1461444805052280

Jin, S.-A. A., & Park, N. (2009). Parasocial interaction with My Avatar: Effects of interdependent self-construal and the mediating role of self-presence in an avatar-based console game, Wii. *CyberPsychology & Behavior, 12*(6), 723–727. doi: 10.1089/cpb.2008.0289

Jordan, N. (in press). Video games: Support for the evolving family therapist. *Journal of Family Therapy.*

Juul, J. (2010). *A casual revolution: Reinventing video games and their players.* Cambridge, MA: MIT Press.

Kim, K., Ryu, E., Chon, M. Y., Yeun, E. J., Choi, S. Y., Seo, J. S., & Nam, B. W. (2006). Internet addiction in Korean adolescents and its relation to depression and suicidal ideation: A questionnaire survey. *International Journal of Nursing Studies, 43*(2), 185–192. doi: 10.1016/j.ijnurstu.2005.02.005

Kirsh, S. J. (2003). The effects of violent video games on adolescents: The over-looked influence of development. *Aggression and Violent Behavior, 8,* 377–389. doi: 10.1016/S1359-1789(02)00056-3

Klimmt, C., & Hartmann, T. (2008). Mediated interpersonal communication in multiplayer video games: Implications for entertainment and relationship man-agement. In E. Konijn, M. Tanis, S. Utz, & S. Barnes (Eds.), *Mediated interper-sonal communication* (pp. 309–330). New York: Routledge.

Klimmt, C., Hefner, D., & Vorderer, P. (2009a). The video game experience as "true" identification: A theory of enjoyable alterations of players' self-perception. *Communication Theory, 19*(4), 351–373. doi: 10.1111/j.1468-2885.2009.01347.x

Klimmt, C., Schmid, H., & Orthmann, J. (2009b). Exploring the enjoyment of playing browser games. *CyberPsychology & Behavior, 12*(2), 231–234. doi: 10.1089/cpb.2008.0128

Kolo, C., & Baur, T. (2004). Living a virtual life: Social dynamics of online gam-ing. *Game Studies, 4*(1), Article 3. Retrieved February 11, 2013, from http:// www.gamestudies.org/0401/kolo

Konijn, E., Bijvank, M. N., & Bushman, B. J. (2007). I wish I were a warrior: The role of wishful identification in the effects of violent video games on aggres-sion in adolescent boys. *Developmental Psychology, 43,* 1038–1044. doi: 10.1037/0012-1649.43.4.1038

LaRose, R., Lin, C. A., & Eastin, M. (2003). Unregulated Internet usage: Addiction, habit, or deficient self-regulation? *Media Psychology, 5,* 225–253. doi: 10.1207/ S1532785XMEP0503_01

Lemmens, J. S., Valkenburg, P. M., & Peter, J. (2009). Development and valida-tion of a game addiction scale for adolescents. *Media Psychology, 12*(1), 77–95. doi: 10.1080/15213260802669458

Lewis, M. L., Weber, R., & Bowman, N. D. (2008). They may be pixels, but they're MY pixels: Developing a metric of character attachment in role-playing video games. *CyberPsychology & Behavior, 11*(4), 515–518. doi: 10.1089/ cpb.2007.0137

Lowood, H. (2006). A brief biography of computer games. In P. Vorderer, & J. Bryant (Eds.), *Playing video games: Motives, responses, consequences* (pp. 27–47). Mahwah, NJ: Lawrence Erlbaum Associates.

Mitchell, E. (1985). The dynamics of family interaction around home video games. *Marriage & Family Review, 8*(1–2), 121–135. doi: 10.1300/J002v08n01_10

Nikken, P., & Jansz, J. (2007). Playing restricted videogames. *Journal of Children and Media, 1*(3), 227–243. doi: 10.1080/17482790701531862

Panelas, T. (1983). Adolescents and video games: Consumption of leisure and the social construction of the peer group. *Youth and Society, 15*(1), 51–65. doi: 10.1177/0044118X83015001004

Pena, J., & Hancock, J. T. (2006). An analysis of socioemotional and task communication in online multiplayer video games. *Communication Research, 33*(1), 92–109. doi: 10.1177/0093650205283103

Peng, W. (2008). The mediational role of identification in the relationship between experience mode and self-efficacy: Enactive role-playing versus passive observation. *CyberPsychology & Behavior, 11*(6), 649–652. do 10.1089/cpb.2007.0229 i:

Poole, S. (2000). *Trigger happy: The inner life of videogames.* London: Fourth Estate.

Ritterfeld, U., Cody, M., & Vorderer, P. (Eds.). (2009). *Serious games: Effects and mechanisms.* New York: Routledge.

Selnow, G. W. (1984). Playing videogames: The electronic friend. *Journal of Communication, 34*(2), 148–156. doi: 10.1111/j.1460-2466.1984.tb02166.x

Sherry, J. L. (2001). The effects of violent video games on aggression. A meta-analysis. *Human Communication Research, 27*(3), 409–431. doi: 10.1093/hcr/27.3.409

Slater, M., Henry, K. L., Swaim, R. C., & Anderson, L. L. (2003). Violent media content and aggressiveness in adolescents: A downward spiral model. *Communication Research, 30*(6), 713–736. doi: 10.1177/0093650203258281

Slater, M. D. (2007). Reinforcing spirals: The mutual influence of media selectivity and media effects and their impact on individual behavior and social identity. *Communication Theory, 17*, 281–303. doi: 10.1177/0093650210375953

Smith, S. L., Lachlan, K., & Tamborini, R. (2003). Popular video games: Quantifying the presentation of violence and its context. *Journal of Broadcasting & Electronic Media, 47*(1), 58–76. doi: 10.1207/s15506878jobem4804_4

Smyth, J. (2007). Beyond self-selection in video game play: An experimental examination of the consequences of massively multiplayer online role-playing game play. *CyberPsychology & Behavior, 10*(5), 717–721. doi: 10.1089/cpb.2007.9963

Steinkuehler, C., & Williams, D. (2006). Where everybody knows your (screen) name: Online games as "third places." *Journal of Computer-Mediated Communication, 11*(4), Article 1. Retrieved February 11, 2013, from http://jcmc.indiana.edu/vol11/issue4/steinkuehler.html. doi: 10.1111/j.1083-6101.2006.00300.x

Tamborini, R., & Skalski, P. (2006). The role of presence in the experience of electronic games. In P. Vorderer & J. Bryant (Eds.), *Playing video games: Motives, responses, and consequences* (pp. 225–240). Mahwah, NJ: Lawrence Erlbaum Associates.

Thalemann, R., Wölfling, K., & Grüsser, S. (2007). Specific cue reactivity on computer game-related cues in excessive gamers. *Behavioral Neuroscience, 121*(3), 614–618. doi: 10.1037/0735-7044.121.3.614

Trepte, S., Reinecke, L., & Behr, K. M. (2009). Creating virtual alter egos or superheroines? Gamers' strategies of avatar creation in terms of gender and sex. *International Journal of Gaming and Computer-Mediated Simulations, 1*(2), 52–76. doi: 10.4018/jgcms.2009040104

Vorderer, P., & Bryant, J. (Eds.). (2006). *Playing video games: Motives, responses, consequences.* Mahwah, NJ: Lawrence Erlbaum Associates.

Wigand, R. T., Borstelmann, S. E., & Boster, F. J. (1985). Electronic leisure: Video game usage and the communication climate of video arcades. *Communication Yearbook, 9,* 275–293.

Williams, D. (2006). Groups and goblins: The social and civic impact of an online game. *Journal of Broadcasting & Electronic Media, 50*(4), 651–670. doi: 10.1207/s15506878jobem5004_5

Williams, D., Caplan, S., & Xiong, L. (2007). Can you hear me now? The impact of voice in an online gaming community. *Human Communication Research, 33,* 427–449. doi: 10.1111/j.1468-2958.2007.00306.x

Williams, D., Ducheneaut, N., Xiong, L., Zhang, Y., Yee, N., & Nickell, E. (2006). From tree house to barracks: The social life of guilds in World of Warcraft. *Games and Culture, 1,* 338–361. doi: 10.1177/1555412006292616

Williams, R. B., & Clippinger, C. A. (2002). Aggression, competition and computer games: Computer and human opponents. *Computers in Human Behavior, 18,* 495–506. doi: 10.1016/S0747-5632(02)00009-2

Wolf, M. J. P., & Perron, B. (Eds.). (2003). *The video game theory reader.* London: Routledge.

Wood, R. T. (2008). Problems with the concept of video game "addiction": Some case study examples. *International Journal on Mental Health and Addiction, 6,* 169–178. doi: 10.1007/s11469-007-9118-0

Wright, T., Boria, E., & Breidenbach, P. (2002). Creative player action in FPS online video games. *Game Studies, 2*(2), Article 4. Retrieved February 11, 2013, from http://gamestudies.org/0202/wright

Yee, N. (2006). The demographics, motivations, and derived experiences of users of massively multi-user online graphical environments. *Presence: Teleoperators and Virtual Environments, 15,* 309–329. doi: 10.1162/pres.15.3.309

12

THE STRUCTURAL TRANSFORMATION OF MOBILE COMMUNICATION

Implications for Self and Society

Scott W. Campbell, Rich Ling, and Joseph B. Bayer

Mobile communication is a relatively new form of interaction. It has only been commonly available in developed countries for the past two decades and in developing countries for less than that. Perhaps because the rise of mobile communication is so recent, the juxtaposition of its use against traditional social practice illuminates issues in a new way. To be sure, mobile communication's explosive growth as an everyday life resource has given us a lens through which we can study both sociological and psychological developments. Despite being a relatively new addition to the media landscape, the assuredness with which we appropriate our mobile devices speaks to well routinized use. When we reach for our phone to fill in what Fortunati (2002, p. 518) calls the "smallest folds" of life, we manipulate them with ease. In addition, at the social level, we increasingly understand that it is expected of us to have a mobile phone. Our friends and family expect us to be available to them, to be socially "on call." Through mobile communication, we become more attached to one another, not to mention to the technology itself. Without the device, it is not uncommon for a user to feel utterly disconnected and psychologically distressed (Vincent, 2006).

As it continues to take root as a multi-channel resource, individuals increasingly rely on mobile communication to stay plugged in outside of their social network as well. Individuals increasingly turn to mobile communication as a way of connecting with society by using it as a resource for news, politics, popular culture, and the like. Thus, the psychological and sociological implications of the technology are becoming progressively united through a consolidated set of processes. For this reason, we argue that explaining mobile communication's role in social life calls for new explanatory frameworks that better integrate psychological and sociological theory.

In this chapter, we will consider the changing nature and implications of mobile communication through a discussion of what is new about the technology in social life. From there, we will review theoretical perspectives from psychology and sociology that complement one another in helping to explain these developments. Along the way, we will identify opportunities for further theoretical extension and integration as scholars continue to make sense of the social implications of mobile communication.

What Is Mobile Communication?

First, a definition for what we mean by mobile communication is in order. Perhaps because of the interdisciplinary nature of this new field, perspectives can vary with regard to the exact nature of mobile communication as well as mobile communication studies. The days of the conventional, narrowly purposed "cell phone" have given way to a new era of multidimensional platforms that support a whole range of information and communication flows, making it impossible to root a definition in a particular artifact. Therefore, we ground our definition in what the hardware, the software, and the communication channels afford, or make possible, as opposed to what these things looks like or conjure up through traditional notions of a wireless telephone.

By mobile communication, we mean how people and groups use devices and services that support mediated communication while the user is in physical motion. The point here is that the technology *can* be used while in motion, not that it always is. There is an important physical dimension to these devices, and usability has changed in important ways over time. In the early days of computing, there were, for example, luggable Kay-Pro and Osbourn computers that were as big as an overstuffed carry-on and weighed even more. Mobile phones at the time were also heavy and awkward devices that were better transported in a car than in our pockets. With time, phones and personal computers (PCs) have slimmed down, and there is even the budding category of pads and tablets that seem to sit somewhere between the phone and the PC in the gadget landscape. Smaller devices have added a spontaneity to our use that was not evident before. In addition, there is a ubiquity associated with mobile communication devices that is important. That is, we are able to assume that others are similarly wirelessly connected and therefore available to us. Thus, mobile communication assumes the ability to move about with devices that allow for spontaneous interaction with others who are similarly equipped.

The nature of mobile-mediated communication has expanded dramatically in recent years. Whereas mobile communication formerly involved calling (and then later) texting, it now might refer to a whole host of channels for interpersonal interaction as well group communication, mass media consumption, information exchange, gaming, and mass self-communication via social media (Castells, 2007). Our definition of mobile communication also includes situations where the user is not actually mobile. Oftentimes, in practice we treat the technology as a portable or even fixed device. The argument here is simply that it offers *the potential* for mediated communication and information exchange while the user is physically in motion, which is important because it shapes our social expectations, and the way that we structure interaction. With that definition in place, we now turn to what is new about the technology, particularly with regard to the role of mobile communication in our psychological orientation and our dealings in society more broadly.

New Developments and Important Questions

Coinciding with the rise of mobile communication and its various social consequences is the emergence of the new field of mobile communication studies. This nascent field is beginning to develop a body of work that follows the contours of how mobile communication is making itself felt in our daily lives. Growing branches in the existing scholarship include studies of mobile communication and social cohesion (Ling, 2008), space and time (Ling & Campbell, 2009), linguistic conventions (Baron & Ling, 2011; Hård af Segerstad, 2005), and the developing world (Chib, 2013; Donner, 2008; Horst & Miller, 2005). Rather than a review of those and other extant themes in the literature, our aim here is to identify and reflect on some of the core questions and concerns on the horizon, particularly with regard to shifting understandings of self and society through mobile communication.

These areas of consideration will be anchored in the central argument that one of the most notable new things about mobile communication is that it is no longer all that new (Goggin, 2011; Ling, 2012). Like the radio, television, and the Internet, it has become an ingrained part of everyday life for many if not most people. This is especially apparent in the developed world where the number of mobile subscriptions actually exceeds the population in many places, indicating that some users have more than one device/subscription (although some subscriptions can be attributed to public entities, e.g. fire department). Even in developing societies it is not uncommon for most people to have access to and use mobile communication as an everyday resource (International Telecommunication Union,

2012). In other words, mobile communication per se is no longer a novelty. It may present novel affordances, apps, and gadgets, but mobile communication itself has joined the realm of other technological advances that have gone from revolutionary to mundane and finally to being expected, such as the watch and the automobile (Ling, 2012).

Following this trajectory, at first, mobile communication was a luxury (Agar, 2003). Then it became "nice to have." Now it is an expectation, with important implications for how we understand ourselves and each other. If people in our lives do not have a mobile device, it becomes *our* problem (Ling, 2012, p. 3; Katz, 2008). We can see this when we are trying to organize an informal social event with a group of people. In the era of landline phones previous to the development of answering machines, getting in touch with people was a chancy affair. Often we had to call back several different times in order to "catch them at home." Others who were willing to take a note were helpful, but there were still lags in connecting. The answering machine helped to bridge this gap since we knew that we could leave a message at the location of the phone being called and, as the technology developed, the owner of the answering machine could call in to hear their messages. However, the lag between our call and the time when our intended interlocutor would call back was not easy to determine. The fact that we are (or at least that we are expected to be) continually outfitted with a mobile phone means that we are almost always available to one another regardless of time and place. The only exceptions are when we do not hear the ringing, our battery is not charged, the phone is in disrepair, or we have forgotten it at home. In addition, we might choose to not answer a call if it comes at an awkward time or we feel uncomfortable talking to the person calling. Beyond voice calls and texts, there is also an increasingly complex set of alternatives that include using social networking sites or a location-based platform for arranging our social lives (e.g., Humphreys, 2007). In Durkheim's (1938) terms, being so highly connected through mobile technology has become something similar to a taken-for-granted *social fact*. Despite the emergence of new features, mobile communication, as a context for being socially connected, is now more of a shared expectation than something new and revolutionary (Ling, 2012).

This movement toward taken-for-grantedness raises important questions about how we got to this point. As such, there is an opportunity for developing theory that explains how mobile communication has become what Berger and Luckman (1967) would describe as a *social institution*, or a structural part of the social environment. Berger and Luckmann argue that understanding the establishment of a social institution can be gleaned by examining the habitualized behaviors that, over time, crystalize and work their way into the rhythms of social life.[1] As new social dynamics become shared experiences, they can become routinized in ways that are both personal and collective, to the extent that they become almost second nature to us as individuals and, in turn, a structured part of the social environment. Therefore, we treat habit as a point of entry for understanding the individual and social processes that have supported mobile communication's transformation into a taken-for-granted aspect of social structure. We do not suggest here that all mobile communication is habitual. Nor do we suggest that habit is the only way of explaining its role in social life. Rather, we recognize habit as a promising avenue for theory building on how mobile communication has become a structural part of it.

With that said, we already know that much of our interaction with technology occurs without full cognitive processing (for a review, see LaRose, 2010). Not surprisingly, there is growing evidence that for many users, certain mobile communication behaviors have become habitualized (Bayer & Campbell, 2012; LaRose, 2010; Oulasvirta et al., 2012; Peters, 2009).[2] Psychologically, habits represent a form of automaticity, or a cued behavior lacking four components: attention, awareness, intention, and control (Bargh, 1994; Gardner, 2012; Orbell & Verplanken, 2010). A mobile phone user can be more or less automatic, regardless of how much they use their device (Bayer & Campbell, 2012; Gardner, 2012). While it shares this in common with other media, the habitualization of mobile communication is distinct.

The mobile phone is an anytime–anywhere resource. Cues for use and our responses to those cues are not restricted to a specific environment. In turn, an individual might develop the habit of checking for texts or Facebook updates when entering an elevator, or texting when they see a funny sign on the street. Alternatively, a person could develop the habit of texting when feeling sad, lonely, or angry. Over time, these cues for mobile communicative behavior—whether physical objects in the environment or discrete states in the mind—become acted on by reflex. They are subconscious links to other social planes. Every habitual mobile user may have a unique and potentially ubiquitous repertoire of cues. Hence, mobile phone behavior can no longer be studied by the mere metric of frequency. Indeed, studies indicate that the frequency of mobile phone usage is often independent from the degree of social and psychological effects (Bayer & Campbell, 2012; Campbell & Kwak, 2011; Walsh et al., 2010, 2011).

Another issue is that, unlike most other habits, mobile communication is characteristically a social activity. Our urge to call or text, and the way that we respond to others who reach out to us in these ways, is a social act. Consequently, new research is needed to understand not only when and where habitual mechanisms are enacted for different users, but how they are enacted *across* users. The reciprocal nature of communication means that habitual processes are not only reinforced by our own personal situation, but that they are contagious. We expect one another to be available when we are excited or angry, and we become concerned when they do not answer their phone. In this sense, mobile communication habits are formed and altered at the collective as well as psychological level. Thus, mobile communication habits and the structural transformation of the technology's role in social life call for explanations that engage with both psychological and sociological processes.

Renewed Bridges Between Sociological and Psychological Theory

Thus far we have argued that mobile communication has transformed into a taken-for-granted part of social life and that one avenue for explaining this transformation is to examine how use of the technology has become routinized in daily affairs. Because the technology is so central to both self and society, and because habits are formed at both individual and collective levels, explanatory frameworks are needed that can bridge between micro and macro levels of social order (Haddon & Kommonen, 2005; Oishi, Kesebir, & Snyder, 2009; Webster, 2009, 2011). In this section we examine steps that have already been taken in this direction and identify opportunities for integrating and extending frameworks for explaining mobile communication's role in social life.

One step toward bridging micro and macro perspectives can be found in the theoretical evolution of micro-sociology, particularly with its interest in collective rituals and social cohesion (Oishi et al., 2009).[3] By bringing the societal-level perspectives of Durkheim (1995) down to the granular level of everyday life experience, Goffman (1967) shows how rituals have become a structured part of social action and foster a sense of togetherness. With this as a foundation, Collins (2004) places more focus on the interactions involved in social rituals as they develop into what he characterizes as ritual interaction chains. These involve a mutually recognized focus on a shared social experience (engrossment) and the development of a common mood (effervescence, to use Durkheim's term). When we give ourselves over to the mood of the situation and share in becoming engrossed, we drop barriers to interaction with our co-participants and share a common experience. It is through these collective processes that we form groups and we grow to trust the other members of the group. Likewise, it is through the recognition of shared status that we drop the barriers to our individuality and begin to identify as part of a social unit. Thus, internal psychological processes as well as social interactions are tightly bound into the situation.

Using this framework, Collins (2004) examines conversation as a ritual interaction. In a conversation there are both psychological and social activities in play. There is this willingness to engage in a mutual social engagement "with its own boundaries and constraints" (p. 23). Further, we have a responsibility to the situation and at the same time we are involved in it with our own personal engagement. Participants must keep the conversation alive by discussing the appropriate topics, giving the appropriate responses, and making the appropriate gestures. We need to work out themes and responses. We need to manage the facade that, following Goffman's ideas, we are "giving off" (1959, p. 108), and we need to interpret the facade and the flow of conversation from our interlocutors. All of these are psychological processes. However, the sum is greater than the parts. The conversation is a social event that is socially constructed and exists in its own right. It draws on culture and on reciprocally constructed understandings. In addition, the conversation can have consequence for the structuring of further interaction between the people involved, and for that matter, people who are not even present. Collins sees these as "rituals calling for cooperation in keeping the momentary focus of attention and thus giving respect both to the persons who properly take part and to the situational reality as something worth a moment of being treated seriously" (2004, p. 24). That is, the conversation is an entity just as the interlocutors are. He considers our orientation toward these social events as the production of self under social constraint, and as such it is a key element in the bridge between the individual and collective.

Both Goffman and Collins emphasized the development of ritual through co-present social interaction, creating an opportunity for Ling (2008) to extend this line of work into the realm of mediation, particularly with regard to mobile communication. According to Ling (2008), mobile communication has become an important resource for ritual interaction chains among close personal ties. It tightens the flows of interaction and aids in the development of distinctive social rhythms (Ling, 2008). This theoretical stream may be a useful starting point for examining how mobile communication habits develop at the social level.

To be sure, the notions of ritualistic and habitual behavior are distinct, one referring to symbolic meaning and the other an automatic orientation. That said, they may be linked in the concrete situation of mobile communication and in ways that are theoretically meaningful. It is possible that socially habitualized mobile communication practices may come out of shared interaction rituals. Some support for this can be found in the notion of *habitus*. In his explication of habitus, Bourdieu (1977) argues that members of a social collective develop shared understandings and practices that, over time, can take on a life of their own and become part of the structure of society. They become ingrained in daily activities and interactions to the extent that individuals fall into these shared understandings and practices without consciously thinking about their original meaning or intent. Arguably, mobile-mediated ritual interaction chains can develop into this type of habitus over time. So far, the research on mobile communication habits has primarily been concerned with explaining behavior that people would like to curb, particularly texting while driving (Bayer & Campbell, 2012). Thus, there is the opportunity for a theoretical contribution by broadening the scope of that line of inquiry to examine whether and how mobile-mediated ritual interaction and habit are related. It is conceivable that habit and ritual interaction are related in ways that shape mobile communication's transformation from something new, to something expected, to something that is now part of self as well as the larger social structure.

Goffman (1959, 1963, 1967; see Jacobsen, 2010) also theorized about habits in ways that point to transcendence from the cognitive to the collective level. He examined the social structure of interaction, arguing that by the end of childhood, many people are conditioned into blasé participation in a clear-cut world of turns and moves. Goffman unveiled the subtext, negotiations, and contracts that uphold social reality—or at least the social reality of his time, which preceded mobile communication. The game has changed with the advent of mobile communication. The full access to our social network is simply a ring (or buzz) away. Our potential social moves are now unlimited; we have gone from checkers to chess. At the same time, we have shown how this game is played in a taken-for-granted manner. Mobile phone users utilize a number of maneuvers to balance both local and virtual interests at once (Ling, 2008). As these uses develop into everyday practices, they become part of the larger mix of media habits (LaRose, 2010).

As researchers pursue habit as an avenue for explaining mobile communication's (now) structural role in social life, they should also keep an eye out for the ways it may undermine or constrain conscious interpersonal goals. On the individual level, it may reduce the number of communicative partners. Alternatively, on the collective level, it may push individuals to go along with social expectations with which they disagree (such as constant availability). As the unconscious mechanisms solidify, individuals lose awareness of agency, but gain communicative efficiency personally and as a member of social units and society. However, this sometimes comes at the expense of attending to one's co-present surroundings, evidenced by research linking texting while driving to a habitual orientation to texting more broadly (Bayer & Campbell, 2012).

Fully developing new explanatory frameworks that integrate the psychological and sociological dimensions of mobile communication is beyond the scope of this chapter. That said, it is within our scope to indicate promising areas that may serve as points of entry for this type of undertaking. The search for bridges between the social and the psychological is obviously not new. As Oishi et al. (2009) point out, "This individual–group discontinuity effect shows that there is a shift in cognition and behavior when people are in groups and that group behavior is not a linear function of individual behavior" (p. 344). Reconciling these levels of human behavior requires researchers to call on established frameworks as well as new interdisciplinary visions.

One possible tool for researchers looking to bridge this gap is structuration theory (Giddens, 1984). Structuration theory provides a framework for understanding how individual behavior interacts with the rules of a social system. Since its inception, communication and technology studies have adapted this framework for understanding the "micro–macro" link in other contexts (see Orlikowski, 2000; Webster, 2011; Whitbred, Fonti, Steglich, & Contractor, 2011; Yates & Orlikowski, 2002). In their recent examination of communication networks, Whitbred et al. (2011) note that according to the structuralist perspective, "As agents (either consciously or subconsciously) behave consistently with existing rules, these same structures are reproduced or reified and continue to have future influence" (p. 408). Their findings provide credence for the duality of structure, or the central idea within structuration theory that individual behavior affects the development of normative rules and vice versa. Such perspectives may be of use to mobile communication researchers going forward given the competing pressures of psychological attachment and societal constraints.

Another opportunity for explaining both micro and macro levels of social change associated with mobile communication is domestication theory.[4] Domestication is a framework for understanding how personal technologies go through transformations in the private realm of use, with emphasis on the individual-level processes of adoption, integration, and conversion of the technology as part of an individual's identity. Domestication theory was originally advanced to explain how computers were transformed from an organizational resource to both a resource and a fixture in the home (Silverstone & Haddon, 1996; Silverstone, Hirsch, & Morley, 1992). It has since been applied to understand mobile communication adoption and usage processes (Haddon, 2003). At the core of domestication theory is the principle that personal technologies go through a series of stages as they develop from just an idea, to something newly acquired, to part of the mix of other objects of everyday life, to part of the user him/herself. These stages are not necessarily linear, meaning the technology can go through several waves of evolution within each of these stages (Ling, 2004).

The transformation of mobile communication into a structured part of social life provides an opportunity to revisit domestication theory (or perhaps what we might call neo-domestication theory since it is not tied to the home) to better account for changes in the socio-technological landscape at the societal as well as personal realm. Mobile communication moves through this conversion process. It moves from being something imagined by the eventual user, through to finding its more or less secure position in our lives, which is characteristically a social process. When used for targeted interaction with peers, rhythms are established making expectations for accessibility more of a shared assumption (Ling, 2008). By extension, we can also think about how "domesticated" technologies gain a critical mass in a society and eventually become assumed ways of facilitating sociation. In this process, there is the individual evaluation of the technology and its place in our personal lives, but there is also a broader social component since technologies with such reach demand our use as a member of society. There are undeniable benefits to, for example, owning a clock or a phone, but we are also expected to be punctual and available (Ling, 2012). Thus, the conversion process from something new to something taken for granted and structured occurs at both micro and macro levels of social order, and extending domestication theory from the micro to the macro level may help to reveal how mobile communication became, and continues to become, a structured part of society.

Concluding Remarks

When we use our mobile device to check for texts, receive a call, access social media, or navigate the web, we are engaging in processes that play out on both psychological and sociological levels. We slip into the interaction using reflexive behaviors as we pull the device out of our pocket or purse. We use familiar behavioral patterns when we start to engage in the texting session or answer the phone. These practices have become well integrated into the flow of events in our daily lives. As the technology's capacity for information management continues to develop, other uses of it are moving in this direction too, creating shared expectations for being connected not only in the private realm, but in public life as well. Not long ago, these affordances for social connection were revolutionary advances. Although they may still be revolutionary, they no longer seem like it to many users. Instead, they are increasingly expected and even taken for granted, much like our reliance on mechanical timekeeping (Ling, 2012). This transformation is meaningful because it represents movement toward a new layer of social structure. Because of the individual and collective dynamics of its use, explaining mobile communication's shift toward a taken-for-granted part of social structure calls for the integration of psychological and sociological perspectives. This chapter helps lay the groundwork for steps to be taken in that direction by identifying points of entry made visible by extant theory, particularly that which bridges micro and macro levels of social order. Future research and theory building will benefit by translating these insights into hypotheses and research questions geared for deeper understanding of how mobile communication has worked its way into the structural realm of social life.

Notes

1 Berger and Luckmann discuss this as a mutually interactive process. Their definition of an institution is the reciprocal typification of habitualized action. Thus, there is an interplay between personal habitualization as well as reciprocal interaction.

2 To be clear, we are not talking about "addiction" here, but rather the extent to which the user puts conscious thought into what they are doing when using the technology.

3 Often when we think of ritual we think of large-scale religious ceremonies. By way of contrast, for Goffman and for Collins, ritual interaction often takes place in the context of everyday life.
4 This approach has roots in the work of Giddens and the scholarly community around him, in particular Leslie Haddon and Roger Silverstone.

References

Agar, J. (2003). *Constant touch: A global history of the mobile phone.* Cambridge, UK: Icon Books.

Bargh, J. A. (1994). The four horsemen of automaticity: Awareness, intention, efficiency, and control in social cognition. In R. S. Wyer, Jr., & T. K. Srull (Eds.), *Handbook of social cognition* (2nd ed., Vol., 3, pp. 1–40). Hillsdale, NJ: Erlbaum.

Baron, N., & Ling, R. (2011). Necessary smileys and useless periods: Redefining punctuation in electronically-mediated communication. *Visible Language, 45,* 45–67.

Bayer, J. B., & Campbell, S. W. (2012). Texting while driving on automatic: Considering the frequency-independent side of habit. *Computers in Human Behavior, 28,* 2083–2090. doi: 10.1016/j.chb.2012.06.012

Berger, P., & Luckmann, T. (1967). *The social construction of reality: A treatise in the sociology of knowledge.* New York: Anchor.

Bourdieu, P. (1977). *Outline of a theory of practice.* Cambridge: Cambridge University Press.

Campbell, S. W., & Kwak, N. (2011). Mobile communication and civil society: Linking patterns and places of use to engagement with others in public. *Human Communication Research, 37*(2), 207–222. doi: 10.1111/j.1468-2958.2010.01399.x

Castells, M. (2007). Communication, power, and counter-power in the network society. *International Journal of Communication, 1.* Retrieved from: http://ijoc.org/ojs/index.php/ijoc/article/view/46

Chib, A. (2013). The promise and peril of mHealth for developing countries. *Mobile Media & Communication, 1*(1) 69–75. doi: 10.1177/2050157912459502

Collins, R. (2004). *Interaction ritual chains.* Princeton, NJ: Princeton University Press.

Donner, J. (2008). Research approaches to mobile use in the developing world: A review of the literature. *The Information Society, 24,* 140–159. doi: 10.1080/01972240802019970

Durkheim, E. (1938). *The rules of the sociological method.* New York: Free Press.

Durkheim, E. (1995). *The elementary forms of religious life.* Glencoe, IL: Free Press.

Fortunati, L. (2002). The mobile phone: Towards new categories and social relations. *Information, Communication, & Society, 5,* 513–528. doi: 10.1080/136911 80208538803

Gardner, B. (2012). Habit as automaticity, not frequency. *The European Health Psychologist, 14,* 32–36. http://www.ehps.net/ehp/issues/2012/v14iss2_June2012/14_2_Gardner.pdf

Giddens, A. (1984). *The constitution of society: Outline of the theory of structuration.* Cambridge: Polity Press.

Goffman, E. (1959). *The presentation of self in everyday life.* New York: Doubleday Anchor Books.

Goffman, E. (1963). *Behavior in public places: Notes on the social organization of gatherings.* New York: The Free Press.

Goffman, E. (1967). *Interaction ritual: Essays on face-to-face behavior.* New York: Pantheon.

Goggin, G. (2011). Telephone media: An old story. In D. Park, N. Jankowski, & S. Jones (Eds.), *The long history of new media: Technology, historiography, and contextualizing newness* (pp. 231–252). New York: Peter Lang.

Haddon, L. (2003). Domestication and mobile telephony. In J. Katz (Ed.), *Machines that become us* (pp. 43–56). New Brunswick, NJ: Transaction.

Haddon, L., & Kommonen, K.-H. (2005). Interdisciplinary explorations: A dialogue between a sociologist and a design group. In L. Haddon (Ed.), *International collaborative research: Cross-cultural differences and cultures of research.* Brussels: COST.

Hård af Segerstad, Y. (2005). Language use in Swedish mobile text messaging. In R. Ling & P. Pedersen (Eds.), *Mobile communications: Renegotiation of the social sphere* (pp. 335–349). London: Springer.

Horst, H. A., & Miller, D. (2005). From kinship to link-up: Cell phones and social networking in Jamaica. *Current Anthropology, 46,* 755–778. doi: 10.1086/432650

Humphreys, L. (2007). Mobile social networks and spatial practice: A case study of Dodgeball. *Journal of Computer-Mediated Communication, 13*(1), article 17. Retrieved from: http://jcmc.indiana.edu/vol13/issue1/humphreys.html

International Telecommunication Union (2012). The world in 2011: ICT facts and figures. Retrieved from: http://www.itu.int/ITU-D/ict/facts/2011/material/ICTFactsFigures2011.pdf

Jacobsen, M. H. (2010). Goffman through the looking glass: From "classical" to contemporary Goffman. In M. Jacobsen (Ed.), *The contemporary Goffman.* New York: Routledge.

Katz, J. (2008). Mainstream mobiles in daily life: Perspectives and prospects. In J. Katz (Ed.), *Handbook of mobile communication studies* (pp. 433–445). Cambridge, MA: MIT Press.

LaRose, R. (2010). The problem of media habits. *Communication Theory, 20,* 194–222. doi: 10.1111/j.1468-2885.2010.01360.x

Ling, R. (2004). *The mobile connection: The cell phone's impact on society.* San Francisco, CA: Morgan Kaufmann.

Ling, R. (2008). *New tech, new ties: How mobile communication is reshaping social cohesion.* Cambridge, MA: MIT Press.

Ling, R. (2012). *Taken for grantedness: The embedding of mobile communication into society.* Cambridge, MA: MIT Press.

Ling, R., & Campbell, S. W. (Eds.). (2009). *The reconstruction of space and time: Mobile communication practices.* New Brunswick, NJ: Transaction Publishers.

Oishi, S., Kesebir, S., & Snyder, B. H. (2009). Sociology: A lost connection in social psychology. *Personality and Social Psychology Review, 13,* 334–353. doi: 10.1177/1088868309347835

Orbell, S., & Verplanken, B. (2010). The automatic component of habit in health behavior: Habit as cue-contingent automaticity. *Health Psychology, 29,* 374–383. doi: 10.1037/a0019596

Orlikowski, W. J. (2000). Using technology and constituting structures. *Organizational Science, 3*, 404–428. doi: 10.1287/orsc.11.4.404.14600

Oulasvirta, A., Rattenbury, T., Ma, L., & Raita, E. (2012). Habits make smartphone use more pervasive. *Personal Ubiquitous Computing, 16*(1), 105–114. doi: 10.1007/s00779-011-0412-2

Peters, O. (2009). A social cognitive perspective on mobile communication technology use and adoption. *Social Science Computer Review, 27*(1), 76–95. doi: 10.1177/0894439308322594

Silverstone, R., & Haddon, L. (1996) Design and domestication of information and communication technologies: Technical change and everyday life. In R. Silverstone & R. Mansell (Eds.), *Communication by design: The politics of information and communication technologies* (pp. 44–74). Oxford: Oxford University Press.

Silverstone, R., Hirsch, E., & Morley, D. (1992). Information and communication technologies and moral economy of the household. In R. Silverstone & E. Hirsch (Eds.), *Consuming technologies: Media and information in domestic spaces* (pp. 15–31). London: Routledge.

Vincent, J. (2006). Emotional attachment and mobile phones. *Knowledge, Technology, and Policy, 19*(1), 39–44. doi: 10.1007/s12130-006-1013-7

Walsh, S. P., White, K. M., Cox, S., & Young, R. M. (2011). Keeping in constant touch: The predictors of young Australians' mobile phone involvement. *Computers in Human Behavior, 27*, 333–342. doi: 10.1016/j.chb.2010.08.011

Walsh, S. P., White, K. M., & Young, R. M. (2010). Needing to connect: The effect of self and others on young people's involvement with their mobile phones. *Australian Journal of Psychology, 62*, 194–203. doi: 10.1080/00049530903567229

Webster, J. G. (2009). The role of structure in media choice. In T. Hartmann (Ed.), *Media choice: A theoretical and empirical overview* (pp. 221–233). New York & London: Routledge.

Webster, J. G. (2011). The duality of media: A structurational theory of public attention. *Communication Theory, 21*, 43–66. doi: 10.1111/j.1468-2885.2010.01375.x

Whitbred, R., Fonti, F., Steglich, C., & Contractor, N. (2011). From microactions to macrostructure and back: A structurational approach to the evolution of organizational networks. *Human Communication Research, 37*, 404–433. doi: 10.1111/j.1468-2958.2011.01404.x

Yates, J., & Orlikowski, W. J. (2002). Genre systems: Structuring interaction through communicative norms. *Journal of Business Communication, 39*, 13–35. doi: 10.1177/002194360203900102

13

THE PLACE WHERE OUR SOCIAL NETWORKS RESIDE

Social Media and Sociality

Kelly Quinn and Zizi Papacharissi

The social life and impact of online media invite intense speculation from the academia and the general public. In an early study of how people make friends online, Parks and Floyd (1996) examined friend-making practices that traversed offline and online, and firmly concluded that the "ultimate social impact of cyberspace will not flow from its exotic capabilities, but rather from the fact that people are putting it to ordinary, even mundane, social uses" (p. 94). Social networks have always been a part of everyday life and sociality. They present the foundational map for how individuals associate socially. Social network sites are platforms that host our networks, and they are part of a long history of architectures, material, virtual, or imagined, that do so. In this context, a social network site is an architecture, that is,

> a networked communication platform in which participants 1) have uniquely identifiable profiles that consist of user-supplied content, content provided by other users, and/or system-provided data; 2) can publicly articulate connections that can be viewed and traversed by others; and 3) can consume, produce, and/or interact with streams of user-generated content provided by their connections on the site.
>
> (Ellison & boyd, 2013, p. 158)

This definition is broad enough to encompass most forms of social media today, and to describe a diverse landscape of socially capable online platforms that is constantly evolving.

Amidst the growing popularity of social media, three grand questions dominate public discourse and speculation about their impact. A first question

189

revolves around the potential of these media to make people more or less social. Decades of research on various media, including net-based ones, reveal that typically, following an initial period of displacement, most people integrate new media into their everyday habitus in a manner that is supportive of their typical routines (e.g., Kraut et al., 1998, 2002; Papacharissi, 2002). More interesting questions for scholars lie in the changing shape of sociality and context for identity that social media afford, pointing to a networked sociality, networked sense of self, and modalities of networked individualism (Papacharissi, 2010; Rainie & Wellman, 2012). A second question then emerges around the social impact of so-called social media, and whether they in fact connect us online by further separating us offline. Aside from the digital dualism that this question introduces, by imposing a false dichotomy between our offline and online interactions (e.g., Jurgenson, 2012; Papacharissi, 2005), this concern is imprecisely premised: All media foster communication, and thus, by definition are social. Moreover, employing the term "social media" implies that some media are inherently social, while others are a-social or, even, potentially anti-social. A more interesting research direction may be pursued along the lines of the changing form of sociality, and the texture it develops as it combines and collapses media and audiences. Finally, a third source of concern forms around questions of how social the spaces rendered by social media are. Setting aside the fact that people render spaces social, more interesting questions for scholars lie in examining the different behaviors distinct social spaces, online and offline ones, invite, and why that is the case.

Social scientists have addressed all of these questions through compelling research focusing on related themes, grouped into three broad categories: sociability, publicity, and privacy. Thus, this chapter examines what research has to say about how we act socially, how we inadvertently or knowingly become public, and how we try to stay private through our use of social network sites. Taking a cue from the seminal Parks and Floyd (1996) study, we explicate the mundane and ordinary, as that is rendered socially through our uses of social media. We organize our review of relevant research on social media to reflect key findings on publicity, sociality, and privacy, as those are enabled through our use of social media. We then provide an overview of theories that have informed these findings and have been further developed as a result of ongoing research in this area. We conclude by considering questions that remain unanswered and important next steps for researchers.

Areas of Inquiry in Social Media Scholarship

Publicity

Profile creation can be considered a rite of initiation for social media use and the first step toward micro-publicity, as individuals literally "write themselves into being" (boyd, 2007b, p. 129) within the media platform. As the locus of social media activity, the profile includes not only biographical details, but also content that has been created or contributed by the profile owner and his or her connections. This might include: visual images in the form of photographs and video clips; links to other Internet content such as websites and new stories; and messages regarding activities, reactions, and commentary in the form of status updates, tweets, and wall posts.

Early research on profiles concentrated on more generalized motives for creation (Haferkamp & Krämer, 2010), but more recently research has centered on the creation of profiles and how personality characteristics are displayed, including such dimensions as narcissism (Buffardi & Campbell, 2010), neuroticism (Amichai-Hamburger & Vinitzky, 2010), extraversion (Correa, Hinsley, & de Zúñiga, 2010), and self-esteem (Christofides, Muise, & Desmarais, 2009). The self-disclosure that takes place through profile creation is seen as important to relationship building (Krasnova, Spiekermann, Koroleva, & Hildebrand, 2010) and, specifically, to the generation of trust (Dwyer, Hiltz, & Passerini, 2007; Golbeck, 2009). The amount of information provided in a profile has been positively correlated to the number connections that an individual has, suggesting that the establishment of common ground and signals are important elements to achieve trust and legitimacy within communities of users (Lampe, Ellison, & Steinfield, 2007).

Because information provided in the profile is under the control of the creator, profile creation is seen as an activity of impression management, a performance of identity (Gilpin, 2010; Krämer & Winter, 2008; Pearson, 2009; Ringrose, 2011) that is at once public and intimate, and which may generate a proximal relationship with the viewer that may or may not exist in reality. As a portrayal of oneself, profiles require cooperation from others for ongoing validation and maintenance (Back et al., 2010; Pearson, 2009). Identity may be idealized (Manago, Graham, Greenfield, & Salimkhan, 2008) or not (Back et al., 2010) or performed in gendered and sexualized ways (Ringrose, 2011; Van Doorn, 2009). The profile can be leveraged to promote or "brand" the self and, when coupled with ongoing practices of identity performativity such as status enhancement, treating connections as fans, and creating content aimed at preserving popularity or drawing attention, becomes a tool of microcelebrity (Senft, 2008; Marwick & boyd, 2011).

Information contained in the profile is not only managed by the owner, it also contributes to how that individual is evaluated by others. The information that is contributed by the profile owner is often deemed unreliable by others, who view information as not necessarily representative of reality (Haferkamp & Krämer, 2010). Alternatively, information generated by others and posted to a profile, such as comments and photos posted by friends, are deemed influential and reliable bases for impression formation (Utz, 2010; Walther, Van Der Heide, Hamel, & Shulman, 2009), as are an individual's visible connections (Tom Tong, Van Der Heide, Langwell, & Walther, 2008). Visual information, and in particular the physical attractiveness of one's connections, has been found to contribute to attractiveness ratings (Walther, Van Der Heide, Kim, Westerman, & Tong, 2008), and importantly relate to how these platforms are used for relationship initiation and maintenance.

Sociality

Sociality, as rendered through the visible articulation of connections, has been the foundation for a significant line of inquiry by social media researchers. Connections, both unidirectional and reciprocal, are a visible sign that a link exists between users of a particular social medium. Displays of reciprocal connection are an implicit verification of identity; they create a mechanism to establish trust and cooperation (Donath, 2007) and also a means to define social position, akin to name dropping in the face-to-face environment (Donath & boyd, 2004). But perhaps more importantly, the list of relationships displays a view of the individual within the context of their own network of relationships (Donath, 2007; Pearson, 2009). The sociality that plays out between these connections is centered on sharing practices (Brandtzæg, Lüders, & Skjetne, 2010; Papacharissi & Gibson, 2011): The sharing of information about oneself in the form of status updates and photos; the sharing of information from third parties such as links to news items and websites; and the sharing of information with respect to others in the form of comments, pokes, and photo tags.

Social media representations of an individual's social network are inescapably flat, meaning that from the user's perspective all relationships hold equal value. This presents challenges for users to differentiate the sharing activities that take place. In the offline world, individuals may use time and space to keep separate portions of their lives which may be incompatible (Donath & boyd, 2004). Online, these contexts become jumbled and decontextualized, with work relationships and personal friendships muddled rather than being contained in separate spaces. This form of technological compression is deemed "context collapse" (Marwick & boyd, 2010) because it entails the merging of audiences of multiple milieux, both real and imagined, into a singular entity. Individuals may manage this assimilation both interpersonally and technologically by utilizing different platforms to engage personal and professional relationships (Quinn, 2013; Wesch, 2009), or by managing identity for specific contexts (DiMicco & Millen, 2007).

Because the visualization of these connections places emphasis on the relationship itself, social media has been a lens for gauging relational quality. Connections in social media are unnuanced, meaning they lack distinction relative to relationship strength, and decontextualized, meaning they lack information on the circumstances of the relationship (Donath & boyd, 2004). Despite these drawbacks, varying measures of social media interactivity have been used to indicate relational strength, drawing on Granovetter's (1973) characterization of relationships as strong and weak ties. The measures used to determine relational strength include such factors as the frequency of contact, bidirectional acknowledgement of the connection, duration of the relationship, and the social homogeneity of those joined in a tie (Baym & Ledbetter, 2009; Gilbert & Karahalios, 2009). Determining relational quality by these types of measures is consistent with the concept of media multiplexity (Haythornthwaite, 2005), a principle which suggests that use of multiple media forms is indicative of stronger relationships; social media use contributes to this pattern of relationship formation (Ledbetter, 2009). Social media use has also been positively correlated to the size and diversity of an individual's network (Hampton, Sessions, & Her, 2011).

The value in one's connections has been framed as social capital by scholars (Lin, 2001; Williams, 2006), and the use of social media to accomplish higher levels of social capital (Ellison, Steinfield, & Lampe, 2007, 2011; Valenzuela, Park, & Kee, 2009) has been an important line of inquiry. The ability to create and maintain weaker ties is considered a potential advantage of social media use, because a relatively larger number of connections can be maintained (Donath, 2007). Correspondingly, the capacity to passively monitor weak connections without significant effort leaves open the possibility that they will become stronger, and thus more valuable, over time (Levin, Walter, & Murnighan, 2010; Pearson, 2009).

It is the totality of one's connections, the network, and its interactive effects that has given rise to new concepts that address traditional conundrums related to sociality, however. "Networked individualism" (Rainie & Wellman, 2012) attends to the enduring tensions between community and individual, and argues that the connectivity enabled through all forms of technology, including social media, enables individuals to operate as connected individuals rather than embedded within groups. "Networked publics" (Ito, 2008) acknowledges the deeply intertwined and embedded nature of engaged audiences, technologies, and media, and suggests that social media has restructured both the interaction space of the public sphere and the imagined community that emerges through the combined interactivity of technology, people, and practices. "Networked privacy" (boyd & Marwick, 2011) addresses the conflict inherent in maintaining privacy while socializing in the public venue of social media and the public-by-default nature of its content; it conceives of privacy as a coordinated and communal quality.

Finally, the nature of social interaction that takes place through these media platforms has prompted examination of the motivations to use social media and the gratifications such media use brings. Individuals use social media platforms to satisfy information needs, to enjoy camaraderie and social connection, as a means of social investigation, for entertainment, and to provide social updating to others (Bumgarner, 2007; Chen, 2011; Park, Kee, & Valenzuela, 2009; Quan-Haase & Young, 2010). Users perceive that social media use is important to meeting social capital needs (Ellison, Vitak, Steinfield, Gray, & Lampe, 2011) and, because self-disclosure is integral to its use, there is recognition that privacy might be compromised due to this powerful social capital pull (Papacharissi & Gibson, 2011; Taddicken & Jers, 2011).

Privacy

The navigational capabilities that enable users to view and traverse the networks of others through hypertext links present a foundational feature of social network sites that support publicity and sociality, but also challenge privacy management for individuals. Typically, a profile viewer can not only scan a visible listing of connections within a profile, but can also jump to the profiles of each of the individuals listed as a connection. The visibility of personal information on those linked profiles may be more or less limited, depending on the privacy settings of the profile owner and the nature of his or her relationship with the viewer. It is this condition of access, however, that has garnered major attention. The related research activity that has been undertaken may be grouped under the umbrella of surveillance and privacy.

The availability of personally identifying profile information and its potential to create privacy threats has seized the imagination of the popular press and scholars alike (e.g., see Debatin, Lovejoy, Horn, & Hughes, 2009; *New York Times*, 2012). There is a tendency to view this form of disclosure within social media use as a binary trade-off between privacy and publicness (Baym & boyd, 2012; boyd, 2007a; Lange, 2007), which has limited appreciation of how these technologies are viewed and used by individuals. More recent work has acknowledged that this trade-off has always been part of sociability (Papacharissi & Gibson, 2011) and is considered as a part of intimacy between family and friends (Taddicken & Jers, 2011). This recognition, that social media use is integrally related to relationship development and maintenance, has been an important step to understanding user behaviors with respect to privacy and has permitted scholars to begin to untangle the "privacy paradox" (Barnes, 2006).

The privacy paradox relates to a perception that there is a significant gap between user privacy preferences (Acquisti & Gross, 2006; Stutzman, Capra, & Thompson, 2011; Tufekci, 2007), which include concerns about privacy breaches and threats, and the lack of privacy enhancing behaviors by users, such as engaging privacy controls and limiting disclosures of personal information (Krasnova et al., 2010). This contradiction has raised important questions related to potential cultural and normative shifts in privacy expectations (Raynes-Goldie, 2010) and the significance of digital literacies in the implementation of privacy technologies (Debatin et al., 2009). Privacy regulation behaviors such as social steganography (boyd & Marwick, 2011), untagging photos (Ahern et al., 2007), the use of aliases (Raynes-Goldie, 2010), and selective disclosure (Schmidt, 2011) are significant to understanding this paradox, as they become adaptive mechanisms to curb intrusions to the private realm, and contribute to how we understand social media use in the context of interpersonal relationships.

The ability to navigate friendship links enables a form of social surveillance (Albrechtslund, 2008; Tokunaga, 2011) as profiles reveal information about their owners about who their friends are, what their interests might be and, perhaps most importantly, recent activities. The ability of individuals to observe the activities of others (Andrejevic, 2004), and especially romantic partners (Marshall, Bejanyan, Di Castro, & Lee, 2013; Tokunaga, 2011), has raised questions about the nature and role of this scrutiny. Though aggregate profile information may be somewhat limited at the discretion of the profile creator, social media platforms have not traditionally permitted discrimination among individual viewers once a connection is established (though Facebook's privacy settings have recently changed to permit greater control in this area). Early studies suggested these surveillance behaviors were of a benign nature, enabling "social searching" (Lampe, Ellison, & Steinfield, 2006) or "social investigation" (Joinson, 2008) to further relationships that had been initiated in offline settings, as they involve "participatory surveillance" (Albrechtslund, 2008) which is mutual and horizontal in nature.

More recently there has been growing concern regarding the surveillance implications of the use of profile information by corporate interests and governments (Fuchs, 2012; Rooksby & Sommerville, 2011). The specter of limitless access to profile information by social media providers has raised questions related to the commodification of personal information and the surveillance potential these technologies possess due to the asymmetrical power relationships between providers, viewers, and profile owners (Fuchs, 2010; Shklovski & Valtysson, 2012).

In summary, the important questions asked through social media research to date have been concentrated in three primary areas. Publicity research has concerned identity practices that are carried out through the use of social media. This includes the examination of the processes and meaning surrounding profile creation and maintenance, the practices of microcelebrity and audience management, and the activities of impression management by profile creators and impression formation by profile viewers. Research in sociality has concentrated on the networks of connection themselves, and the habits and routines that are evidenced within these complex systems of relationship. Research in this area includes analysis of relationship differentiation and measurement, valuation of the network as a potential resource source, and the gratifications of social media use. Privacy and surveillance comprise the third dimension of social media research to date and has keyed on the nature of self-disclosure. The apparent discrepancy between privacy concerns related to social media use, a lack of privacy enhancing behaviors, and concern that these media enable both benign and more malignant forms of surveillance has raised important questions related to how these media forms are understood and employed.

Primary Theories

As researchers examine the use of social media and its impact on sociality, a few key theories have emerged as critical foundations to scholarly interpretation. The following sections provide detail on the predominant theoretical lenses that have been employed in each of the three research dimensions of publicity, sociality, and privacy and surveillance.

Publicity

Interpretations of the publicity dimensions of social media use have been largely derived from a symbolic interactionist perspective of identity management, that is, that the self is a product of interaction rather than being a fixed entity. Goffman's (1973) dramaturgical metaphor of the presentation of self as a performance has been quite powerful with respect to identity research in social media, as his suggestion that individuals perform their identities within a bounded area resonates with social media features such as profiles and update feeds. The symbolic interactionist interpretation of self-presentation is both managed and idealized, and it is important to recognize that it is accomplished with cooperation and assistance from co-actors, activities, and a stage/setting. This makes the presentation of self contextual and referential, which resonates with the types of interaction that is played out through the milieu of social media and its inherent visibility of connection networks, profiles, and activity displays.

Identity as performance also assumes the presence of an audience, and implies use of a front and backstage, a place where the performance can be knowingly contradicted because barriers to the audience's perceptions are erected. The imagined audience (Brake, 2012; Litt, 2012) is a second prevailing metaphor that scholars of social media and publicity have employed. A "mental conceptualization of the people with whom we are communicating" (Litt, 2012, p. 331), the imagined audience is distinct from an actual audience, with whom visibility and exchange is possible. Social media relegate an audience to invisibility, as its size, composition, boundaries, accessibility, and cue availability are altered and difficult to determine with any accuracy (Litt, 2012). While actual and imagined audiences may be comprised of members both known and unknown to the individual, it is misalignment between these two conceptions of audience that has received consideration in the form of context collapse (Marwick & boyd, 2010; Wesch, 2009) and impression formation (Walther et al., 2008).

Sociality

The individual networks of social media users have been conceptualized with the framework of more traditional notions of community, along the lines of previously argued ideas of community as "personal" (Bender, 1978) and "imagined" (Anderson, 1991). Social networks have also been theorized to represent an individual's intersecting social spheres (Simmel, 1955), which emphasizes an individual's relational contexts, and also as having relational foci that might include individuals, places, social positions, activities, or groups (Feld & Carter, 1998). This network imagery has somewhat limited versatility for social media research, however, because an individual's entire network may not be represented within a single social media platform. Thus more newly developed models such as networked individualism (Rainie & Wellman, 2012; Wellman et al., 2006) and community as process (Fernback, 2007) may hold more promise.

The architecture of social media sites positions the individual user at the center of a system, an ecosystem, which is comprised of nodes (other individuals in the system) and edges (the relationships between individuals). Various strains of network theory have been employed to look at the individual relationships that are articulated through social media. Granovetter's (1973) characterization of interpersonal relationships as being made up of "strong," "weak", and "absent" ties has strongly influenced how researchers conceive of the relationships that are visualized through social media. Media multiplexity theory (Haythornthwaite, 2005; Haythornthwaite & Wellman, 1998) builds on this characterization and proposes that media use is a characteristic of the strength of the relationship: Those in stronger relationships use more media with greater frequency to connect with one another than those in weaker relationships. This theory has enabled researchers to connect social media use to relational strength (Baym & Ledbetter, 2009; Ledbetter, 2009) and also to growth in network size and diversity (Hampton et al., 2011).

Social capital theory (Lin, 2001) underscores much of the research involving motivation for social media use, and connects it to sociability. Social capital theory acknowledges that one's network of relationships provides the framework for the production of capital, and that investment in social relations is the mechanism with which individuals gain advantage (Lin & Erikson, 2008). In other words, individuals engage in activities that deliberately build access to social capital resources with the expectation that they will be able to collect those resources at some point in time. Thus, social media use is seen as integral to social capital formation (Ellison, Steinfield, & Lampe, 2007), but also gives weight to its ability to support weak relationships that may provide value in the future (Levin, Walter, & Murnighan, 2010).

Finally, the user-centered focus of uses and gratifications theory (see Katz, Blumler, & Gurevitch, 1974, and Ruggiero, 2000, for history) has provided a foundation for questions related to the motivations for social media use. Uses and gratifications is an approach that dates to the earliest empirical mass communication research of Lazarfeld, Hertzog, and Lasswell (Katz, Blumler, & Gurevitch, 1974). The underlying premise is that individuals use media, either purposefully or unintentionally, as a means to fulfill cognitive and emotional needs such as surveillance, information and learning, entertainment, personal identity, parasocial interaction, companionship, and escape (Lin, 2002). Early media studies proposed that media use fulfilled functions of personal relationships, personal identity, surveillance, and diversion (McQuail, Blumler, & Brown, 1972), and that gratifications could be derived from media content, exposure to the medium, or the social context that typifies the exposure (Katz et al., 1974). Because the same set of media materials is capable of serving a multiplicity of uses and gratifications, uses and gratifications theory has been productive from a research standpoint as it enables the ability to view social network sites from both a profile owner's and profile viewer's perspective.

Privacy and Surveillance

The theoretical understanding of how social media use and privacy intersect is grounded in an understanding that privacy is maintained by a selective control of access to the self (Altman, 1975). Because social media are seen primarily as tools of communication, researchers have keyed on theories of privacy regulation (Altman, 1975) and communication privacy management (Petronio, 2002) to explain how privacy, sociality, and social media use overlap. Privacy regulation theory (Altman, 1975) focuses broadly on the linkage between privacy and disclosure, a process that is intertwined with relationship development. Communication privacy management theory (Petronio, 2002) considers privacy regulation as a rule-based system that is used to manage accessibility to private information; hence, communication privacy management is a negotiated process, between an individual and others, that establishes how information will be kept and managed. Both of these perspectives underscore a dialectical process between openness and closedness, and researchers have interpreted social media user behaviors in this same binary public/private dichotomy.

More recently, the concept of contextual integrity (Nissenbaum, 2010) has provided a framework to understand privacy as a normative process governed by information contexts, actors, information types, and transmission principles which govern the constraint and flow of information. This perspective has enabled researchers to understand that threats to privacy occur when these norms are violated, or when information flows in ways that contradict the integrity of its context. This perspective has more utility for social media researchers as it provides a basis to disentangle seemingly contradictory concepts such as the privacy paradox.

In summary, social media researchers have largely drawn on traditional media theories to interpret user behaviors and activities in social media platforms. The identity practices of publicity have been based in symbolic interactionist perspectives, with identity seen as performance and the audience viewed at once as imagined and real. Research in sociality was initially grounded in more traditional notions of community; however, the tenets of network theory have shaped more recent interpretations of sociality in terms of the social capital resources that are provided through social media use. This utilitarian approach has been further reinforced by uses and gratifications perspectives, which contextualize media use by its functions and the needs its use fulfills. The study of privacy and surveillance has utilized frameworks supported by privacy regulation and boundary management theories, which has led to a forced binary public/private interpretation of social media use.

While providing a framework to interpret these new technologies, the use of these more traditional theories also places constraints on how behaviors and actions are interpreted and understood because they attempt to locate these media within existing scholarly frameworks. The danger in this approach is to visualize these new media forms as merely new forms of old media and not as enabling new forms of sociality and interaction. The next section will outline some new directions for social media research to confront, as scholars continue in the quest to understand the impact of these technologies on sociality and social life.

Next Steps

The future of social media research is at once challenging and limitless, and should be guided by the research that has not yet been undertaken in meaningful ways. One area that deserves more exploration is the temporal dimensions of social media use, both with users of various ages as well as usage over time. The majority of social media studies have examined populations of young adults, whether through convenience or because this user demographic has the deepest and widest penetration of social media use. However, research on older adults (Madden, 2010) and children (O'Keeffe & Clarke-Pearson, 2011) suggest that social media use among other age groups is growing rapidly. It will be important to consider how social media use among each of these generational groups may differ with their related levels of life experience, and also how usage patterns of each group changes over time and with life experience. The temporal dimensions of life experiences also provide interesting intersections with social media use. Future research might consider how social media use and life stages interconnect with identity performance and play, for example, and examine how identity representations in profiles and postings might change at varying points in life. Alternatively, the impacts of social media use on the processes of friendship and relational maintenance might be examined, along with how these might contribute to relational elasticity over lifelong relational processes.

Social media platforms are growing smaller and increasingly visual as recent entrants such as Pinterest and Instagram have joined with longer-standing platforms such as YouTube and Flickr in the social media milieu. Yet, the visual aspects of social media engagement have been largely under-explored. As these more ocular platforms gain prominence, it will become important to understand the communicative and social qualities that make them attractive to users, qualities that extend beyond traditional notions of sharing and entertainment. Understanding how these media forms contribute to information search and retrieval, satisfy curiosity, and enhance sociality will further our awareness of how interactions are shaped by these technologies and how the technologies, in turn, are shaped by social practices.

We have also seen a surge in social media platforms that operate in tandem with one another, such as Instagram, FourSquare, and Spotify. The growing use of mobile platforms to access these technologies intersects with interoperability as well, creating new opportunities for norms of social behavior to be extended and altered. As these social media forms converge, complement, and substitute for one another, so does their impact on sociality and social interaction. The importance of understanding these processes and interaction effects will intensify as these technologies proliferate and become more pervasive.

Finally, the social, cultural, and opportunity divides that result from social media engagement, or the lack thereof, and the literacies that are required for social media use are significant, if poorly understood to date. Recent research has demonstrated that those with lower digital skill levels report fewer privacy enhancing behaviors while using social media sites than those with greater skills (boyd & Hargittai, 2010), and that higher levels of Internet skills predict certain types of social media use (Hargittai & Litt, 2011). When coupled with research relating increased social capital resources with social media use (Ellison, Steinfield, & Lampe, 2007, 2011), these findings raise the potential that the implications of digital exclusion and a lack of digital skills may be more complex and significant than previously understood.

Conclusion

In conclusion, as a locus of social activity, social media continue to gain in relevance and import in everyday sociality. Research on the relationship between social media and sociality has received significant attention, yet faces substantial future opportunities to demonstrate its continued and symbiotic evolution. We have yet to determine how norms of sociality will be stretched and remediated through social media use or how conceptions of relationships will change if the ability to stay connected, if only weakly, persists. Yet, these are aspects of consequence to our personal, professional, and social relationships. To date, research has been concentrated on three dimensions of social media practice: publicity, sociality, and privacy and surveillance. Future research programs should key on the temporal dimensions of life experience and social media use, the visual aspects of social media platforms, the effects of various social media platforms interacting in tandem, and the social, cultural, and opportunity divides that result from a lack of social media literacy skills and engagement.

References

Acquisti, A., & Gross, R. (2006). Imagined communities: Awareness, information sharing, and privacy on the Facebook. In G. Danezis & P. Golle (Eds.), *Privacy enhancing technologies* (pp. 36–58). Cambridge, UK: Springer-Verlag. doi: 10.1007/11957454_3

Ahern, S., Eckles, D., Good, N. S., King, S., Naaman, M., & Nair, R. (2007). Over-exposed? Privacy patterns and considerations in online and mobile photo sharing. *Proceedings of the SIGCHI Conference on Human Factors on Computing Systems—CHI '07* (p. 357). New York: ACM Press. doi: 10.1145/1240624.1240683

Albrechtslund, A. (2008). Online social networking as participatory surveillance. *First Monday, 13*(3), 1–11. Retrieved from http://firstmonday.org/article/view/2142/1949

Altman, I. (1975). *The environment and social behavior: Privacy, personal space, territory, crowding.* Monterey, CA: Brooks/Cole Publishing.

Amichai-Hamburger, Y., & Vinitzky, G. (2010). Social network use and personality. *Computers in Human Behavior, 26*(6), 1289–1295. doi: 10.1016/j.chb.2010.03.018

Anderson, B. (1991). *Imagined communities: Reflections on the origin and spread of nationalism* (Rev. ed.). London: Verso.

Andrejevic, M. (2004). The work of watching one another: Lateral surveillance, risk, and governance. *Surveillance & Society, 2*(4), 479–497.

Back, M. D., Stopfer, J. M., Vazire, S., Gaddis, S., Schmukle, S. C., Egloff, B., & Gosling, S. D. (2010). Facebook profiles reflect actual personality, not self-idealization. *Psychological science, 21*(3), 372–374. doi: 10.1177/0956797609360756

Barnes, S. B. (2006). A privacy paradox: Social networking in the United States. *First Monday, 11*(9), 1–12. Retrieved from http://firstmonday.org/ojs/index.php/fm/article/view/1394/1312

Baym, N. K., & boyd, d. (2012). Socially mediated publicness: An introduction. *Journal of Broadcasting & Electronic Media, 56*(3), 320–329. doi: 10.1080/08838151.2012.705200

Baym, N. K., & Ledbetter, A. (2009). Tunes that bind: Predicting friendship strength in a music-based social network. *Information, Communication & Society, 12*(3), 408–427. doi: 10.1080/13691180802635430

Bender, T. (1978). *Community and social change in America.* New Brunswick, NJ: Rutgers University Press.

boyd, d. (2007a). Social network sites: Public, private, or what? *Knowledge Tree, 13*, 1–7. Retrieved from http://kt.flexiblelearning.net.au/tkt2007/?page_id=28

boyd, d. (2007b). Why youth (heart) social network sites: The role of networked publics in teenage social life. In D. Buckingham (Ed.), *MacArthur Foundation series on digital learning—youth, identity, and digital media volume* (pp. 119–142). Cambridge, MA: MIT Press.

boyd, d., & Hargittai, E. (2010). Facebook privacy settings: Who cares? *First Monday, 15*(8), 1–17. Retrieved from http://firstmonday.org/ojs/index.php/fm/article/view/3086

boyd, d., & Marwick, A. E. (2011). *Social steganography: Privacy in networked publics.* Boston, MA. Retrieved from http://www.danah.org/papers/2011/Steganography-ICAVersion.pdf

Brake, D. R. (2012). Who do they think they're talking to? Framings of the audience by social media users. *International Journal of Communication, 6*, 1056–1076.

Brandtzæg, P. B., Lüders, M., & Skjetne, J. H. (2010). Too many Facebook "friends"? Content sharing and sociability versus the need for privacy in social network sites. *International Journal of Human-Computer Interaction, 26*(11–12), 1006–1030. doi: 10.1080/10447318.2010.516719

Buffardi, L. E., & Campbell, W. K. (2010). Narcissism and social networking web sites. *Personality and Social Psychology Bulletin, 34*, 1303–1314. doi: 10.1177/0146167208320061

Bumgarner, B. (2007). You have been poked: Exploring the uses and gratifications of Facebook among emerging adults. *First Monday, 12*(11). Retrieved from http://firstmonday.org/htbin/cgiwrap/bin/ojs/index.php/fm/article/view/2026/1897

Chen, G. M. (2011). Tweet this: A uses and gratifications perspective on how active Twitter use gratifies a need to connect with others. *Computers in Human Behavior, 27*(2), 755–762. doi: 10.1016/j.chb.2010.10.023

Christofides, E., Muise, A., & Desmarais, S. (2009). Information disclosure and control on Facebook: Are they two sides of the same coin or two different processes? *Cyberpsychology & Behavior: The Impact of the Internet, Multimedia and Virtual Reality on Behavior and Society, 12*(3), 341–345. doi: 10.1089/cpb.2008.0226

Correa, T., Hinsley, A. W., & de Zúñiga, H. G. (2010). Who interacts on the web?: The intersection of users' personality and social media use. *Computers in Human Behavior, 26*(2), 247–253. doi: 10.1016/j.chb.2009.09.003

Debatin, B., Lovejoy, J. P., Horn, A.-K., & Hughes, B. N. (2009). Facebook and online privacy: Attitudes, behaviors, and unintended consequences. *Journal of Computer-Mediated Communication, 15*(1), 83–108. doi: 10.1111/j.1083-6101.2009.01494.x

DiMicco, J. M., & Millen, D. R. (2007). Identity management: Multiple presentations of self in Facebook. *Proceedings of the 2007 International ACM Conference on Supporting Group Work—GROUP '07* (p. 383). New York: ACM Press. doi: 10.1145/1316624.1316682

Donath, J. S. (2007). Signals in social supernets. *Journal of Computer-Mediated Communication, 13*(1), 231–251. doi: 10.1111/j.1083-6101.2007.00394.x

Donath, J., & boyd, d. (2004). Public displays of connection. *BT Technology Journal, 22*(4), 71–82. doi: 10.1023/B:BTTJ.0000047585.06264.cc

Dwyer, C., Hiltz, S. R., & Passerini, K. (2007). Trust and privacy concern within social networking sites: A comparison of Facebook and MySpace. *Proceedings of the Thirteenth Americas Conference on Information Systems.* Keystone, CO.

Ellison, N. B. & boyd, d. (2013). Sociality through social network sites. In W. H. Dutton (Ed.), *The Oxford handbook of Internet studies* (pp. 151–172). Oxford, UK: Oxford University Press.

Ellison, N. B., Steinfield, C., & Lampe, C. (2007). The benefits of Facebook "friends": Social capital and college students' use of online social network sites. *Journal of Computer-Mediated Communication, 12*(4), 1143–1168. doi: 10.1111/j.1083-6101.2007.00367.x

Ellison, N. B., Steinfield, C., & Lampe, C. (2011). Connection strategies: Social capital implications of Facebook-enabled communication practices. *New Media & Society.* doi: 10.1177/1461444810385389

Ellison, N. B., Vitak, J., Steinfield, C., Gray, R., & Lampe, C. (2011). Negotiating privacy concerns and social capital needs in a social media environment. In S. Trepte & L. Reinecke (Eds.), *Privacy online: Perspectives on privacy and self-disclosure in the social web* (pp. 19–32). Berlin & Heidelberg: Springer Berlin Heidelberg. doi: 10.1007/978-3-642-21521-6

Feld, S., & Carter, W. C. (1998). Foci of activity as changing contexts for friendship. In R. G. Adams & G. Allan (Eds.), *Placing friendship in context* (pp. 136–152). Cambridge: Cambridge University Press.

Fernback, J. (2007). Beyond the diluted community concept: A symbolic interactionist perspective on online social relations. *New Media & Society, 9*(1), 49–69. doi: 10.1177/1461444807072417

Fuchs, C. (2010). studiVZ: Social networking in the surveillance society. *Ethics and Information Technology, 12*(2), 171–185. doi: 10.1007/s10676-010-9220-z

Fuchs, C. (2012). The political economy of privacy on Facebook. *Television & New Media, 13*(2), 139–159. doi: 10.1177/1527476411415699

Gilbert, E., & Karahalios, K. (2009). Predicting tie strength with social media. *Proceedings of the 27th International Conference on Human Factors in Computing Systems—CHI '09* (pp. 211–220). doi: 10.1145/1518701.1518736

Gilpin, D. R. (2010). Working the Twittersphere: How public relations practitioners use microblogging for professional identity construction. In Z. Papacharissi (Ed.), *The networked self: Identity, community and culture on social network sites* (pp. 232–250). New York: Routledge.

Goffman, E. (1973). *The presentation of self in everyday life.* Woodstock, NY: Overlook Press.

Golbeck, J. (2009). Trust and nuanced profile similarity in online social networks. *ACM Transactions on the Web, 3*(4), 1–33. doi: 10.1145/1594173.1594174

Granovetter, M. S. (1973). The strength of weak ties. *American Journal of Sociology, 78*, 1360–1380.

Haferkamp, N., & Krämer, N. C. (2010). Creating a digital self: Impression management and impression formation on social network sites. In K. Drotner & K. C. Schrøder (Eds.), *Digital content creation: Perceptions, practices and perspectives* (pp. 129–146). New York: Peter Lang.

Hampton, K. N., Sessions, L. F., & Her, E. J. (2011). Core networks, social isolation, and new media. *Information, Communication & Society, 1* (July 2012), 130–155.

Hargittai, E., & Litt, E. (2011). The tweet smell of celebrity success: Explaining variation in Twitter adoption among a diverse group of young adults. *New Media & Society, 13*(5), 824–842. doi: 10.1177/1461444811405805

Haythornthwaite, C. (2005). Social networks and Internet connectivity effects. *Information, Communication & Society, 8*(2), 125–147. doi: 10.1080/13691180 500146185

Haythornthwaite, C., & Wellman, B. (1998). Work, friendship, and media use for information exchange in a networked organization. *Journal of the American Society for Information Science, 49*(12): 1101–1114. doi: 10.1002/ (SICI)1097-4571(1998)49:12<1101::AID-ASI6>3.3.CO;2-S

Ito, M. (2008). Introduction. In K. Varnelis (Ed.), *Networked publics* (pp. 1–14). Cambridge, MA: MIT Press.

Joinson, A. N. (2008). Looking at, looking up or keeping up with people? In *Proceedings of the Twenty-Sixth Annual CHI Conference on Human Factors in Computing Systems—CHI '08* (pp. 1027–1036). New York: ACM Press. doi: 10.1145/1357054.1357213

Jurgenson, N. (2012). When atoms meet bits: Social media, the mobile web and augmented revolution. *Future Internet, 4,* 83–91.

Katz, E., Blumler, J. G., & Gurevitch, M. (1974). Uses and gratifications research. *The Public Opinion Quarterly, 37*(4), 509–523.

Krämer, N. C., & Winter, S. (2008). Impression management 2.0. *Journal of Media Psychology: Theories, Methods, and Applications, 20*(3), 106–116. doi: 10.1027/1864-1105.20.3.106

Krasnova, H., Spiekermann, S., Koroleva, K., & Hildebrand, T. (2010). Online social networks: Why we disclose. *Journal of Information Technology, 25*(2), 109–125. doi: 10.1057/jit.2010.6

Kraut, R., Kiesler, S., Boneva, K., Cummings, J., Helgeson, J., & Crawford, A. (2002). Internet paradox revisited. *Journal of Social Issues, 58*(1), 49–74.

Kraut, R., Patterson, M., Lundmark, V., Kiesler, S., Mukophadhyay, T., & Scherlis, W. (1998). Internet paradox: A social technology that reduces social involvement and psychological well-being? *American Psychologist, 53,* 1017–1031.

Lampe, C., Ellison, N. B., & Steinfield, C. (2006). A face(book) in the crowd. *Proceedings of the 2006 20th Anniversary Conference on Computer Supported Cooperative Work—CSCW '06* (p. 167). New York: ACM Press. doi: 10.1145/11808 75.1180901

Lampe, C. A. C., Ellison, N., & Steinfield, C. (2007). A familiar face(book): Profile elements as signals in an online social network. *Proceedings of the SIGCHI Conference on Human Factors in Computing Systems—CHI '07* (p. 435). New York: ACM Press. doi: 10.1145/1240624.1240695

Lange, P. G. (2007). Publicly private and privately public: Social networking on YouTube. *Journal of Computer-Mediated Communication, 13*(1), 361–380. doi: 10.1111/j.1083-6101.2007.00400.x

Ledbetter, A. M. (2009). Patterns of media use and multiplexity: Associations with sex, geographic distance and friendship interdependence. *New Media & Society, 11*(7), 1187–1208. doi: 10.1177/1461444809342057

Levin, D. Z., Walter, J., & Murnighan, J. K. (2010). Dormant ties: The value of reconnecting. *Organization Science, 22*(4), 923–939. doi: 10.1287/orsc.1100.0576

Lin, C. A. (2002). Perceived gratifications of online media service use among potential users. *Telematics and Informatics, 19*(1), 3–19.

Lin, N. (2001). Building a network theory of social capital. In N. Lin, K. Cook, & R. S. Burt (Eds.), *Social capital: Theory and research* (pp. 3–29). New York: Aldine De Gruyter.

Lin, N., & Erikson, B. (2008). Theory, measurement, and the research enterprise on social capital. In N. Lin & B. Erikson (Eds.), *Social capital: An international research program* (pp. 1–24). Oxford: Oxford University Press.

Litt, E. (2012). Knock, knock. Who's there? The imagined audience. *Journal of Broadcasting & Electronic Media, 56*(3), 330–345. doi: 10.1080/08838151.2012.705195

Madden, M. (2010). *Older adults and social media.* Washington, DC: Pew Internet & American Life Project. Retrieved from http://pewinternet.org/~/media//Files/Reports/2010/Pew Internet - Older Adults and SocialMedia.pdf

Manago, A. M., Graham, M. B., Greenfield, P. M., & Salimkhan, G. (2008). Self-presentation and gender on MySpace. *Journal of Applied Developmental Psychology, 29*(6), 446–458. doi: 10.1016/j.appdev.2008.07.001

Marshall, T. C., Bejanyan, K., Di Castro, G., & Lee, R. A. (2013). Attachment styles as predictors of Facebook-related jealousy and surveillance in romantic relationships. *Personal Relationships, 20*(1), 1–22. doi: 10.1111/j.1475-6811.2011.01393.x

Marwick, A. E., & boyd, d. (2010). I tweet honestly, I tweet passionately: Twitter users, context collapse, and the imagined audience. *New Media & Society, 13*(1), 114–133. doi: 10.1177/1461444810365313

Marwick, A. E., & boyd, d. (2011). To see and be seen: Celebrity practice on Twitter. *Convergence: The International Journal of Research into New Media Technologies, 17*(2), 139–158. doi: 10.1177/1354856510394539

McQuail, D., Blumler, J. G., & Brown, J. R. (1972). The television audience: A revised perspective. In D. McQuail (Ed.), *Sociology of mass communications* (pp. 135–165). Harmondsworth: Penguin.

New York Times. (2012, November 6). Daily report: Tech and media companies resist proposal to strengthen online privacy protections for children. Retrieved from http://bits.blogs.nytimes.com/2012/11/06/daily-report-tech-and-media-companies-resist-proposal-to-strengthen-online-privacy-protections-for-children/

Nissenbaum, H. (2010). *Privacy in context: Technology, policy and the integrity of social life.* Stanford, CA: Stanford Law Books.

O'Keeffe, G. S., & Clarke-Pearson, K. (2011). The impact of social media on children, adolescents, and families. *Pediatrics, 127*(4), 800–804. doi: 10.1542/peds.2011-0054

Papacharissi, Z. (2002). The virtual sphere: The internet as a public sphere. *New Media & Society, 4*(1), 9–27. doi: 10.1177/14614440222226244

Papacharissi, Z. (2005). The real/virtual dichotomy in online interaction: A meta-analysis of research on new media uses and consequences. *Communication Yearbook, 29*, 215–238.

Papacharissi, Z. (2010). A networked self. In Z. Papacharissi (Ed.), *A networked self: Identity, community and culture on social network sites* (pp. 304–318). New York: Routledge.

Papacharissi, Z., & Gibson, P. L. (2011). Fifteen minutes of privacy: Privacy, sociality, and publicity on social network sites. In S. Trepte & L. Reinecke (Eds.), *Privacy online: Perspectives on privacy and self-disclosure in the social web* (pp. 75–89). Berlin & Heidelberg: Springer Berlin Heidelberg. doi: 10.1007/978-3-642-21521-6_7

Park, N., Kee, K. F., & Valenzuela, S. (2009). Being immersed in social networking environment: Facebook groups, uses and gratifications, and social outcomes. *Cyberpsychology & Behavior, 12*(6), 729–733. doi: 10.1089/cpb.2009.0003

Parks, M. R., & Floyd, K. (1996). Making friends in cyberspace. *Journal of Communication, 46*(1), 80–97. doi: 10.1111/j.1083-6101.1996.tb00176.x

Pearson, E. (2009). All the World Wide Web's a stage: The performance of identity in online social networks. *First Monday, 14*(3). Retrieved from http://firstmonday.org/ojs/index.php/fm/article/viewArticle/2162/2127

Petronio, S. (2002). *Boundaries of privacy: Dialectics of disclosure.* Albany, NY: State University of New York Press.

Quan-Haase, A., & Young, A. L. (2010). Uses and gratifications of social media: A comparison of Facebook and instant messaging. *Bulletin of Science, Technology & Society, 30*(5), 350–361. doi: 10.1177/0270467610380009

Quinn, K. (2013). We haven't talked in 30 years! Relationship reconnection and Internet use at midlife. *Information, Communication & Society, 16*(3), 397–420. doi: 10.1080/1369118X.2012.756047

Rainie, L., & Wellman, B. (2012). *Networked: The new social operating system.* Cambridge, MA: MIT Press.

Raynes-Goldie, K. (2010). Aliases, creeping, and wall cleaning: Understanding privacy in the age of Facebook. *First Monday, 15*(1), 1–8. Retrieved from http://firstmonday.org/htbin/cgiwrap/bin/ojs/index.php/fm/article/view/2775/2432

Ringrose, J. (2011). Are you sexy, flirty, or a slut? Exploring "sexualization" and how teen girls perform/negotiate digital sexual identity on social networking sites. In R. Gill & C. Scharff (Eds.), *New femininities: Postfeminism, neoliberalism and subjectivity* (pp. 99–116). London: Palgrave.

Rooksby, J., & Sommerville, I. (2011). The management and use of social network sites in a government department. *Computer Supported Cooperative Work (CSCW), 21*(4–5), 397–415. doi: 10.1007/s10606-011-9150-2

Ruggiero, T. E. (2000). Uses and gratifications theory in the 21st century. *Mass Communication and Society, 3*(1), 3–37. doi: 10.1207/S15327825MCS0301_02

Schmidt, J. (2011). (Micro)blogs: Practices of privacy management. In S. Trepte & L. Reinecke (Eds.), *Privacy online: Perspectives on privacy and self-disclosure in the social web* (Vol. 12, pp. 159–173). Berlin & Heidelberg: Springer Berlin Heidelberg. doi: 10.1007/978-3-642-21521-6_12

Senft, T. M. (2008). *Camgirls: Celebrity and community in the age of social networks*. New York: Peter Lang.

Shklovski, I., & Valtysson, B. (2012). Secretly political: Civic engagement in online publics in Kazakhstan. *Journal of Broadcasting & Electronic Media, 56*(3), 417–433. doi: 10.1080/08838151.2012.705196

Simmel, G. (1955). *Conflict and the web of group-affiliations*. Translated by K. H. Wolff & R. Bendix. Glencoe, IL: The Free Press. (Original works published in 1908 and 1922, respectively.)

Stutzman, F., Capra, R., & Thompson, J. (2011). Factors mediating disclosure in social network sites. *Computers in Human Behavior, 27*(1), 590–598. doi: 10.1016/j.chb.2010.10.017

Taddicken, M., & Jers, C. (2011). The uses of privacy online: Trading a loss of privacy for social web gratifications? In S. Trepte & L. Reinecke (Eds.), *Privacy online: Perspectives on privacy and self-disclosure in the social web* (pp. 143–156). Berlin & Heidelberg: Springer Berlin Heidelberg. doi: 10.1007/978-3-642-21521-6

Tokunaga, R. S. (2011). Social networking site or social surveillance site? Understanding the use of interpersonal electronic surveillance in romantic relationships. *Computers in Human Behavior, 27*(2), 705–713. doi: 10.1016/j.chb.2010.08.014

Tom Tong, S. T., Van Der Heide, B., Langwell, L., & Walther, J. B. (2008). Too much of a good thing? The relationship between number of friends and interpersonal impressions on Facebook. *Journal of Computer-Mediated Communication, 13*(3), 531–549. doi: 10.1111/j.1083-6101.2008.00409.x

Tufekci, Z. (2007). Can you see me now? Audience and disclosure regulation in online social network sites. *Bulletin of Science, Technology & Society, 28*(1), 20–36. doi: 10.1177/0270467607311484

Utz, S. (2010). Show me your friends and I will tell you what type of person you are: How one's profile, number of friends, and type of friends influence impression formation on social network sites. *Journal of Computer-Mediated Communication, 15*(2), 314–335. doi: 10.1111/j.1083-6101.2010.01522.x

Valenzuela, S., Park, N., & Kee, K. F. (2009). Is there social capital in a social network site?: Facebook use and college students' life satisfaction, trust, and participation. *Journal of Computer-Mediated Communication, 14*(4), 875–901. doi: 10.1111/j.1083-6101.2009.01474.x

Van Doorn, N. (2009). The ties that bind: The networked performance of gender, sexuality and friendship on MySpace. *New Media & Society, 12*(4), 583–602. doi: 10.1177/1461444809342766

Walther, J. B., Van Der Heide, B., Hamel, L. M., & Shulman, H. C. (2009). Self-generated versus other-generated statements and impressions in computer-mediated communication: A test of warranting theory using Facebook. *Communication Research, 36*(2), 229–253. doi: 10.1177/0093650208330251

Walther, J. B., Van Der Heide, B., Kim, S.-Y., Westerman, D., & Tong, S. T. (2008). The role of friends' appearance and behavior on evaluations of individuals on Facebook: Are we known by the company we keep? *Human Communication Research, 34*(1), 28–49. doi: 10.1111/j.1468-2958.2007.00312.x

Wellman, B., Quan-Haase, A., Boase, J., Chen, W., Hampton, K., Díaz, I., & Miyata, K. (2006). The social affordances of the internet for networked individualism. *Journal of Computer-Mediated Communication, 8*(3). doi: 10.1111/j.1083-6101.2003.tb00216.x

Wesch, M. (2009). YouTube and you: Experiences of self-awareness in the context collapse of the recording webcam. *Explorations in Media Ecology, 8*(2), 19–34.

Williams, D. (2006). On and off the 'net: Scales for social capital in an online era. *Journal of Computer-Mediated Communication, 11*(2), 593–628. doi: 10.1111/j.1083-6101.2006.00029.x

14

BLOGGING

Carmen D. Stavrositu

Restricted to a handful of tech-savvy users initially, blogging has been rising to prominence as a media activity since the early 2000s. The emergence of free and easy to use blogging platforms has led to the realization that ordinary people can create media content to cater to their own needs and motivations, and to facilitate connections with similar others. By recent estimates, there are about 181 million blogs in the entire "blogosphere," or world of blogs (Nielsen, 2012). In the U.S. alone, there are an estimated 31 million bloggers, with the actual number of blogs produced being around 42 million (Rampton, 2012).

Situated at the intersection of private and public realms, blogs permeate most every aspect of social life. Individuals have adopted this medium to voice themselves on issues of personal or public concern, participate in public discourse, create and/or maintain their identities, embark in self-transformation journeys alone or along with others, and join communities of bloggers with similar interests and concerns, among other activities.

Several blog genres have emerged over time, but they can be subsumed under two main categories—personal journal-type blogs and filter blogs. These two blog genres share several structural similarities. Specifically, they both feature the distinctive reverse chronological order of blog entries, or posts (Herring, Scheidt, Bonus, & Wright, 2004), and they both embed tools for connectivity such as commenting tools or blogrolls (i.e., lists of links to other blogs). However, these two types of blogs share some important differences as well, particularly in their content focus. With personal home pages as their predecessors, personal journal-type blogs are centered around blog authors' internal universe, and typically record their personal thoughts, feelings, and experiences (Blood, 2002; Herring et al., 2004; Wei, 2009). Such blogs explore topics that are personally relevant, important, and meaningful, and may include daily experiences, trials and tribulations, personal hobbies and interests, or emotional experiences triggered by life events. For this reason, early on, many perceived blogs to be akin to personal diaries (e.g., Lawson-Borders & Kirk, 2005; McNeill, 2003). In contrast, filter blogs revolve around events that are external to the blogger. Examples include politics, social and economic issues, or science, among others. Such blogs may focus on disseminating information about new scientific discoveries, interpreting mainstream news coverage, or simply pontificating and providing opinion about various issues of public interest.

This chapter will focus on personal journal-type blogs for two reasons. First, it is estimated that a vast majority of the English blogosphere consists of this type of blog (Heacock, 2011; Herring, Scheidt, Kouper, & Wright, 2006). Second, the personal nature of these blogs is more aligned with the focus of the present volume on media and social life, as opposed to filter blogs, which can and often do attract mass audiences, rivaling the reach of some mainstream media outlets (Heacock, 2011).

The chapter will first review extant literature examining blogging from different theoretical perspectives. Particular attention will be paid to the driving forces behind blogging and its perceived outcomes. Based on this review, the chapter will conclude by pointing to limitations in current blogging scholarship and suggesting possible avenues for future research.

Theoretical Perspectives in Blogging Research

Like most research on emerging technologies, blogging research is diffused across multiple academic disciplines. Consequently, the study of blogging is guided by theory stemming from communication, psychology, and interaction science, among others.

Across these disciplines, the most important questions about blogging have dealt with the reasons behind people's blogging activity and the outcomes likely to emerge from it. In what follows, this chapter will synthesize the literature on blogging as it pertains to personal journaling in particular, by highlighting its uses and effects.

Why Do People Blog? Uses and Gratifications of Blogging

As is the case following the inception of most new communication mediums, blogging scholarship was first and foremost fueled by inquiries into individuals' motivations to blog and the uses they put the new medium to. This research, more or less explicitly couched under the uses and gratifications perspective (Rubin, 1984), rests on the premise that individuals are active consumers of media fare, rather than passive and powerless recipients of media messages. What's more, in the context of blogging, users are simultaneously consumers of media and content producers alike (Hollenbaugh, 2011; Papacharissi, 2007). In light of these considerations, the uses and gratifications approach has naturally become one of the most consistently employed theoretical approaches in blogging research, seeking to understand why users are driven to a medium that so dramatically recasts their role in the communication process.

Generally, research exploring the uses and gratifications of blogging points to personal motivations and individual differences based on demographic, personality, or individual dispositions, as important drivers of blogging activity.

Motivations

In one of the earliest studies on blogging motivations, Nardi, Schiano, Gumbrecht, and Swartz (2004) identified five motives for blogging—documenting one's life, providing commentary and opinions, expressing deeply felt emotions, articulating ideas through writing, and forming and maintaining relationships. Jung, Youn, and McClung (2007) highlighted four such motives—entertainment, self-expression, professional advancement, and passing time. Likewise, Fullwood, Sheenan, and Nicholls (2009) inferred three main reasons for blogging from a content analysis of MySpace blogs—self-expression, networking, and identity construction and management—while Hollenbaugh (2011) reported that users participate in blogging in order to help/inform, archive/organize, pass time, get feedback, as well as engage in social connection, exhibitionism, and professionalism. Lastly, based on a survey of women bloggers in particular, Stavrositu and Sundar (2012) suggested three main motivations for blogging—exploring oneself, connecting with others, and bringing about change.

Individual Differences

Research on the uses and gratifications of blogging further indicates that differences in personal blogger demographics, personality, or individual dispositions are related to blogging use and motivations. For example, Pedersen and Macafee (2007) suggested that female bloggers have a stronger focus on personal content as well as a more pronounced orientation towards the social aspects of blogging, as opposed to males, whose main emphasis is on informational content. Women also show less technical sophistication and a greater preference for anonymity compared to men. Further, Guadagno, Odkie, and Eno (2008) reported that whereas all bloggers tend to score fairly high in openness to experience and neuroticism, the neuroticism trend is particularly salient among women bloggers. Moreover, according to a study by Stefanone and Jang (2008), extraversion and self-disclosure traits are related to blogging for relationship maintenance. These trends are consistent with broader social media usage

211

patterns indicating that social media use is positively predicted by extraversion and openness to experience, but negatively predicted by emotional stability (Correa, Willard, & Gil de Zúñiga, 2010).

In sum, the above review of the literature suggests that while bloggers do report taking up blogging for habitual or ritualized use, it most often appears to be an instrumental activity that is at once self- and other-centered. Indeed, blogging is no more a platform for the self (e.g., exploring and expressing oneself, documenting one's life) than it is one for social activity (e.g., relationship maintenance, social connection). Personal and demographic characteristics relate to these instrumental motivations in ways that are consistent with other social media use trends. As we will see in the following section, these self- and other-centered uses of blogs translate to a host of blogging outcomes of significant psychological import for the user.

Blogging as Positive Technology: Outcomes and Consequences

Prevailing blogging scholarship has identified self-disclosure, that is, the voluntary provision of personal information about one's thoughts, feelings, experiences, and/or needs (Derlega & Chaikin, 1977), as a core practice in personal journal-type blogging (e.g., Rains & Keating, 2011; Jang & Stefanone, 2011). In fact, this type of blogging owes its very existence to users' self-disclosure, and would cease to exist as a medium in its absence. From expressing one's feelings related to a recent divorce or a disappointing job interview, to detailing the intense experience of a cancer diagnosis or one's hopeful healing journey, bloggers routinely disclose personal details about their lives.

Self-disclosure via blogging is both a self-centered (intrapersonal) and other-centered (interpersonal) endeavor. At the intrapersonal level, blogging allows users to engage in dialogues with oneself, which materialize in bloggers' reflections on their personal life events and experiences. By virtue of its "publicness" and interactive capabilities, however, blogging is also a quintessentially interpersonal activity. Indeed, the act of self-disclosure is hardly just an egocentric process; research has long established its value as a catalyst for relationship formation and maintenance (Altman & Taylor, 1973).

This two-fold core practice of personal journal-type blogs fulfills several key functions and leads to several of psychological outcomes. Among these are identity construction/management, sense of agency, sense of community, and overall psychological well-being.

Identity Construction

Identity construction is an obvious function of blogging, given that it revolves around users' habitual self-disclosure and self-presentation (Bortree, 2005). Identity formation is a process that all individuals are consciously or unconsciously partaking in on a continual basis. However, some scholars suggest that in the blogosphere, identity construction is perhaps most prominent among adolescent users who are still actively negotiating their identities, as well as among users with socially stigmatized characteristics. For example, studies have indicated that identity construction via blogging is quite common among teenagers who adopt this medium to explore, make sense of, and come to terms with struggles particular to adolescence, such as sexuality, physical appearance, and overall self-identity, all within a relatively consequence-free environment (Bortree, 2005; Huffaker & Calvert, 2005). Similarly, research suggests that users also commonly turn to blogging to affirm and work through parts of themselves that they are largely silent about in real life, such as mental health issues (Sundar, Edwards, Hu, & Stavrositu, 2007) or sexual orientation (Rak, 2005).

Furthermore, identity construction via blogging can have potentially lasting and powerful implications for users. Gonzales and Hancock (2008) reported that when individuals present themselves in public computer-mediated venues in ways that are uncharacteristic of them (e.g., an extraverted online presentation by introverted individuals), they tend to internalize the trait presentation, signaling a tangible identity shift. This finding is reminiscent of Turkle's (1984) early observations of identity construction in multi-user dungeons (MUDs), whereby shy users, unshackled by the social inhibitions present in real life, adopted much more assertive personae that frequently led to healthy disinhibition in their offline personalities as well.

Sense of Agency

By affording regular individuals the opportunity to create content and express themselves, blogging is part of a host of web 2.0 technologies that can also afford users a strong sense of agency (Sundar, 2008)—that is, the feeling of having a competent, confident, and assertive voice (Stavrositu & Sundar, 2012). In the context of blogging, sense of agency is primarily the result of two parallel mechanisms—one psychological, the other technological. On the one hand, with each new blog post or reply to a reader comment, bloggers routinely engage in the act of expressing their voice and asserting themselves. With each new blog post or reply, bloggers reflect on or pontificate about themselves and the world around them. This frequent reiteration of one's voice, then, unsurprisingly serves to boost one's competence, confidence, and assertiveness, or *sense of agency*. On the other hand, the public nature of blogging apparent in blog visibility metrics (e.g., site visits) communicates to bloggers implicit reassurance or approval (Rains & Keating, 2011), and thus enables them to gain external validation of their voice. Stavrositu and Sundar (2012) demonstrated that awareness of site metrics pertinent to the number of blog visitors further translates to bloggers' heightened sense of agency as the amount of these metrics increases.

Sense of Community

Similarly, there are parallel psychological and technological mechanisms that work in tandem to imbue users with a heightened sense of community. Building on the work of McMillan and Chavis (1986), *virtual sense of community* has been defined as users' feelings of membership and belonging, identity, influence, and attachment with each other in computer-mediated contexts (Blanchard, 2008).

On the one hand, scholars have examined bloggers' self-disclosure as a means for establishing connection and perceived community. This area of research is generally built on the principles and assumptions of *social penetration theory*, positing that the purpose of self-disclosing is to establish intimacy (Altman & Taylor, 1973). In fact, research suggests that even though self-disclosure via blogging is typically non-directed due to the medium's "broadcast" nature, bloggers tend to adopt traditional interpersonal norms, routinely expecting acknowledgment, reciprocity, and perceived personalness in interpersonal exchanges (e.g., Jang & Stefanone, 2011). Additionally, Ko and Kuo (2009) found direct evidence that self-disclosure behaviors predict bloggers' perceived social capital (i.e., social integration, social bonding, and social bridging).

On the other hand, from a human–computer interaction (HCI) research perspective, characteristics of the blogging platforms themselves have been invoked as powerful tools with psychological outcomes (Sundar, 2008). Specifically, mainly via its embedded commenting functions, blogging often materializes in continued dialogues between bloggers and readers, leading to the emergence of veritable online communities (Rheingold, 1993). For example, studies have found that comments received by a blog boost bloggers' perceived sense of community and social support, especially when the number of comments is high (Stavrositu & Sundar, 2012), or when they are supportive and encouraging (Miura & Yamashita, 2007; Rains & Keating, 2011).

Psychological Health

Couched under the journaling-effects literature in clinical and social psychology, blogging research has further examined the health benefits of self-disclosure and expressive writing in personal blogs. It has been long documented that translating emotions into words, particularly about distressing life events and experiences, yields important psychological benefits (see Pennebaker & Chung, 2011; Wright & Chung, 2001). In the context of cancer blogging, for example, Chung and Kim (2008) found

214

that for cancer patients, blogging serves an emotion-management function. Similarly, Rains and Keating (2012) found that making public disclosures about health via blogging leads to meaningful improvements in well-being. While there is no one clear mechanism to explain the link between expressive writing and therapeutic benefits, venting and catharsis or simply gaining self-awareness through writing have been invoked as potential routes to psychological well-being (e.g., Kerner & Fitzpatrick, 2007; Pennebaker & Beall, 1986). In fact, many bloggers report that they undertake the practice of writing in a blog mainly as a means for "letting off steam" and achieving catharsis, as well for working through personal issues (Nardi et al., 2004).

As previously noted, however, blogging further affords users social connection. Even though people who keep a personal diary may very well hold "the belief that some symbolic other person may 'magically' read their essays" (Pennebaker & Chung, 2011, p. 423), with blogging, social feedback becomes tangible and explicit (Nagel & Anthony, 2009). Consequently, some people have argued that engaging in expressive writing publicly via blogging yields an additional boost in therapeutic benefits. For example, in a study with teenagers suffering from socio-emotional difficulties, Boniel-Nissim and Barak (2011) found that, overall, expressive writing about socio-emotional issues in a blog was far superior to writing on a standalone computer, which mimicked diary-writing. Further, teens assigned to a blogging condition that allowed for feedback/comments experienced the most dramatic decrease in distress levels. Likewise, Baker and Moore (2008a, 2008b, 2011) provided evidence for positive psychosocial changes in bloggers (as opposed to non-bloggers) over time, stemming from both the act of self-expression through writing and the ensuing social support structures. Finally, Ko and Kuo (2009) showed that, in general, blogging about personal feelings, emotions, behaviors, and experiences had a positive impact on subjective well-being via perceived social capital. More recent research with similar patterns of findings (Jung, Song, & Vorderer, 2012; Rains & Keating, 2011) suggests that active and frequent use of personal journal-type blogs leads to perceived social support, which ultimately serves to maximize psychological well-being while minimizing feelings of loneliness.

Psychological Empowerment

Lastly, psychological empowerment, another indicator of well-being, has often been touted as the ultimate benefit of blogging. Indeed, the promise of personal empowerment has been a regular fixture in discussions regarding the anticipated impacts of blogging ever since the medium's inception (Blood, 2002; Herring et al., 2004; Nagel & Anthony, 2009; Stefanone & Jang, 2008). It was not until recently, however, that this early prediction has been empirically substantiated. In a study of female bloggers, in particular, Stavrositu and Sundar (2012) found that specific user motivations for personal journal-type blogging (e.g., explore oneself, social connection) activate bloggers' perceived sense of community to ultimately imbue users with a deep sense of psychological empowerment.

In sum, as evident from the preceding review of the literature, personal journal-type blogging has been shown to yield important psychological benefits for bloggers. Because of this, blogging provides a fitting embodiment of what Botella et al. (2012) have labeled as "positive technology." The emerging *positive technology* field of research combines the principles and objectives of *positive psychology* with the affordances of information and communication technologies (ICTs) to investigate ways in which technology can elicit positive human development and experiences, and maximize well-being in individuals, organizations, and society at large (Botella et al., 2012).

Limitations and Future of Directions in Blogging Research

One aspect of research on blogging that becomes immediately apparent upon surveying the prevailing literature is its predominant focus on the salutary outcomes of blogging (e.g., sense of community, psychological well-being, etc.), with fewer studies exploring its bleak consequences. For instance, the phenomenon of hostile and abusive commenting has received relatively little attention in scholarly research, despite its frequent mentions in popular media (e.g., Adams, 2012; Nakashima, 2007; Valenti, 2007). Similarly, some scholars have expressed concerns regarding the excessive self-focus that user-driven technologies, including blogging, can engender (Cohen, 2006; McNeill, 2003). Some researchers have gone as far as to suggest that these technologies are partly responsible for the prevalent sense of entitlement and for the "narcissism epidemic" in contemporary society (Twenge & Campbell, 2009). Further, despite persistent evidence of the community-building function of blogging and its ensuing psychological benefits, Turkle (2011) cautions against the seductiveness of new communication technologies which, she says, threaten to deteriorate the quality of our interpersonal relationships in a range of settings. With these considerations in mind, blogging scholarship could arguably benefit by more directly examining these potential negative facets of blogging. Blogging research could also extend its inquiries beyond active blogs into the myriad of abandoned and defunct blogs. By many accounts, these blogs outweigh active blogs (see Perseus, 2003), though little is known about the reasons behind their extinction.

The study of blogging puts the media user center stage, unlike any other medium before it. Not only are users "active users" when it comes to blogging, but their activity is the core ingredient of blogging. Indeed, more user-centered than previous technologies, blogs not only encourage but depend on user activity. Not surprisingly, then, as evident from the preceding synthesis of the blogging literature, the majority of blogging scholarship to date has focused primarily on bloggers, or blog authors. Blogging, nonetheless, can be simultaneously conceptualized as reading or commenting, in addition to authoring original blog posts. In fact, though not particularly common for personal journal-type blogs (Heacock, 2011), readership of blogs can, and at times does, reach mass-audience proportions, with certain blog posts attracting comments in the thousands. In order to gain a more rounded understanding of blogging, future research would do well to pay more attention to the motivations for and benefits of blogging for blog readers and commenters, in addition to blog authors. For example, research examining the role of narratives in shaping health-related outcomes suggests that presenting information in narrative formats is far superior to non-narrative modes of information delivery, contributing more effectively to shifts in health knowledge, attitudes, and behavioral intentions (e.g., Murphy, Frank, Chatterjee, & Baezconde-Garbanati, 2013). This line of research points to the potentially beneficial implications of reading about health in personal journal-type blogs which revolve around individual narratives.

From a methodological standpoint, blogging scholarship could further benefit from a stronger emphasis on experimentally controlled examinations. Survey methodology is well suited for inquiries related to perceived motivations and outcomes of blogging; experimental studies, however, can help establish causal patterns, as well as pinpoint unambiguously the specific aspects of the blogging activity that can be implicated in the myriad of blogging outcomes previously discussed.

Lastly, microblogging, or short-form blogging (e.g., Twitter), provides a new testing ground for blogging research findings. For example, the observed therapeutic benefits of blogging could be tested in the context of microblogging platforms as well given existing evidence in the journaling-effects literature suggesting that writing duration matters little in deriving such benefits. Specifically, studies have found that even very brief periods of expressive writing (i.e., two minutes per day) can proffer health benefits comparable to those emerging from longer periods of writing (Burton & King, 2008). In light of this evidence, future research could explore whether the amount of writing allowed by microblogging platforms can facilitate outcomes similar to those seen in traditional blogging. Such research can help integrate the blogging and microblogging scholarship, as well as delineate the boundaries of the two writing platforms.

Conclusion

The primary goal of this chapter was to provide an overview of the main questions and theoretical perspectives guiding blogging research, of the emerging main findings of this scholarship, as well as of potential directions for future research. As illustrated throughout the chapter, users are driven by a variety of psychological needs and motivations and are impacted by the practice of blogging in several significant ways. Much more remains to be understood, however, about the nature and outcomes of blogging. Initially feared by many to be a mere technological fad, blogging has withstood the test of time in the face of many new technological innovations since its inception, and it is clearly here to stay. Consequently, it is imperative that research builds on existing findings and perhaps extensions of this technology (e.g., Twitter) to further our understanding of this platform. In addition to the specific lacunae that it could address, as identified in this chapter, future blogging scholarship should also attempt to integrate the distinct theoretical perspectives employed in this arena in compelling and cohesive ways. Moreover, going forward, it is imperative that scholars do not merely apply existing media theories to blogging inquiries, but strive to expand the theoretical boundaries of blogging scholarship. This would in fact benefit not only blogging research, but also research on other web platforms that encourage user content creation and self-expression.

References

Adams, M. (2012, April 26). Health blogger threatened with jail time for advocating Paleo diet that cured his diabetes. *NaturalNews.com*. Available at http://www.naturalnews.com/035691_dieticians_free_speech_nutrition_advice.html

Altman, I., & Taylor, D. A. (1973). *Social penetration: The development of interpersonal relationships*. New York: Holt, Rinehart & Winston.

Baker, J. R., & Moore, S. M. (2008a). Distress, coping, and blogging: Comparing new MySpace users by their intention to blog. *Cyberpsychology and Behavior, 11*(2), 81–85. doi: 10.1089/cpb.2007.9930

Baker, J. R., & Moore, S. M. (2008b). Blogging as a social tool: A psychosocial examination of the effects of blogging. *Cyberpsychology and Behavior, 11*(6), 747–749. doi: 10.1089/cpb.2008.0053

Baker, J. R., & Moore, S. M. (2011). An opportunistic validation of studies on the psychosocial benefits of blogging. *Cyberpsychology, Behavior, and Social Networking, 14*(6), 387–390. doi: 10.1089/cyber.2010.0202

Blanchard, A. L. (2008). Testing a model of sense of virtual community. *Computers in Human Behavior, 24*(5), 2107–2123. doi:10.1016/j.chb.2007.10.002

Blood, R. (2002). *The weblog handbook: Practical advice on creating and maintaining your blog*. Cambridge, MA: Perseus.

Boniel-Nissim, M., & Barak, A. (2011). The therapeutic value of adolescents' blogging about social-emotional difficulties. *Psychological Services, 1541*–1559. doi: 10.1037/a0026664

Bortree, D. S. (2005). Presentation of self on the web: An ethnographic study of teenage girls' weblogs. *Education, Communication, and Information Journal, 5*(1), 25–40. doi: 10.1080/14636310500061102

Botella, C., Riva, G., Gaggioli, A., Wiederhold, B. K., Alcaniz, M., & Baños, R. M. (2012). The present and future of positive technologies. *CyberPsychology, Behavior, and Social Networking, 15*(2), 78–84. doi: 10.1089/cyber.2011.0140

Burton, C. M., & King, L. A. (2008). The effects of (very) brief writing on health: The 2-minute miracle. *British Journal of Health Psychology, 13,* 9–14. doi: 10.1348/135910707X250910

Chung, D. S., & Kim, S. (2008). Blogging activity among cancer patients and their companions: Uses, gratifications, and predictors of outcomes. *Journal of the American Society for Information Science and Technology, 59,* 297–306. doi: 10.1002/asi.20751

Cohen, K. R. (2006). A welcome for blogs. *Continuum: Journal of Media & Cultural Studies, 20*(2), 161–173. doi: 10.1080/10304310600641620

Correa, T., Willard, A., & Gil de Zúñiga, H. (2010). Who interacts on the web? The intersection of users' personality and social media use. *Computers in Human Behavior, 26,* 247–253. doi: 10.1016/j.chb.2009.09.003

Derlega, V. J. & Chaikin, A. L. (1977). Privacy and self-disclosure in social relationships. *Journal of Social Issues, 33*(3), 102–115. doi: 10.1111/j.1540-4560.1977.tb01885

Fullwood, C., Sheehan, N., & Nicholls, W. (2009). Blog function revisited: A content analysis of MySpace blogs. *CyberPsychology & Behavior, 12,* 685–689. doi: 10.1089/cpb2009.013

Gonzales, A. L., & Hancock, J. T. (2008). Identity shift in computer-mediated environments. *Media Psychology, 11,* 167–185. doi: 10.1080/15213260802023433

Guadagno, R. E., Odkie, B. M., & Eno, C. A. (2008). Who blogs? Personality predictors of blogging. *Computers in Human Behavior, 24,* 1993–2004. doi: 10.1016/j.chb.2007.09.001

Heacock, R. (2011, November). Blogging Common releases overview of English blogosphere. *Blogging Common,* Berkman Institute for Internet and Society. Available at http://bloggincommon.org/2011/11/10/blogging-common-releases-overview-of-english-blogosphere/

Herring, S. C., Scheidt, L. A., Bonus, S., & Wright, E. L. (2004). Bridging the gap: A genre analysis of weblogs. *Proceedings of the Thirty-Seventh Hawaii International Conference on System Sciences (HICSS-37).* Los Alamitos: IEEE Press.

Herring, S. C., Scheidt, L. A., Kouper, I., & Wright, E. (2006). A longitudinal content analysis of weblogs: 2003–2004. In M. Tremayne (Ed.), *Blogging, citizenship, and the future of media* (pp. 3–20). London: Routledge.

Hollenbaugh, E. E. (2011). Motives for maintaining personal journal blogs. *Cyberpsychology, Behavior, and Social Networking, 14*(1/2), 13–20. doi: 10.1089/cyber.2009.0403

Huffaker, D. A., & Calvert, S. L. (2005). Gender, identity, and language use in teenage blogs. *Journal of Computer-Mediated Communication, 10*(2), 00. doi: 10.1111/j.1083-6101.2005.tb00238.x

Jang, C. Y., & Stefanone, M. A. (2011). Non-directed self-disclosure in the blogosphere. *Information, Communication & Society, 14*(7), 1039–1059. doi: 10.1080/1369118X.2011.559265

Jung, T., Youn, H., & McClung, S. (2007). Motivations and self-presentation strategies on Korean-based "Cyworld" weblog format personal homepages. *CyberPsychology, Behavior, & Social Networking, 10,* 24–31. doi: 10.1089/cpb.2006.9996

Jung, Y., Song, H., & Vorderer, P. (2012). Why do people post and read personal messages in public? The motivation of using personal blogs and its effects on users' loneliness, belonging, and well-being. *Computers in Human Behavior, 28,* 1626–1633. doi: 10.1016/j.chb.2012.04.001

Kerner, E. A., & Fitzpatrick, M. R. (2007). Integrating writing into psychotherapy practice: A matrix of change processes and structural dimensions. *Psychotherapy: Theory, Research, Practice, Training, 44,* 333–346. doi: 10.1037/0033-3204.44.3.33

Ko, H. C., & Kuo, F. Y. (2009). Can blogging enhance subjective well-being through self-disclosure? *CyberPsychology & Behavior, 12*(1), 75–79. doi: 10.1089/cpb.2008.0163

Lawson-Borders, G., & Kirk, R. (2005). Blogs in campaign communication. *American Behavioral Scientist, 49,* 548–559. doi: 10.1177/0002764205279425

McMillan, D. W., & Chavis, D. M. (1986). Sense of community: A definition and theory. *Journal of Community Psychology, 14*(1), 6–23. doi: 10.1002/1520-6629(198601)14:1<6::AID-JCOP2290140103>3.0.CO;2-I

McNeill, L. (2003). Teaching an old genre new tricks: The diary on the Internet. *Biography: An Interdisciplinary Quarterly, 26*(1), 24–48. doi: 10.1353/bio.2003.0028

Miura, A., & Yamashita, K. (2007). Psychological and social influences on blog writing: An online survey of blog authors in Japan. *Journal of Computer-Mediated Communication, 12,* 1452–1471. doi: 10.1111/j.1083-6101.2007.00381.x

Murphy, S. T., Frank, L. B., Chatterjee, J. S., & Baezconde-Garbanati, L. (2013). Narrative versus nonnarrative: The role of identification, transportation, and emotion in reducing health disparities. *Journal of Communication, 63*(1), 116–137. doi: 10.1111/jcom.12007

Nagel, D. M., & Anthony, K. (2009). Writing therapy using new technologies—The art of blogging. *Journal of Poetry Therapy, 22*(1), 41–45. doi: 10.1080/08893670802708001

Nakashima, A. (2007). Sexual threats stifle some female bloggers. *The Washington Post.* Available at http://www.washingtonpost.com/wpdyn/content/article/2007/04/29/AR2007042901555.html

Nardi, B. A., Schiano, D. J., Gumbrecht, M., & Swartz, L. (2004). Why we blog. *Communications of the ACM, 47* (12), 41–46. doi: 10.1145/1035134.1035163

Nielsen (2012). *State of the media: The social media report.* Available at http://www.nielsen.com/us/en/reports/2012/state-of-the-media-the-social-media-report-2012.html

Papacharissi, Z. (2007). Audiences as media producers: Content analysis of 260 blogs. In M. Tremayne (Ed.), *Blogging, citizenship, and the future of media* (pp. 21–38). New York: Routledge.

Pedersen, S., & Macafee, C. (2007). Gender differences in British blogging. *Journal of Computer-Mediated Communication, 12*(4), 1472–1492. doi: 10.1111/j.1083-6101.2007.00382.x

Pennebaker, J. W., & Beall, S. K. (1986). Confronting a traumatic event: Toward an understanding of inhibition and disease. *Journal of Abnormal Psychology, 95,* 274–281. doi: 10.1037//0021-843X.95.3.274

Pennebaker, J. W., & Chung, C. K. (2011). Expressive writing and its links to mental and physical health. In H. S. Friedman (Ed.), *Oxford handbook of health psychology* (pp. 417–437). New York: Oxford University Press.

Perseus (2003). The blogging iceberg—of 4.12 million hosted weblogs, most little seen, quickly abandoned. Available at http://www.perseus.com/blogsurvey/thebloggingiceberg.

Rains, S. A., & Keating, D. M. (2011). The social dimension of blogging about health: Health blogging, social support, and well-being. *Communication Monographs, 78,* 511–534. doi: 10.1080/03637751.2011.618142

Rains, S. A., & Keating, D. M. (2012). Health blogging: An examination of the outcomes associated with making public, written disclosures about health. *Communication Research.* Advance online publication. doi: 10.1177/0093650212458952

Rak, J. (2005). The digital queer: Weblogs and Internet identity. *Biography, 28*(1), 166–182. doi: 10.1353/bio.2005.0037

Rampton, J. (2012, July). Blogging stats 2012. *Blogging.org.* Available at http://blogging.org/blog/blogging-stats-2012-infographic/

Rheingold, H. (1993). *The virtual community: Homesteading on the electronic frontier.* New York: HarperCollins.

Rubin, A. (1984). Ritualized and instrumental television viewing. *Journal of Communication, 34*(3), 67–77. doi: 10.1111/j.1460-2466.1984.tb02174

Stavrositu, C., & Sundar, S. S. (2012). Does blogging empower women? Exploring the role of agency and community. *Journal of Computer-Mediated Communication, 17,* 369–386. doi: 10.1111/j.1083–6101.2012.01587.x

Stefanone, M. A., & Jang, C. Y. (2008). Writing for friends and family: The interpersonal nature of blogs. *Journal of Computer-Mediated Communication, 13,* 123–140. doi: 10.1111/j.1083-6101.2007.00389.x

Sundar, S. S. (2008). Self as source: Agency and customization in interactive media. In E. Konijn, S. Utz, M. Tanis, & S. Barnes (Eds.), *Mediated interpersonal communication* (pp. 58–74). New York: Routledge.

Sundar, S. S., Edwards, H. H., Hu, Y., & Stavrositu, C. (2007). Blogging for better health: Putting the "public" back in public health. In M. Tremayne (Ed.), *Blogging, citizenship, and the future of media* (pp. 83–102). New York: Routledge.

Turkle, S. (1984). *The second self.* New York: Simon and Schuster.

Turkle, S. (2011). *Alone together: Why we expect more from technology and each other.* New York: Basic Books.

Twenge, J. M., & Campbell, W. K. (2009). *The narcissism epidemic: Living in the age of entitlement.* New York: Free Press.

Valenti, J. (2007, April 6). How the web became a sexists' paradise. *The Guardian.* Available at http://www.guardian.co.uk/g2/story/0,,2051394,00.html

Wei, L. (2009). Filter blogs vs. personal journals: Understanding the knowledge production gap on the Internet. *Journal of Computer-Mediated Communication, 14*(3), 532–558. doi: 10.1111/j.1083-6101.2009.01452.x

Wright, J., & Chung, M. C. (2001). Mastery or mystery? Therapeutic writing: A review of the literature. *British Journal of Guidance & Counselling, 29,* 277–291. doi: 10.1080/03069880120073003

INDEX

For Product Safety Concerns and Information please contact our EU
representative GPSR@taylorandfrancis.com
Taylor & Francis Verlag GmbH, Kaufingerstraße 24, 80331 München, Germany

www.ingramcontent.com/pod-product-compliance
Lightning Source LLC
Chambersburg PA
CBHW071419050326
40689CB00010B/1899